My Nine Lives

LEON FLEISHER

AND ANNE MIDGETTE

Doubleday   *New York   London   Toronto   Sydney   Auckland*

MY
NINE
LIVES

A Memoir of Many Careers in Music

ⅅⅅ
DOUBLEDAY

Copyright © 2010 by Leon Fleisher

All rights reserved. Published in the United States by Doubleday, a division of Random House, Inc., New York, and in Canada by Random House of Canada Limited, Toronto.

www.doubleday.com

DOUBLEDAY and the DD colophon are registered trademarks of Random House, Inc.

Book design by Maria Carella
Title page photo: collection of Leon Fleisher

Library of Congress Cataloging-in-Publication Data
Fleisher, Leon.
My nine lives : a memoir of many careers in music /
Leon Fleisher and Anne Midgette.—1st ed.
p. cm.
1. Fleisher, Leon. 2. Pianists—United States—Biography.
I. Midgette, Anne. II. Title.
ML417.F56A3 2010
786.2092—dc22
[B]   2010012735

ISBN 978-0-385-52918-1

To the memory of my father, Isidor Fleisher,
and my brother, Raymond Fleisher,
who made so many sacrifices so I could live these lives;
and my mother, Bertha Fleisher,
who dreamed of them first.

CONTENTS

MY NINE LIVES

INTRODUCTION

My twelfth birthday present from my mother and father was a recording of Brahms's first piano concerto in D Minor. My family didn't have many records, apart from a few by Enrico Caruso—a staple in American homes in those days—but my parents knew this one was something out of the ordinary. The soloist was my teacher, the great Artur Schnabel, whose playing even then was legendary and bore the seal of absolute authority: after all, in his youth in Vienna he had met Brahms, and heard him play, and even gone on a picnic with him. And the conductor was the brilliant Hungarian taskmaster George Szell.

The Brahms D Minor concerto is a huge work. In those days of 78 rpm records, it took up seven or eight disks. I put the first disk on the record player and lowered the needle, and a dark roll of timpani poured out of the big horn of the speaker, like the thunder of Thor. There followed a defiant cry from the massed forces of the orchestra, as if shaking a fist at the lowering heavens. The hair on my head stood up. That opening did something to me that no other music had done before. I wore out the first side of that recording. It took me about a week even to get to side 2, where the piano actually makes its entrance.

For weeks I ate, slept, and breathed that piece. Even for a child prodigy, the Brahms D Minor is a tall order. It calls for two-fisted piano playing and emotions that you might think are beyond the compass of a child. But I loved it so much I couldn't stay away. Within a year or so, I was working on making it my own. I was probably a little young. It's smart, though, to learn very difficult repertory when you're young. That way, you get it in your fingers, and in your DNA, before you realize just how hard it really is.

From the moment I first heard it, I dreamed of playing the Brahms D Minor with a full orchestra, with George Szell conducting. And when I began learning it, actually playing it myself, I dreamed even harder. Dreaming helps. My dreams were fulfilled. The Brahms D Minor concerto became my talisman. I played it in my debut with the New York Philharmonic, when I was sixteen. I played it when I won the Queen Elisabeth Competition in Brussels. And I played it, finally, with George Szell. We even recorded it together. Some people call our recording a classic.

If my story is about anything, it's about being very careful when your dreams come true. The Greek myths are full of tales of heroes cut down in the arrogance of their prime, taught humility by a blow from the gods. It sounds melodramatic. But such things really can happen. They happened to me. I was at the peak of my career, ready to conquer the world, and whether or not I was guilty of hubris, the thunder of Thor came down and hit me where I lived. When I was thirty-six years old, I mysteriously lost the use of two fingers on my right hand. The fourth and fifth finger started cramping, curling up, until they were firmly lodged against my palm. When the gods want to get you, they know right where to strike: the place it will hurt the most. I thought I would never play again.

Was it in my head? Was it some bigger malady? No one was able to tell me what was wrong. I looked. I looked in more places than I might have thought possible. I was willing to try anything to get the use of my hand back: treatments, therapy, medications, spiritual healers, you name it.

I wasn't especially noble in my affliction. I shut down. I acted out in all kinds of ways, of which I am not particularly proud. Inwardly, I railed against my situation; outwardly, I hid from it, turning away from friends and family, trying to prove however I could that I was still vital. I grew my hair, grew out my beard, and began tooling around on a Vespa. I didn't have any other tools to help me deal with what had happened. It was hard to find words for the dark cloud that hovered over me: of anguish, of dejection, of rage. I fell into a deep depression. At my lowest point, I seriously considered killing myself.

But I didn't kill myself. I stayed alive. And, just as I was stuck with being alive, I was stuck with my love of music. Something about it was still sustaining, and still worthwhile. So I embarked on a quest to make a life in music, in any way I could.

It wasn't the first time I'd found myself setting out on a new career.

I always say I've had more careers than a cat has lives. Even before I lost the use of my hand, my life with the piano never seemed to be a straightforward process. First, I was a child prodigy, playing Beethoven concertos in my native San Francisco; but that ended when Schnabel himself took me on as a student, on the condition that I give no more concerts. After years of study with him, I was ready to take the world by storm after my New York Philharmonic debut at sixteen, but after a couple of years of concert activity, the engagements seemed to peter out. Not until I became the first American to win the prestigious Queen Elisabeth Competition in Brussels, at twenty-three, did I develop a piano career that had staying power. Then came the disaster with my hand, and it seemed that chapter was over.

But after the catastrophe, I slowly found my way to other careers in music. I became a conductor, working with other musicians to make the sounds I could no longer make myself. I developed as a teacher, learning to use words to communicate the truths in the pieces I loved, which I had once expressed with my fingers alone. Somehow, my experience of music became richer the more I explored other ways of relating to it.

I didn't fully realize, as I lived them, how much these different careers were opening me up to new experiences and approaches I had never even dreamed of. I, the clean-cut piano soloist, took on the appearance of a long-haired hippie. I, the interpreter of Brahms, began conducting contemporary music that was unlike anything I had previously encountered in my musical life: thorny scores and avant-garde operas. I, the hard-nosed rationalist who spent hours a day sitting at the piano practicing, began visiting faith healers, practitioners of Eastern medicine, gurus, and quacks, in search of a cure. I, the acolyte of the great Schnabel, began seeking out other piano teachers and experimenting with different techniques to see if anything could cast some light on my condition.

Because call me obsessive-compulsive, call me stubborn, call me inspired, I never stopped looking for a way to make my right hand work again. And I never stopped testing it on the keyboard, every day, to see if my symptoms were abating.

Every day. For thirty years.

In the meantime, the world was moving forward. Medical science was making advances. Repetitive strain injuries became a subject of study. So did injuries to instrumentalists. Once, we were told it was all in our heads. Now, it seemed, inflicting the same unnatural set of movements over and over on your body could lead to severe consequences if you weren't careful—or if you were just unlucky. I began hearing of other pianists with hand problems, violinists who couldn't finger, horn and flute players who lost the ability to purse their lips. I began hearing of a neurological condition that could be aggravated by repeated movement or triggered by stress or trauma.

Therapists and doctors, practitioners of Western and holistic healing alike, were becoming more adept at dealing with such injuries. And after all the years of searching, of suffering, some of the principles of recovery began to take hold. I gradually realized that my hand might not regain its full former strength. But that didn't mean that I couldn't, with the help of healing techniques, and the full force of my will, begin to use it.

I turned to Rolfing, a massagelike technique. The practitioner identified pressure points where years of tension were stored, and slowly brought my frozen muscles back to life. I turned to Botox, a deadly poison that doctors running an experimental program at the National Institutes of Health suggested might help numb the muscles that had been pulling at my fingers, so the rest of my hand could get on with it.

And I turned to my inner resources, the part of me deep within that knew that, somehow, someday, I was going to be able to play with two hands again.

My right hand began to open.

One morning, in the privacy of my home, with the sun streaming through the windows, I went and sat at my keyboard. I flexed my fingers. I heard, in my inner ear, the thunder of Thor.

And I began playing, with both hands, the Brahms D Minor concerto, at the point where the long orchestral introduction ends and the piano finally makes its entrance.

I was sixty-six years old, and I was about to begin another new career.

CHAPTER 1

CHILD
PRODIGY

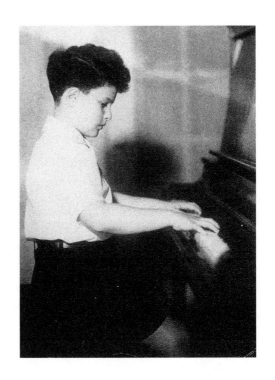

*At age seven or eight, around the time of my first
solo recital.* (Author's collection)

For Mr. Shorr, it wasn't a good lesson until he made me cry.

Lev Shorr was my piano teacher. Slender, with a bald spot on top of his head, he sported a cane that he didn't need and wore pince-nez—glasses that attached to the bridge of his nose with a spring—and even, incredibly enough, spats. He looked as though he had stepped out of an illustration for a men's haberdashery. He was like James Mason, but with a Russian accent.

Mr. Shorr was a prodigy maker. He was also a pianist of some distinction, and he dressed the part. He was the pianist of the San Francisco Symphony; he accompanied Yehudi Menuhin, a local boy, when he was in town. But his real reputation ultimately derived from his students. There was a huge concentration of so-called child geniuses around San Francisco in those days. Shorr had taught Menuhin's sisters, Hephzibah and Yalta. He taught a girl named Laura Dubman, who gave her debut recital at the age of five and was supposed to be a rising piano talent (she later worked at MGM and taught Katharine Hepburn how to look like she was really playing the piano as Clara Schumann in *Song of Love*). He taught Ruth Slenczynska, who was really a big deal for a while, until she had a nervous breakdown in her teens that put her career on hiatus for a few decades. He later taught Stephen Kovacevich, who went on to be a star soloist in the generation after mine. And he taught me.

His manner was just as taut and crisp and old school as his appearance. In lessons, he focused on technique. "Technique" meant, of course, Russian technique, the classic approach for virtuosos: for Mr. Shorr, that was the only technique there was. Our fingers were to be curved over the keys and raised and lowered like little hammers. Physiologically, this approach, widespread as it is, doesn't actually make sense, and I suspect Mr. Shorr might have done harm to some players, although many of his students did go on to careers all over the world. It wasn't much fun, though. If you played a clinker, he all but rapped you on the fingers with his cane. He never actually did that, but you felt he might. When I was six or seven and trying with all my might to please him, it wasn't long before tears of frustration would rise to the surface.

But he wasn't an unkind man. He could also be rather paternalistic. Not that he would exactly comfort me when I began to cry, but after it happened he invariably took me out to lunch, for lamb chops. There was obviously method to his madness. He didn't succeed in molding me to the Russian technique, but to this day I have retained a marked love of lamb chops.

I can't actually remember a time when I wasn't playing the piano. I started when I was four years old, and my whole life came very quickly to revolve around the instrument—an upright piano, in the living room of whatever San Francisco apartment we happened to be living in at the moment. We moved around a lot. The piano was my mother's idea. My parents didn't have any real connection to music, but for my mother the instrument represented, as it did for many immigrants, a gateway to a new and better world.

My father, Isidor Fleisher, was straight off the boat. He was born in Odessa, and his family emigrated to the United States with him when he was thirteen to join his brother, who had gone on ahead and established himself. He met my mother one summer night on the Lower East Side of Manhattan, when the sweltering heat had driven everyone out of their apartments and up onto the rooftops and fire escapes in search of a breath of fresh air. Those were different days.

My mother was born in Chelm, a little town in Poland that is known, in Jewish folklore, as a center of foolishness. The traditional stories about the stupidity of the Chelmers have been taken up and elaborated by authors like Sholem Aleichem and Isaac Bashevis Singer; you could call them the original Polish jokes. They say that when God created the world, he sent out an angel with two bags, one filled with wisdom and one with foolishness: the latter, being heavier, dragged the angel down, snagged on a mountaintop, ripped open, and spilled its contents all over Chelm. Thereafter, the Chelmers were an idiosyncratic bunch. For instance, the city fathers decided one day that they wanted trees in front of the courthouse—so the Chelmers picked up the courthouse and moved it into the forest. My mother, of course, wanted nothing to do with that sort of silliness.

My parents didn't have a lot of formal education. My father was a milliner. He made ladies' hats, little pillboxes, out of straw. I have no idea where he learned to do that. He came out to San Francisco at the behest of an uncle, who was manufacturing hats for the navy. I'm quite sure the navy hats were only the remotest preparation for what my father ended up doing in San Francisco. Somewhere along the way, he lost the c in his last name, because while his brothers and sisters all went by "Fleischer," my immediate family has always been plain "Fleisher." Perhaps he wanted something that sounded more American. He had a little shop on Geary Street, catty-corner to the Clift Hotel. One day he came home quite excited because a lovely red-headed girl had come in and bought one of his hats and then told him that her name was Lucille Ball. That really perked him up. He didn't have that kind of clientele all the time, but he became successful enough to open a second shop on Fillmore Street. My mother ran that one.

My mother, Bertha, was a strong, strong personality. I think she was part Tartar: dark skin, firm features, and stubborn. She was also a little bit crazy. She was fixated on getting the best for her family, and she would do whatever it took to achieve that end. She was certainly driven. She came over to America on her own, at the age of twenty, and she married my father two years later. Even without education, she was keenly aware that there were higher things in life. In her later years, she would sit and read Emerson by the hour; she appeared to find great comfort in that. For her, that was just one example of the kinds of things that could enrich one's life and bring some kind of peace and tranquillity and satisfaction. Music, evidently, was another. One of my early publicity biographies states that she was a singer herself. That's complete nonsense. I suspect that someone asked her a question in such a way that by omission she allowed this misapprehension to continue.

She certainly had big dreams for me. I was going to be either the first Jewish president or a great concert pianist. It's fortunate that my talents were apportioned in such a way that I was able to fulfill at least one of those goals. It doesn't always work out that way.

The piano was purchased for my brother, Ray, five and a half years older than I, who started lessons when he was around nine years old. In those days—the early 1930s—teachers, like doctors, made house calls; they came to you. Ray would come home from school and the teacher would arrive, and I would curl up in a corner of the big sofa in the living room and listen to my brother's lesson. After the teacher left, Ray would go out and play in the park with his friends, and I would go to the piano and redo his entire lesson, copying everything the teacher had asked of him. It wasn't long before my parents decided to switch the lessons to me. That's how it all began. At least, that's how the story goes in our family.

My first teacher was a woman named Lillian Lanier, who taught me the notes and keys, but it was soon obvious to everyone that I needed more of a challenge. Mr. Shorr was supposed to be the best in San Francisco, so off to Mr. Shorr I went. I was, of course, too special to go to regular school like other children. I was enrolled briefly in kindergarten, but it seemed like such a waste of time. We had to take naps every afternoon on straw mats on a hard floor, and I objected to this fairly strenuously. Certainly my mother saw the whole project as detracting from precious hours I might otherwise have spent practicing. Accordingly, I was withdrawn from kindergarten after two weeks and set up with a succession of private tutors in a range of subjects, which constituted my formal education for the rest of my childhood. I've long thought of entitling my autobiography *I Was a Kindergarten Dropout.*

So for the rest of my childhood, my brother, Ray, was the one who went to school and had friends and a normal life. And I was the one who practiced. I can't say it was a happy childhood. Since my mother worked, I was supervised by governesses, like a woman named Muriel Fraser, who was with us for several years. She was a rather uncompromising figure. She used to wallop me with wooden coat hangers across the back of my legs when I wasn't good. She became a nun after she left us.

San Francisco had a considerable musical life when I was a child, even if most of its institutions—the symphony, the opera—were relatively new. Compared with Los Angeles, it was downright cosmopolitan. The San Francisco Symphony was founded in 1911, and the San Francisco Opera in 1923; they both moved into the brand-new War Memorial Opera House in 1932, when I was four. But opera in San Francisco went back a lot farther than that. A notorious episode in American opera history was the 1906 Metropolitan Opera tour that placed Enrico Caruso in San Francisco at exactly the moment of the great earthquake and the ensuing fire, an experience that left the tenor shaken and traumatized and that he used as a reason never to return to San Francisco. Not everyone on the tour had the same reaction. Alfred Hertz, the star conductor on that tour (he described the earthquake as sounding like a "mezzo forte roll on a cymbal or gong"), ultimately developed such a rapport with the city that he settled there in 1915 (the year San Francisco hosted the World's Fair) as the second-ever music director of the fledgling San Francisco Symphony and stayed there for the rest of his life.

Hertz was as bald as a billiard ball, with a formidable dark, bushy beard that was salt-and-pepper gray by the time I knew him and round wire-framed glasses: a bona fide representative of the great European tradition, straight out of the concert halls of Gustav Mahler. His appearance was also notoriously easy to caricature (Caruso left a drawing of him among his affectionate send-ups of his Met Opera colleagues). Crippled as a child by what they used to call infantile paralysis—that is, polio—he walked with a cane for all of his adult life, but this did not diminish his notable vigor. He had a loud laugh, an ear for a joke, and an eye for a pretty girl. "Come for dinner, stay for breakfast!" he used to say, laughing, while his wife, Lilly, made derogatory noises in the background.

He was also a formidable and renowned musician. In the early years of the twentieth century he led a number of world premieres at the Metropolitan Opera, as well as the first American performances of Strauss's *Der Rosenkavalier* and *Salome*. (The opera, based on the Oscar Wilde play and depicting Salome kissing John the Baptist's severed head, created such a scandal in 1907 that it was withdrawn and not performed again until 1934.) Even more notorious, though, was the first American production of Richard Wagner's *Parsifal*. This was a monumental event—front-page news for many American papers—because Wagner had forbidden the performance of the work anywhere other than his own theater in Bayreuth, so the Met's doing it was tantamount to sacrilege in the eyes of many European music lovers. Mind you, the Met production didn't take place until 1903, twenty years after Wagner's death, but the prohibition was actively upheld by Wagner's acolytes, first and foremost his widow, Cosima. Cosima Wagner's clout in Europe was such that after Hertz conducted that *Parsifal*, he never conducted in an opera house in Germany again.

Europe's loss (and the Met's, after Hertz left the company in 1915 over artistic differences with its director) was San Francisco's gain.

Hertz's stature was such that he was able to attract a whole new caliber of player to San Francisco, both as soloists and as orchestra players. The violinist Louis Persinger, for instance, was the concert-master of the Berlin Philharmonic before Hertz lured him to take that position at the San Francisco Symphony. With this kind of musician on its roster, the San Francisco Symphony quickly developed into a serious professional orchestra. It was also, to Hertz's credit, the first American orchestra to admit women as anything other than harpists. And the presence of so many good musicians doubtless contributed to the child-prodigy boom in San Francisco in the 1920s and 1930s. There were a striking number of talented children performing around the city. Persinger himself taught Menuhin, Ruggiero Ricci, and Isaac Stern, among others.

Hertz was also forward-looking. He was committed to education and outreach—words that didn't have as much currency in the classical music world in those days as they do now—and was happy to explore new ways of reaching audiences. In 1922, for example, he was the only conductor willing to gamble on leading a motley series of outdoor orchestra concerts with the brand-new Los Angeles Philharmonic in the Hollywood Hills—the first season of the Hollywood Bowl, a summer series he continued to lead for years as it rapidly became a popular fixture of the country's musical life. He was also eager to explore recording and radio. The San Francisco Symphony became one of the first American orchestras to make commercial recordings, starting in the 1920s. And after he retired from the symphony in 1930, he continued to lead a pioneering series of regular radio broadcasts. He went on in the late 1930s to found the orchestra of the Northern California Chapter of the Works Progress Administration, the WPA.

More to the point, as far as my own story is concerned, was Hertz's eye for young talent. Three young artists were his particular protégés in his San Francisco years. There was Menuhin, who, of course, got everyone's attention in San Francisco when he was young. There was the conductor Leslie Hodge, who led a number of the

WPA Orchestra concerts. And there was me. Most of my first orchestral concerts—at the advanced age of eight and nine years old—were with that WPA orchestra, often performing in schools. I used to play the first or third movement—never, for some reason, the slow movement—of Beethoven's B-flat concerto, the second concerto. They didn't want to tax a child's powers of concentration by making me play, or the students listen to, the whole thing.

In the meantime, the San Francisco Symphony had run into financial difficulties after Hertz left—this was, after all, the beginning of the Great Depression—and had to suspend operations for the 1934–35 season. Finally some of San Francisco's leading citizens managed to convince the French conductor Pierre Monteux to come and resurrect it. This was, arguably, even more of a coup than securing Hertz had been two decades before. Monteux was one of the great French conductors. He had led some of the most important orchestras in the world: the Boston Symphony, the Concertgebouw. He had been the conductor of the legendary Ballets Russes, and conducted the world premiere of Stravinsky's "Rite of Spring" in Paris in 1913, an event that has gone down in music history for having incited a veritable riot among the audience confronted with these horrible modern dissonances and raw rhythms. (Today, of course, "The Rite of Spring" is a classic; a mere twenty-seven years after its premiere, Disney was accompanying it with animated dinosaurs in *Fantasia*.)

A short, tubby man with a tremendous walrus mustache, Monteux immediately became beloved in San Francisco. He and his wife, Doris, had two French poodles, and when he walked them in the city people used to hang out of the cable cars to greet him. Sometimes, the story goes, the conductors used to salute him with the opening notes of Beethoven's Fifth Symphony.

Monteux, too, had an eye for young talent—he gave Isaac Stern his orchestral debut with the San Francisco Symphony in 1936, when Stern was sixteen. And he took a great, avuncular interest in me. He was generous enough to call me the "pianistic find of the century," something that has been so abundantly quoted in the years since he said it that I half suspect it of being apocryphal. In my later years, I am constantly encountering people filled with wonderful humorous anecdotes about me and my life. These are tarnished only by the fact that I have no memory of these events whatsoever. They say that I said it. Whether or not you believe them is up to you.

My mother certainly had a hand in my meeting these distinguished conductors. She was eager to show off her gifted son to anybody who might be able to further his career. She was altogether enterprising in moving me along. When I was no more than five or six, she took me to the War Memorial Opera House to hear a recital by the great composer-pianist Sergei Rachmaninoff. I think we sat in the last balcony, miles from the stage. I remember nothing about the concert, but after it was over, when the encores started, my mother grabbed me by the hand and swiftly negotiated a labyrinthine network of passages and stairways until we had made our way backstage and ended up standing in the wings, right next to the curtain by which the great man walked on and off stage. The encores went on and on. Rachmaninoff was always called back for lots of encores; it was his custom to signal that they were over by playing his famous Prelude in C-sharp Minor, which everyone in the audience knew would be the last one. I was struck that when he emerged into the view of the public, walking out to the piano, he moved very slowly, but when he came offstage again, as soon as he was safely hidden from view behind the curtain, he walked with striking briskness. After the fourth or fifth encore—well before the C-sharp Minor prelude had made its appearance—he noticed me, and came over to where we were standing. He was a very tall man. He pointed his finger almost in my face and said, in a heavy Russian accent, "You pianist?"

I looked up into his face, which was like a map of Russia, crisscrossed with crevasses and ravines and great plains. Speechless, I could only nod my head.

"Ah," said Rachmaninoff, looking down at me. "Bad business. Bad business."

And with these edifying words of advice, he strode back out on stage for the next encore.

Rachmaninoff didn't want to be a performing pianist. He wanted to stay home and compose. He couldn't, though, because he had to make a living. The year I met him was the year he wrote the "Rhapsody on a Theme of Paganini," which would be the first piece of his I would play and which was featured on one of my first commercial recordings. But he wasn't quite as encouraging to me as my mother had hoped.

I gave my first public recital when I was eight years old, at the San Francisco Community Playhouse. Mr. Shorr prepared me strenuously for the great event. I remember that he had me play a Toccata in A by an obscure eighteenth-century composer named Domenico Paradies, who was fated to be remembered principally for this single movement from his sixth keyboard sonata. But my further memories of that occasion are hazy. There's a reason for this, since as I was proceeding from the darkness of backstage out into the bright lights in front of the audience, my mother reached out her hand and whipped the glasses from my face. She wasn't going to have her precious son reveal any imperfections to the audience. The rest of the evening passed, quite literally, in a blur.

Though my mother read books on Mozart to prepare her for life with her wunderkind, she wasn't solely responsible for my moving ahead. A talented little boy has a way of attracting people as a kind of project. A publicity agent named Julie Medlock began working with us and got a certain amount of press about me in the papers. This, in turn, occasioned some interest at Temple Emanu-El, where, although we didn't actually attend services, we had a membership so I could use the gym facilities and the pool. The cantor there, Reuben Rinder, played an active role over the years in San Francisco's musical life. It was he who allegedly suggested to the seven-year-old Isaac Stern that he might want to switch instruments from piano to violin; he also had a hand in finding sponsors for both Stern and Menuhin among the wealthier members of the congregation (though Stern's parents were so careful to have their gifted child lead a normal life that his sponsor thought he wasn't serious enough about his music and, with a singular lack of prescience, dropped him). One of the temple's congregants, a woman named Amy Goldsmith, thought Cantor Rinder might take an interest in me, too; the cantor knew both Hertz and Monteux, and that's how my first meeting with both of those eminent conductors was set up.

Hertz's verdict, after hearing me play a few times, was that I should have more training in the German school—which represented the ne plus ultra of musical attainment at that time, as well as the German-born maestro's own natural predilections. Accordingly, I started working with a sequence of interim teachers. I studied for a short period with a Danish virtuoso named Gunnar Johansen, an eccentric and rather brilliant composer-pianist who ended up as a champion of the maverick Ferruccio Busoni, also a composer-pianist, who sought to discover a new musical language in his experimental, often symbol-laden works. I always looked forward to my lessons with Johansen, because he lived across the bay, in Oakland, and having a lesson meant taking the ferry across. The San Francisco Bay Bridge was just being completed—it opened in late 1936, six months before the Golden Gate Bridge—and there was a huge amount of ferry traffic: hundreds of crossings every day, boats steaming across the harbor carrying thousands of people, passing the steamships from China, and the freighters, under the raucous cries of the gulls. It was all too exciting for words.

But Johansen wasn't really set up to be a long-term teacher. In 1937, Hertz met a young refugee from Germany named Ludwig Altman. Actually, Lilly Hertz met him by chance at a dance recital in which Monteux's daughter was performing; Altman evidently said something she interpreted as being mildly disparaging about the Monteux clan, and she took this as a sign of allegiance to her own husband. Hertz and Monteux were quite friendly; nonetheless, Monteux was Hertz's successor, and Lilly, who was fiercely loyal, took props for her husband where she could find them. She invited Altman over, where he impressed Hertz with his performance of a Brahms sonata, and Hertz thereafter set about finding what opportunities he could for a penniless émigré. Altman eventually became the organist for Temple Emanu-El, where he stayed for many years. But Hertz also recommended him as my teacher, and for a year he came to our apartment on Fulton Street almost every day.

Altman was a lovely, gentle man, short, stocky, and mild-mannered. His whole approach was different from the Russian-hammer school I had been drilled in. He spoke about a loosening of physical tension, a relaxation at the instrument. He helped my playing lose some of the vinegar it had developed under Shorr. He also talked about things like expressivity, and even larger concepts: the nobility and the transcendence of music and how it was the expression of the good in people. He spoke of mythology, the gods, the Holy Grail, awakening a sense of idealism and yearning and seeking: the kind of things that give a young person a sense of purpose, of goals in life.

I loved working with him, and I covered a tremendous amount of repertory in that year: Liszt, Bach's "Well-Tempered Clavier," Mendelssohn's "Variations sérieuses." And of course we did some Beethoven sonatas. I was up for anything. I had a huge musical appetite. I could memorize a Beethoven sonata overnight, a feat that astonished Altman no end. He had a quiet sense of humor. I remember him coming for a lesson one day when I had a cold. He asked how my cold was, and I said it was bad. "Oh, that's good," he said. "If the cold is doing badly, that means you're doing better. You'll be fit as a fiddle in no time."

"Fit as a piano!" I said, laughing.

Altman, though, wasn't the teacher my two conductor mentors really wanted for me. They both thought I should study with the great pianist Artur Schnabel. Schnabel was already a legend, seen by many as the greatest living exponent of the German repertoire. He specialized in Mozart, Schubert (he was the first pianist to perform most of Schubert's sonatas in public), and particularly Beethoven (he was the first pianist to record all thirty-two of the Beethoven sonatas). In place of flashy showmanship he offered, in his performances, a kind of deep spiritual, musical understanding, a constant level of inspiration. There was not a single phrase that did not speak in the most eloquent way. He was also a renowned teacher and a personal friend of the Hertzes.

The only problem was that he wouldn't take any students under the age of sixteen. When the idea of working with me was presented to him, he kindly but firmly said no: a nine-year-old like me wasn't able to understand his language or the level of abstraction on which he talked. He wasn't the kind of teacher who worked on technique with youngsters; his lessons were about ideas, penetrating into the depths of music. So he politely declined.

Schnabel, however, came regularly to San Francisco to perform. After his concerts, he would dine with the Hertzes at their home on Sea Cliff and then play bridge. Dining at the Hertzes was a mixed blessing. Lilly Hertz had been a singer before she married Alfred—a pretty terrible singer, to judge from the few times I heard her hooting away at Strauss's song "Traum durch die Dämmerung," with her silver ringlets quivering around her face—but she represented none of the excesses generally associated with the breed. That is, far from enjoying the luxuries of life, she was a devout Christian Scientist, and she didn't really think even food was all that necessary. She was always on the lookout for Alfred's health by doing things like forbidding him to drink coffee, which he dearly loved. And her portions, when she served meals, were so modest that guests were well advised to eat before they came. Still, Schnabel and his wife, Therese—who was herself an extraordinary musician and singer, far out of Lilly's league—were regular guests.

Lilly, not altogether unlike my mother, thought she knew what was best for people. She was always advising Ludwig Altman about prospective brides. In my case, she was convinced that what would be best was to study with Schnabel. Thus, she hatched a plan. In the spring of 1938, Schnabel was coming through town to play with the symphony under Monteux. Schnabel might decline to work with me when approached in a letter, but surely he would not be so uncivil as to refuse to hear me if I was actually in the room with him, and once he heard me—so Lilly thought—there was no question but that he would accept. The trick was to figure out how to get me there. The Hertzes' home had a basement garage with an entrance into the house, and on the appointed night my mother and I were snuck in through this access while the couples were still at table. Moving stealthily, speaking in whispers, I was set up in my place at the grand piano, so that when the doors to the dining room were opened after the meal, preparatory to the bridge game, there I was.

Schnabel was a consummate gentleman: an august, stocky figure, short yet solid, with a halo of close-cropped white hair shining around his head. And Lilly Hertz had been quite right. He was too polite to show the door to an adorable nine-year-old boy.

"Isn't it rather late for you to be up?" he asked me, with a smile. Then he graciously took a seat and submitted to the inevitable.

So I played for Artur Schnabel.

I started with the cadenza to the Beethoven B-flat concerto, which I had played so often in WPA concerts. The B-flat concerto is called the second of Beethoven's five concertos, though it was actually written first (one of the many vagaries of musical cataloguing); in any case, it's an early work. The cadenza is another matter. A cadenza, in a concerto, is an elaborate solo passage inserted near the end of a movement, and in the late eighteenth century, when Beethoven wrote his B-flat concerto, it was nearly always improvised. Later, though, composers began writing out cadenzas, and Beethoven, in the early 1800s, went back and committed to paper some cadenzas for his earlier concertos. The B-flat cadenza, therefore, has considerably more maturity—and technical range, starting with a miniature fugue—than the body of the concerto. Not only is it showy, but it gets very satisfyingly stormy in places, and it comes to a resounding finish.

I then played the third of Liszt's Petrarch sonnets, which are piano transcriptions of pieces he originally wrote as songs and later, in their piano version, incorporated into his large-scale compendium "Années de pèlerinage," Years of Pilgrimage, a musical autobiography depicting the vignettes and landscapes of three years of his life. Sonnet 123 is an evocation of the beauty of the poet's beloved, Laura, after her death; Liszt's music takes the dreamy, aching, wistful vision of the original into sound, sweet and intense and otherworldly. There's a place where the tune comes back high in the treble, kind of like angels speaking. Liszt is a composer of many moods and is well known for pieces of breathtaking virtuosity, but this piece, by contrast, shows his poetic side, a musical world Altman's lessons had started to open for me. It was a fine piece for a kid. It ignited the imagination. I put my whole heart into playing it.

Schnabel listened, and nodded, and smiled, revealing even teeth stained from many years of smoking cigars.

Then he asked me to sight-read.

Schnabel had devoted many years to producing a definitive edition of Beethoven's thirty-two piano sonatas. After some rummaging, the Hertzes located the volume that he was looking for, a yellow-bound score of the second sonata, Op. 2, No. 2. Schnabel opened it to the third movement and placed it before me on the piano.

My veins were filled with adrenaline. I had just played my heart out. With every atom of my nine-year-old being, I wanted to study with Artur Schnabel. I could memorize a sonata overnight. But I was an atrocious sight reader. For the life of me, I couldn't navigate the unfamiliar notes on the page in front of me.

So Schnabel gently sat down beside me on the piano bench and showed me how the piece should go. The great Artur Schnabel, sitting next to me, was playing a Beethoven scherzo, giving a lilt to its light-hearted opening, moving on into more darkly shaded areas, returning to the lilt, playing light as air and with a twinkle in his eye. It was one of the most extraordinary musical experiences of my short life.

Then he got up and signed the cover of the score and gave it to me as a souvenir. And sight-reading or no sight-reading, he invited me to come to Italy that summer, to study with him at his vacation home.

Thus I began ten years of work with one of the great hearts and minds of music.

Schnabel had one condition: no more performances. It was a small enough price to pay to be admitted into what I saw, even then, as the Elysian Fields of Schnabel's elect. I gave my farewell performance in San Francisco at the age of nine in the spring of 1938, with Hertz conducting me in the final movement, yet again, of the Beethoven B-flat concerto.

By now I was an old hand. I came out on stage and bowed and sat at the piano. Silence fell over the hall. The final movement of the B-flat concerto opens with the piano alone, playing a sprightly, rollicking, slightly off-kilter tune and leading the whole orchestra in after it. There was only one problem: I couldn't remember how the piece began.

I must have been the picture of poise: a little boy with curly hair and wide dark eyes behind his round glasses, dressed in short pants and a crisp white shirt, bowed in concentration over the piano. But inside, I was consumed with sheer terror. How, how, how? How does it start? The silence lengthened, ominously. When you're on stage, a few seconds of silence feels like an eternity. This was considerably more than a few seconds, and I felt it pressing down on my shoulders.

Finally, in panic, I had an idea: maybe if I just put my fingers up on the keyboard, they'd know what to do. I lifted my hands slowly to the keyboard (the audience was surely, by this point, deeply impressed by my precocious genius). And by a miracle, it worked. By themselves, on their own, my fingers found the right configuration of black and white keys, and I let them go. Before I knew it, they had jumped into the opening theme, and the orchestra soon came galloping up behind them, and the performance was, as it usually was, a great success.

So I ended my first career.

CHAPTER 2

STUDENT
OF
SCHNABEL

With Artur Schnabel at Lake Como, 1938.
(Author's collection)

My mother had had enough.

First, she had had to acquire a steamer trunk and pack up for a whole summer in Europe with her nine-year-old son. Then there was traveling across the country to New York, and there was almost missing the boat to Italy when the taxi cab broke down in the Holland Tunnel on the way to the New Jersey port where we embarked, so that we had to be towed out. There was the voyage over. That part wasn't so bad. We traveled on the *Conte di Savoia*, a flagship of the Italian Line, an exceptionally beautiful ocean liner that strove to bring a resort climate to its passengers. For me, of course, being on an ocean liner was exciting beyond words. The *Conte di Savoia* had a gyroscope device in a forward hold that was supposed to regulate the vessel and stop it from rocking too much in high seas. That was pretty fascinating to a nine-year-old boy.

For my mother, things didn't get any easier once we landed, arriving in a country where she had no knowledge of the language. Not that that fazed her; still, there was a lot to be done. There was traveling up to Tremezzo, a little town on Lake Como's steep, tree-clad western shore (a journey that was accomplished by a whole armada of pianos for Schnabel's students, transported up from Milan every summer). There was setting up temporary accommodations in a strange place—a hotel in the little town of Cadenabbia, just north of Tremezzo—and then there was spending several months there, with no real activity of her own. And there was keeping tabs on her son, who could be quite a handful, when he wasn't occupied with his practicing or taking lessons with the Greatest Musician in the World.

At times, I think, she got a little fed up.

One afternoon we were taking a walk along the lake, which snakes like an inverted Y through the green foothills beneath the looming Alps. The road ran right along the water, past outdoor tables and docks and a little place where you could rent rowboats. And there was Stefan Schnabel, the Great Man's son, preparing to go out for a row with Sylvia Kunin, one of his father's more comely students.

Stefan was an actor. He had been appearing at the Old Vic, in London, ever since the Schnabels had settled on London as their winter residence, after the family left Berlin in 1933 in response to the rising tide of anti-Jewish policies. (Schnabel had seen the writing on the wall as his engagements gradually dried up. The last straw was a call from the director of a Brahms festival who had booked Schnabel well in advance, shamefacedly informing the pianist that his presence would no longer be required. Schnabel set his jaw and quipped, "Though I may not be pure-blooded, I am fortunately cold-blooded," after which he left Germany forever.) Stefan was the spitting image of his father, though a good bit taller. At the Old Vic, he appeared with Olivier in *Hamlet* (in the tiny role of Lucianus) and got to know George Bernard Shaw, and he went on to work in America on radio (in Orson Welles's "War of the Worlds," among other things), in Hollywood, on Broadway, and on the soap opera *The Guiding Light* for seventeen years. But that summer afternoon on Lake Como, his immediate ambition was to go out on the lake with Sylvia and make out.

My mother, however, had other plans. Seeing the rowboat ready to embark, she more or less picked me up, deposited me in the vessel, and said, "Here, take him with you. Give him a ride."

Stefan was less than thrilled at having me suddenly injected into the middle of his date with Sylvia. He started rowing with somewhat bad grace, leaving my mother behind us, liberated, on the lake's western shore. I can't remember if I did anything to provoke him. But I do remember that when we got nearly across the lake, by Bellagio, he picked me up unceremoniously by the scruff of the neck and dumped me in the water.

Well. My mother may have been fed up with me, but she was like a mother tiger when someone attacked her cub. The next day, she marched up to Schnabel and gave him an earful about his son's behavior toward her precious charge. She certainly wasn't shy about expressing herself, Great Man or no Great Man. Schnabel was very charming to her, though his twinkling smile was, I think, mainly occasioned by his profound amusement at the whole incident.

There was no lasting bad blood between me and Stefan. In a group photo from that summer, he is standing behind me, one arm around Sylvia's waist, with his bare foot on my shoulder keeping me in my place.

I was, of course, the youngest of all the students. Next oldest was Noel Mewton-Wood, a British sixteen-year-old with technique to burn—now forgotten because he killed himself at thirty-one, drinking poison after his closest friend (doubtless his lover, though one didn't say so in those days) died of a ruptured appendix. Closest to me, though, was Maria Curcio, nineteen, another of Schnabel's younger protégés, who had been working with him for several years. Sparkling, warm, petite, and very Italian, she took me under her wing as a kind of surrogate big sister, as she would later do to most of the world's greatest pianists, who came to play for her and get her feedback in her studios in Holland and London throughout her long life.

There were plenty of others. There was the lovely Helen Fogel, already an established concert artist at twenty-seven, who was soon to marry Schnabel's oldest son, Karl Ulrich. There was Karl Ulrich himself, a wonderfully gifted pianist, tall and gentle, with kind eyes behind wire-rimmed glasses, who would act as my second teacher for many years. There was Sylvia from the rowboat, who later decided her hands were too small for piano and became a producer of television shows about classical music. There was Peter Diamand, a former schoolmate of Stefan's who had also fled Berlin, now Schnabel's imperturbable amanuensis. Bucktoothed, skinny, and bespectacled, he had a Leslie Howard–like charm, wit, and gentleness that had women flocking around him wherever he went; he later married Maria Curcio, ran the Edinburgh Festival, and dallied with Marlene Dietrich and another Maria: Callas.

There was Konrad Wolff, a German Jewish lawyer who loved music so intensely that he finally quit the law and devoted himself to it full time. Wolff had come so late to piano—in part because of his father's opposition to his studies—that there was no question of his becoming a professional pianist. But he was encyclopedically knowledgeable about music and already had the makings of the fine teacher and significant musicologist he would become, serving as a chronicler of Schnabel's lessons for future generations.

There was Schnabel's illegitimate daughter, who showed up in his life one year with a son in tow and was warmly welcomed into the family. There were a handful of other students from around Europe.

And there was me.

I turned ten that summer on Lake Como. I learned to ride a bicycle there, wobbling down the narrow roads—and once, when a truck came up beside me, freaking out and falling so hard that I needed stitches on my chin from a doctor who was slightly inebriated from his lunchtime wine. I still have the scar to show for it.

And I started on a journey of learning about music from the source of the German piano tradition.

There's a genealogy of pianists and their teachers, like the "begat"s in the Bible. Beethoven taught Carl Czerny, who became famous for his exercises for improving piano technique. Czerny taught a whole roster of notable students, including Franz Liszt and Theodor Leschetizky. Leschetizky, a brilliant teacher, taught Paderewski, the phenomenally popular virtuoso of the late nineteenth and early twentieth century who became prime minister of his native Poland, and he taught the young Artur Schnabel. And Schnabel, of course, taught me.

So in the family tree of teacher-student relationships, I am in a line going back to Beethoven.

That isn't all that extraordinary, though. Leschetizky is the weak link in that chain. He taught everybody. I've called him a "teaching ho." There are thousands of descendants of Beethoven walking the streets of this planet today as a result of Leschetizky and his unstinting labors. So I can't really claim to be anything special on that account.

Schnabel was solid and short—he stood all of five foot four—with a mischievous smile and an ineffable personal magnetism. Like many other Europeans of that generation who came to English later in life, he spoke slowly and carefully, letting the words roll around in his mouth as if savoring their taste. He sounded like Richard Burton with a German accent. "First hear, then play," he would say. To some people, it sounded backward: he must have meant it the other way round. But he was being absolutely precise. What he meant was that we needed to form an idea of what we wanted the music to sound like before even touching our fingers to the keys. You must have in your inner ear the exact sound you're going for. Once you put down a note without purpose or without intention, you can't retrieve it. Then you are left having to build the rest of your performance on an accident.

His aphoristic style and his precise diction only emphasized the sense that what he was offering you was the pure distillation of piano wisdom. His teaching method was to give you a whole lifetime's worth of experience about whatever piece you brought in. Once. It was up to you to figure out what to make of it.

Schnabel wasn't a flashy virtuoso. He was simply the greatest musician at the keyboard I've ever heard. His playing had an irresistible élan—what the Germans call Schwung—as if he were grabbing you and twirling you in a dance. For many musicians, the beats in a measure can become aggressive, downward events, like nails driven into a coffin. Bang, bang, bang, bang. One! Two! Three! Four! For Schnabel, they were an upward impetus, like springs, launching you forward to the next point. His playing defied gravity in that way. It caught you up and didn't let you down until the piece was over. Some people felt he had a tendency to rush, because his playing was so inexorably propelled by this sense of forward motion.

His performances were never about him. They were all about the composer. In an era when the cult of personality was still flourishing, Schnabel was insistent that a performer serve the score. He abhorred any kind of showmanship. Indeed, his programs—a whole evening of Beethoven or Schubert, without a single crowd-pleasing bonbon like a Chopin mazurka or Liszt operatic paraphrase—were often considered boring, particularly in the United States, where he was long seen as something of an acquired taste. He certainly didn't pander to his listeners. Once he told his wife that he felt sorry for the audience during a recital he gave of Beethoven's Diabelli Variations. He was the one enjoying it, and he was the one getting paid, while his listeners, who had paid to hear it, had to sit through it and suffer.

His wife, Therese, the singer, played a considerable role in Schnabel's musical formation. She was six years older and a head taller than her husband, with a sharp-faced look that belied her inner warmth, and she was an extraordinary musician herself. Schnabel used to say that everything he had learned about music he learned from Therese; I don't think he was just being gallant. In her prime, she had a rich contralto—Richard Strauss wrote the song "Traum durch die Dämmerung" for her—and though that wasn't much in evidence by the time I met her, she still taught a number of students (including the British tenor Peter Pears). She and her husband had often performed together in the early years of their marriage, particularly specializing in Schubert lieder (Schnabel also composed a number of songs for her himself). And she listened with a sharp ear to his playing. There's a story about Schnabel, relatively late in his career, obsessively practicing "Träumerei," one of the best-known sections of Robert Schumann's piano cycle "Kinderszenen"—a piece so easy that it can be played by intermediate piano students. Suddenly, from another part of the house, Therese shouted, "Artur—you've got it! You've been playing it wrong for forty years!" What's notable, of course, is not only that Therese was attuned to such minute details but that Schnabel was so intently revisiting the piece in the first place.

But that was Schnabel's attitude. He wanted to penetrate to the heart of a score and understand what the composer really wanted. He was most interested in works that allowed him to keep asking questions, probing, exploring—"music," as he used to say, "that is better than it can be performed." Early in his career, he had a fairly large repertory, including plenty of Chopin and Liszt. By the time I met him, though, he was focusing mainly on Mozart, Beethoven, and Schubert, simply because he thought they were the best. Beethoven remained his calling card. He played all thirty-two of the sonatas in a series of concerts in Berlin in 1927, the centennial of Beethoven's death, and while he wasn't the first pianist to perform them as a cycle, he was certainly the first to record them, a project that took him about ten years. He also prepared the edition of the sonatas I mentioned before: the printed scores, that is, with his own exhaustive annotations as well as Beethoven's own markings. Schnabel's comments are in slightly smaller type.

"You are not a pianist," Leschetizky once told Schnabel. "You are a musician." It was rather an ambiguous compliment, but it wasn't off the mark. Pianists, in Leschetizky's parlance, came out of the nineteenth-century tradition of solo virtuosos, which involved a lot of glamour and glitz, performances that showcased technical feats and fireworks, and performers who weren't above modifying a composer's score with their own embellishments to enhance their own effect. Schnabel, by contrast, really cared only about the music. Leschetizky, accordingly, gave him pieces like the subtle, dreamy sonatas of Franz Schubert—sonatas that, at the time, virtually nobody performed. He called them "food for a musician." Schnabel became a veritable Schubert pioneer, the first to offer much of his piano music in any serious way in public performance.

Soloists didn't play chamber music, either—that was something for people who weren't good enough to play alone. But Schnabel played chamber music all the time. He formed his first professional trio in 1902. It was a smashing success, and over the years until the 1930s there were to be four different incarnations of the Schnabel Trio, including such luminaries as the violinist Carl Flesch and the cellist Gregor Piatigorsky. As I said, Schnabel also accompanied his wife in song recitals, an activity that many solo pianists used to consider beneath them. At a performance shortly before their marriage in 1905, they programmed the Hugo Wolf song "Mein Liebster ist so klein," my beloved is so small, which Therese sang with a pointed grin at her accompanist. The audience ate it up.

But Schnabel's main interest was his own composing. For his entire life, he thought of himself as primarily a composer, not a pianist. His music is startling. You might think he would have emulated the Classical composers he loved, but Schnabel the composer was very much a child of his time. He actually did play some contemporary music, especially earlier in his career. He was certainly friends with a number of contemporary composers, starting in the days when he and Richard Strauss played skat—Strauss's favorite card game and lifelong passion—in the early years of the century in Berlin. In the 1940s, he became very close to the Czech émigré Ernst Krenek and the American composer Roger Sessions. (Sessions once asked him why he didn't play the music of Arnold Schoenberg, since he admired it so much. Schnabel's response was that he played only music that was problematic for him, and Schoenberg's was not.) And there is a picture of him and Paul Hindemith on the floor, heads to the ground, watching one of Hindemith's less-known passions: his model trains, passing them on their tiny tracks.

Given all this, it is less surprising that Schnabel's music is so very much a product of the twentieth century. It is advanced, sophisticated, intense, and almost entirely atonal. It's wonderful, passionate music, and it's huge. His second symphony lasts an hour; some of his five string quartets—a core part of his output, each of them an outburst of humanity—are forty-five minutes long. Unfortunately, whether because his music is too challenging, is too long, or lacks the right champions, Schnabel as performer has trumped Schnabel as composer in the eyes of posterity, and his music, these days, is largely neglected.

More proof that Schnabel was more a musician than a pianist is that he wasn't really concerned with piano technique per se. This was one reason he didn't work with children: he didn't want to spend time teaching the basic mechanics. He expected his students to have mastered the mere physical requirements of playing already. He might give a suggestion if I was having trouble with a particular passage—if he saw that my intention was good but that I couldn't figure out how to reproduce the sound I was going for. He'd say, Hold your hand this way, or, Try this fingering, or, Use your arm. But he didn't go into much more detail than that, and he certainly didn't offer any tips about how to practice. What he really wanted to talk about was the music itself. Technique was almost beside the point.

Indeed, Schnabel's own playing was far from note-perfect. There's a story that when his original Beethoven sonata recordings were being remastered for transfer to LP, a technician decided to patch up the missed notes in the repeated sections by splicing the master tape, duplicating passages Schnabel had played accurately and inserting them to cover up the sections where he had not. There are plenty of repeats in the Beethoven sonatas, so the technician figured that since the notes were the same, there was no problem. But Schnabel never repeated a passage with the same shadings of meaning or nuance, and the patchwork that resulted from the technician's labors had lost all relation to the artist's conception of the piece. The technician was told by his boss, in no uncertain terms, to "put those goddamn clinkers back!"

At the age of ten, I still needed a certain amount of instruction in the basics, so Schnabel always assigned me to other teachers—his students and former students, and especially his son Karl Ulrich—in addition to his own lessons. In the group lessons, precisely because he talked so little about technique, our eyes were always glued to his hands on the keyboard whenever he played to demonstrate something for us. My hands gradually loosened and relaxed, my fingers losing their tension and yet extending farther across the keys, through watching what he did.

Once, when I was in my teens, I got to hear Schnabel rehearse the Adagio of Mozart's piano concerto K. 467 (nicknamed "Elvira Madigan" because of its use on the soundtrack of a now forgotten Swedish film of that name in the 1960s) with the Chicago Symphony. It's an angelic theme, and the way Schnabel played it, it was suspended in midair. It sounded like the language of the spheres. It involved silence, and an expressivity that was somehow universal. That was Schnabel's power. He was able to achieve that with just about anything he played. Hearing that rehearsal, even knowing Schnabel's playing, at that point, fairly intimately, I felt as if the top of my head were being lifted off. I had an actual loss of balance. It was one of the most moving experiences of my life, and in a way that rehearsal has guided my life ever since. This, for me, is what music is about.

Summer days in Lake Como. Two or three times a week, we would climb the two hundred steps up to the Villa Ginetta, the Schnabels' home, perched above the opulent gardens of Tremezzo's Grand Hotel. In the ground-floor living room, its windows open to the sun but swathed in heavy velvet drapes to dampen the echo off the room's white marble, were two Bechsteins, Schnabel's piano of choice. Schnabel always taught with two pianos. Generally, the students would play one, and he would sit and comment, and elucidate, at the other (though if one of us was working on a concerto, the second piano might function as a stand-in for the orchestra, with another student playing the orchestral parts). Schnabel's lessons were all group lessons: everyone heard everything. It was an eminently reasonable way to teach, because it meant you got a far wider exposure to repertoire than you would have in a private lesson. You got the feedback not only on what you were playing but on what everybody else was playing, and thus you began to get an overview of music.

Furthermore, no student ever brought the same piece twice. The way Schnabel taught, there was no point, because he said what he had to say about the piece when you played it for him, and you were expected to absorb that. And he could say a lot. The first time I played Beethoven's "Les Adieux" sonata for him—that's Op. 81a, No. 26 of the thirty-two—we stayed on the opening Adagio, three lines of music, for three and a half hours.

It was a tremendous amount of information to take in. We didn't have any pocket recorders in those days to capture what he said, and every word was pure gold. We'd desperately try to write it all down, sitting hunched over our scores scribbling away with our pencils. He found that an amusing sight because, as he pointed out, his comments were directed at a specific student's performance of the piece, and if another student played it for him, he might say something quite different. It was true, too, that if you did bring him a piece a second time, after an appropriate interval had passed—say, a year or two—he usually had completely different things to say about it.

That didn't matter. We wanted it all. We would stagger out of the lessons like drunkards, reeling from the excitement, the information, the inspiration. I felt transported out of myself. It was a high far beyond anything else in my experience—even performing. It took you onto a different plane. It was very heady stuff.

It wasn't all in exalted musical jargon, either. Far from it. A lot of feelings were discussed. We talked about the meaning of musical markings like "maestoso" (Italian for "majestically," the marking on the opening of the Brahms D Minor concerto) or "marziale" (martial or military, a directive Liszt gives in both of his concertos), and that led us to ideas about heroism. We also talked about music that was plaintive or sad. The focus was on seeking and defining sentiment while avoiding sentimentality. This was a key distinction. Sentimentality was equated with bathos. It cheapened noble feeling. The point was to be clear and honest and exact.

Schnabel conveyed his meanings in images that were especially powerful to a child. At one point in a Brahms piece, he said the playing should be like liquid gold. In the third movement of Beethoven's Opus 109, a set of variations, he said that one of the variations was like juggling balls of cotton. In the middle of that movement, there's an empty octave, the same note played in upper and lower registers, with no notes in between to fill in the chord. Schnabel said that was like a deathly stare, because it was startling and hollow. All of this brought the music alive for me in a new way.

I was absorbing everything like a sponge. I first brought to Schnabel Schubert's sonata in A Major, D. 664. (Schubert's music was catalogued in 1951 by a musicologist named Otto Deutsch, and therefore each of his pieces has a "D" number indicating its approximate position in the chronology of his short life. Deutsch was following the example of Ludwig, Ritter von Köchel, who published a catalogue of Mozart's music in 1862; Mozart's pieces are all indicated with "K" numbers, the "Köchelverzeichnis," or Köchel listing.) I later worked on the Liszt A Major concerto, some Chopin, a few Beethoven sonatas, and a large amount of Brahms.

In short, I was being schooled in what Schnabel thought of as great music. And learning Beethoven, Mozart, Schubert directly from the master gave me an exalted sense of myself as a musician: whatever anyone else said, I had the true Word, straight from the source. By some standards, it was a slightly one-sided diet. Schnabel had decided tastes. I remember he enjoyed Bartók when a student brought his works to a lesson. But it was years before I was introduced to the sensuality and color of some of the great French composers, like Ravel. I played some Debussy for Schnabel, but he didn't enjoy it. He wanted music built on logical structures and underpinnings rather than music that wafted past in an expressive haze. And he didn't have much time for the Russian school at all. I recall his distress when I assaulted him in one lesson with Rachmaninoff's "Rhapsody on a Theme of Paganini," and then when I had the effrontery to bring the same piece in again a year later, because I had been too lazy to learn anything new, he was really quite unhappy with me. "Why do you bring this to me!" he said. "You know I don't like this music!"

Yet though Schnabel could be strict, I don't recall him ever saying a destructive word. His teaching style had evidently changed considerably over the years. There were two great North American piano talents who went to study with Schnabel in the early 1930s, when he taught at the conservatory in Berlin: Aube Tzerko and Leonard Shure. Their tales of his teaching, which I heard years later, described a person I didn't know. Schnabel, in his Berlin classes, was sarcastic, disdainful, and imperious. "He could be brutally cruel and unbelievably kind," Leonard once said; a year into his work with Schnabel, he could barely play at all. Schnabel left terrible psychological imprints on these people: Aube developed some kind of hand problem and never performed much. Both of them, though, became sought-after teachers who practiced the kind of aggressive tough-love approach they had gotten from Schnabel, cultivating a worshipful, distant love-hate relationship with their students.

I don't know what made Schnabel change. I can't believe it was just the sunshine of Italy and the beauty of Lake Como that transformed him as a human being. But to us, he was twinkle-eyed and smiling. He might become impatient if we were slow to grasp what he was saying, but he was never cruel. And those of us who worked with him in this later stage of his life, in Italy and, later, in New York, followed this later model and became much more supportive, embracing teachers.

The lesson would last as long as it needed to; there was no fixed time, but it seldom ended before two in the afternoon. Afterwards, there was a certain amount of decompression. Some of the older students would join Schnabel for a game of tennis, which Schnabel loved; access to the tennis courts of the Grand Hotel was one of the perks of the Villa Ginetta. Schnabel was also a passionate hiker, though he saved most of his excursions for his annual vacation in Switzerland in August. There were meals on the terrace; there were walks with the Schnabel family dog, Mecki (or Mackie). One afternoon, when I was out walking with Schnabel, I, a city child, saw a live pig for the first time; Schnabel had to tell me what it was. Of course, we also had to practice.

Schnabel had a little more time than usual to compose that summer. The group of students was smaller than it had been in Tremezzo summers past. It was the summer of 1938, a summer of brewing unease. Schnabel's native Austria had been annexed by Germany in the spring, and now the international powers were trying to pacify the megalomania of Hitler, who was about to annex part of Czechoslovakia in the fall. That summer Mussolini issued his Manifesto of Race, which deprived Jews of their Italian citizenship. Schnabel didn't know it, but it was to be his last summer in Tremezzo for many years. Within a year, Schnabel and his family had settled in New York.

So when the summer ended, my mother and I went to New York, too.

My mother, at this point, had one goal in life: to help further my studies. She was ready to do whatever it took. When we first met Schnabel, we learned that he charged the enormous sum of $50 a lesson. There was no way my family could afford that. My mother had promptly marshaled her resources and sent out feelers through a network of friends, and had managed to locate a patron for me. His name was James David Zellerbach, and he was the head of Crown Zellerbach, which was the largest papermaking corporation in the country. It was a big fortune. J.D. agreed to sponsor my student years with Schnabel. He gave my mother a monthly stipend, and that took care of the cost of my lessons and other things related to our needs. Before he met me, I don't think J.D. had much connection to music at all, but after getting involved with us he began to take a more and more active interest—not so much in me as in music in general. He eventually became the president of the board of the San Francisco Symphony, as well as the American ambassador to Italy. I like to think I made his life a little more colorful by bringing music into it.

Money was one thing; geography was another. My mother saw that I clearly needed to be near Schnabel, and Schnabel, when he was in the country, was in New York. Therefore we were going to settle in New York. Of course, there was the slight difficulty that my father's business, the source of our family income, which he had built up over so many years, was in San Francisco. This wasn't an obstacle for my mother. For a year or so, she and I lived in an apartment on West Seventy-ninth Street while she and he tried to figure out a solution that would bring the whole family together. The solution was really very simple, from my mother's point of view. My father closed up his shops in San Francisco and he and Ray, who was in high school, came to New York. My father would have liked to start another store in New York, but everything was so different there that he ended up going into a factory, making hats for someone else. Eventually he started his own factory, which was a grueling amount of work. I was quite aware that all of this change and upheaval in our family life was my responsibility. It was a heavy burden for a ten-year-old.

My brother, Ray, however, fit right into his new surroundings. I don't think he minded too much that I got all the attention in the family. It left him free to do what he wanted. He was a star of the basketball team, so he had a huge circle of friends, both boys and girls, while I was cloistered with my practicing and my lessons and my tutors and had no friends at all. I was actually useful to my brother. After he and my father arrived, we settled in an apartment on the Grand Concourse, in the Bronx; it was on the fifth floor, and Ray had a girlfriend who lived across the street, a couple of floors lower down. In the summer, when everyone lived with open windows, he would have me play the theme from Tchaikovsky's "Romeo and Juliet," while he sat in the window communicating with his girlfriend by means of gestures, pantomiming, Listen, this is for you. It was very *West Side Story*.

For me, the most significant thing about the apartment on the Grand Concourse was that for the first time I had the use of a grand piano at home. Zellerbach, of course, helped us rent it.

Moving to New York also meant that we acquired a new layer of relatives. My father's whole family was in New York: my grandparents and five aunts and uncles, all of whom, as I mentioned before, were Fleischers, with a c. We saw them with a certain amount of regularity while I was growing up. At family gatherings, I was inevitably treated to a chorus of "Play something for us, play something" from Uncle Herbie, Aunt Rose, and the other relatives. I would oblige, rather grudgingly. Finally, once, I offered them Brahms's Variations and Fugue on a Theme by Händel, a piece that lasts more than twenty-five minutes. I don't think they ever asked me to play again after that.

After a couple of years, we moved from the Bronx back to Manhattan, to West 177th Street in Washington Heights, an apartment that became our final family domicile. We lived in the last building before the highway and the river. In winter, the wind coming off the Hudson was so strong and fierce you could lean into it and it would practically bear you up. My mother would fight with it every day, coming back the four long blocks from Fort Washington Avenue, laden with shopping bags bearing the day's groceries. When I looked out my bedroom window, the George Washington Bridge took up half the view, and then New Jersey beyond it, with the whole Hudson River and downtown Manhattan spreading out to my left. During the war years, there were blackouts, so the land and water were in deep shadow, though there were still stray lights around, winking out of the blackness.

I remember the outbreak of war very well. It was my first-ever trip to Baltimore. Hannah Zellerbach, the wife of my patron, was from Baltimore; she was on the East Coast visiting her family, and she had invited us to come down and see her and play for her family. It was a wonderful place. They lived out in Hunt Valley, north of Baltimore, in horse country, with gently rolling hills and those splintered log fences around the horse pastures. It was a brisk, almost cold Sunday afternoon in early December, and we took a long walk through the drifts of fallen leaves rustling underfoot. When we got back to the house, the news was on the radio that the Japanese had bombed Pearl Harbor.

By 1942, my brother Ray had enlisted. He joined the army. He became a pathologist's assistant, so he wasn't actually an infantry-man, but he did end up on Okinawa, which was, of course, a big, big battleground. He also, just before he shipped out, got married. Flo was a really beautiful woman, and she and Ray were very much in love, but the occasion was less than celebratory. Flo was not at all what my mother had in mind for her eldest son. She had grown up in our neighborhood and she had a pronounced New York accent. I once asked her if she liked Chinese food, and her response was, "I don't eat that gawbage." It was all a little lowbrow for my high-minded mother, and the occasions when we visited Flo in Ray's absence were more dutiful than enthusiastic. At least they were for my parents. Flo had two very attractive sisters, and I liked seeing them just fine.

Meanwhile, Ray's departure meant that I was left home alone with my parents. It didn't make that much difference to my daily life. I had always taken the brunt of the family's attention.

My days had a fixed plan. I would get up in the morning and practice from about nine to twelve. I was terrible about it. I used to read books while I was practicing, propping a book on the music rack while I went through mindless exercises, my whole focus on "The Gold Bug" or "The Purloined Letter." (Edgar Allan Poe was a particu-lar favorite of mine.) The door to the living room had glass panes, so my mother could see through, and when I heard her coming down the hall to check on me, I would quickly slip the book under the leg that was away from the door, where she couldn't see it. She caught me a couple of times, though, and it was always a big production. I was given to understand that after all the sacrifices she and the fam-ily were making for me, I was causing her to suffer terribly with my willful ways. Once, she bit her fingers until she drew blood, and held them out to show me just what I was inflicting on her. I worked even harder to keep the book hidden after that.

Then I'd have lunch. Around one, a tutor would show up to lead me through the basic subjects: literature and history and French. My mother seemed to always choose radical, left-leaning people as my tutors. They were really very stimulating, enlivening young men. I remember two slender ones who looked like Bolsheviks from central casting. Communism, of course, was a popular movement in a certain segment of Jewish intellectual New York, and these young men were bursting with social idealism, particularly the one who led me through the works of Shakespeare. I was about twelve when I got to Shakespeare. I remember the frisson I felt when I discovered the word *bastard* in a Shakespeare text. I had heard the word on the street, but to find it in a literary work gave it a new glow of legitimacy. Not long thereafter, at the dinner table, in the full flower of my new discovery, I looked across at my big brother—this was while he was still in high school—and called him a bastard. Ray responded by hauling off and slugging me. He had evidently failed to understand that I had really intended the word in the exalted, Shakespearean sense.

At four, my lessons were over and I had a few hours of free time. The nearest park was several blocks away, and once I got old enough that I could be trusted to make my way safely there and back, I would go and just hang out there for a couple of hours. I loved the feeling of being on my own and free of all the rules that bound my life, although I didn't always know what to do with myself. I didn't have any friends whom I could visit. The neighborhood kids gathered in the park; they all knew one another from school, while I was just this outsider who appeared for a couple of hours in the afternoon. Fortunately, I was rather athletic. I wasn't the last to be chosen for teams for whatever game was going to be played at the moment. My mother didn't want me to play softball, for fear that I would hurt my hands, but when she wasn't around I disregarded her worries; I could swing a bat pretty well. There was also a Ping-Pong table in the park, which some really

wonderful players used to frequent; at least one of them went on to
compete at the international level. So my Ping-Pong game got pretty
good. When I was in my early teens, we got a puppy named Brownie,
and she became my companion on park outings and gave me someone
else to be with. And then there was flirting with girls. As I got older,
there was always a certain amount of that.

Then I went home for dinner, around six o'clock, and there would
be a couple more hours of practicing—or Edgar Allan Poe, depending
on which side of the door you were on—with Brownie at my feet,
before bed.

It's not true, though, that I was entirely without friends. My closest
tie in those years was to Konrad Wolff, the musicologist I had met at
Schnabel's lessons on Lake Como, who moved to Washington Heights
around the same time we did (after a brief stint in a French intern-
ment camp courtesy of the Vichy government). Konrad was twenty
years older than me, but that didn't get in the way of our talking about
music for hours, discussing things that Schnabel had said or trying
out repertory for four-hand piano. It was Konrad who introduced me
to the music of Gustav Mahler, through a four-hand arrangement of
the Mahler First, which in the years before recording was invented
was a standard way of approaching symphonies, and also helped me
improve my sight-reading skills. Konrad was a cherubic figure, filled
with love and enthusiasm about every aspect of music, with a delightful sense of humor. He was married to the photographer Ilse Bing,
who had been a tremendously acclaimed figure in Europe between the
wars but who couldn't find work after they moved to America in 1941;
for a while, she ended up grooming dogs. Ilse used to ride a bicycle all
over Manhattan; I remember encountering her once in Times Square,
miles from our neighborhood. It was hard to imagine two less congru-
ous people than her and Konrad, but their marriage endured. So did
my friendship with Konrad, which continued to the end of his life.

I had other lessons as well. Schnabel thought it was important
that I get a grounding in music theory. He started me right at the top,

sending me to his good friend Roger Sessions. Sessions was a fiercely intelligent composer who had one foot in the composing traditions of Europe but produced intricate, even dramatic American works and was a cornerstone of the American music scene. (It was once said of him that "everybody loves Roger Sessions except the public.") He was virtually the only notable American composer of his generation not to have studied with Nadia Boulanger. American graduate students flocked to New York to work with him. He didn't have a lot of experience, though, with eleven-year-olds. It didn't help that I was inattentive and less than assiduous in trying to learn what he assigned me. Once, he told me to reharmonize a Bach chorale. I happened to find an old dusty Peters edition that contained hundreds of Bach chorales for four hands, and I rejoiced at my luck and copied one of them down to present to Sessions at my next lesson. It was immediately obvious what I had done, and Sessions, who was really a very sweet man, peered at me with a strange expression.

I suppose Sessions must have decided that he couldn't do anything more with me, for I was soon studying with a different composer. This was Paul Dessau, a leading German composer who spent the war years in America and not long after the war went back to the nascent East Germany, as much out of political conviction as national pride. He had met Bertolt Brecht in California, and went on to become a frequent collaborator of his, writing music for a number of his plays, setting his poems as songs, and using his work as a basis for two (now little-known) operas. I worked with Dessau for a couple of years in the brief period before he went back to Berlin in 1948. For me, one of his most notable characteristics was his habit of eating a whole raw lemon, peel and all, during our lessons. The music world in those days was peopled with individuals of strong character.

On some days, of course, there were lessons with Schnabel, which superseded everything else.

Schnabel had taken up residence at the Peter Stuyvesant Hotel, on Eighty-sixth Street and Central Park West, with windows overlooking

Central Park. His living room couldn't fit two grand pianos, so we students would play on a Steinway and he would sit at a simple upright
piano. The sounds he got out of that upright—which he called a
"noodleboard"—were infinitely more beautiful than anything we could
manage to coax out of the grand piano. One of his great precepts,
and that of his teacher Leschetizky, was beauty of tone. There was a
photograph of Leschetizky that he kept in his teaching room, with
an inscription in German: To Artur, in memory of good and difficult
lessons. (The German word *Stunde* means both lessons and hours; the
wordplay was intentional on Leschetizky's part.)

As I got older, there were more and more students closer to my
age. Claude Frank, three years older than I, came into the Schnabel
studio in the 1940s; we remained colleagues, competitors, and friends
for the rest of my life. Hilda Banks, a girl about my age who was
very talented, brought in unusual pieces like Bartók's Opus 14 suite
for piano. Plenty of established professionals would also look in on
lessons for what amounted to refresher courses: people like Clifford
Curzon and Rudolf Firkusny, both noted pianists who had studied
with Schnabel in Berlin. Or Fabien Sevitzky, the nephew of the great
conductor Serge Koussevitzky, who paid him a large sum of money
not to use the family name in his own professional appearances. Or
Vitya Vronsky and Victor Babin, who were acclaimed for decades as
the greatest piano duo of all time. Victor, during the war, sported the
crisp uniform of a captain in the U.S. Army.

Lessons with Schnabel, however, were never a weekly affair. He
was playing all over the country throughout the war years, although
he dissolved ties with his managers in 1943; he conducted his own
business affairs, and retained a distaste for managers, for the rest of
his life. "People know how to reach me," he said, and they did: they
would write to him in New York and ask him to perform, and he
would write back and tell them what his fee was (generally $750), and
it was a gentleman's agreement, and that was that. The lack of a manager didn't seem to diminish his performing activities all that much.

And his summer vacations remained sacred: he and Therese spent two summers on a ranch in New Mexico, which satisfied their desire for hiking opportunities and mountain air, as well as space and time for him to compose. As a result, I'd say he gave no more than fifteen lessons a year. And when he was gone, he assigned me to one of his acolytes to make sure that my studies continued unbroken and that I was working in the right direction.

For a while, I worked with the brilliant, high-strung Aube Tzerko. I enjoyed those lessons a lot, and not only because Aube was a fine teacher. I would ride up to his apartment in the Bronx for a lesson, and after our session at the piano—we did a lot of Chopin études, which in their challenging complexity are hardly what you might think of as summertime fare—he would take me down to the public tennis courts by the elevated tracks and teach me how to play tennis. He was very energetic and vocal, but the more sarcastic or disdainful aspects he would later manifest as a teacher to many of his students hadn't yet appeared. Of course, because I was Schnabel's student at the time, he might have been gentler with me.

For one summer, I studied with Schnabel's daughter-in-law, Helen Fogel. She was awfully nice, and I think I might have had a bit of a crush on her. Actually, I had a crush on pretty much every female I met. I have always been eminently crushable.

But my main auxiliary teacher during my years with Schnabel, from the very beginning, was his son Karl Ulrich, whom we called Ruli. He was a wonderful pianist and a wonderful teacher, and a very kind man. As a pianist, he naturally had trouble breaking out of his famous father's shadow, but he was never hostile about it; he admired and venerated his father all his life. His attempts to forge his own identity did make him a rather idiosyncratic player, though, since he often bent over backward to come up with his own distinctive solution to a problem his father had already solved.

Since his father didn't work on technique, some of his unusual or imaginative techniques also derived simply from watching him play and trying to figure out how he did what he did. His trills, for instance, were extraordinary. A trill is an embellishment over a held note that involves playing the note in rapid alteration with the note next to it, so that you get the effect of a vibration or vibrato. There are two principal kinds of trills. Most commonly, a player hits two adjacent keys with extraordinary agility and speed, so that it sounds a little bit like a telephone bell, with both notes more or less equal. Just as valid, though, is the kind of trill where one note predominates. You do that by playing the main note with the thumb, which is always going to be louder. Karl Ulrich would have me practice that by playing both notes together and then starting to lift the alternate finger so that it sounded a fraction later, so that you start out by playing an interval and gradually separate it out into two distinct, alternating tones.

Ruli was a wonderful teacher for a young person. He was most imaginative and gallant, and he was also filled with a kind of ethical integrity. He was a tremendous role model for me, and my lessons with him—which lasted for a good five years—were very meaningful.

I didn't have total freedom in what I played. I was assigned certain pieces. There were good periods and there were fallow periods. A good period was the Liszt A Major concerto. A fallow period was César Franck's *Symphonic Variations* for piano and orchestra. It was a style of writing that was totally new to me, and for the life of me I couldn't manage to learn it. It was full of accidentals (sharps and flats, that is—usually the black keys on the piano) and for some reason I couldn't keep track of them. I would learn two bars one day, and the next day I'd go back to the keyboard and it was as if I'd never seen the music before. The piece had some nice piano writing, some nice tunes, but Franck's style was just so strange to me, after the classics.

My performing career was on hold. That was, as I said, a condition of my working with Schnabel, though I did give an occasional house concert or small recital, just to keep in touch with the feeling of going out on stage and playing for people. But the first time this prohibition was a real wrench for me was when I was twelve or thirteen and my old mentor Pierre Monteux asked me to come to San Francisco and play Gershwin's Concerto in F with the orchestra. I was thrilled. After a few years of intense study with Schnabel, I felt it was time to take the stage again. Bursting with excitement, I informed him of the offer at our next lesson—only to encounter a brick wall. Schnabel wouldn't budge. If I played the concerto, he said, it would mean an end to our lessons. Looking back, I think he was quite right. For one thing, the piece was musically incompatible with the track I was on; it would have been a huge stylistic detour. For another, the chances are good that it would have been a big success—a little kid playing a big showy concerto—and have led to more of the same. However much fun it would have been to do it, it wasn't what I needed at that point in my development. I had to tell Monteux no.

My contact with Monteux, however, remained constant. Monteux's second avocation was teaching. In 1943 he had founded a school for conductors up at his wife's childhood home in Hancock, Maine, envisioned as a continuation of the conducting courses he led in the 1930s in France. In the early years, facilities were pretty spare, and there were, of course, no orchestras to be had in Hancock, Maine, so Monteux invited me and another protégé of his, Vera Franceschi, to come up for the summer and act as a substitute orchestra. We would play four-hand arrangements of the orchestral masterpieces, and the students would conduct us. "Make a meeztake sometimes," Monteux would remind us in his strong French accent, sotto voce, a smile dancing across his plump pink face behind the walrus mustache.

For a long time, the Monteux school was my summer camp. Actually, I went to another summer camp when I was younger, a regular camp in Maine called Kamp Kohut, where I did things like archery and tennis. It was probably Zellerbach's idea, and he almost certainly paid the camp fees. I think the adults in my life were concerned about my psychological and emotional growth—what today might be termed my ability to play with others—given my extremely sheltered childhood. Kamp Kohut drew heavily from a New York population and happened to have some musical connections as well; I attended it together with Walfredo Toscanini, the conductor's grandson. One weekend, the great man himself, Arturo Toscanini, came up to the camp with his family to visit him. Since I was the camp's resident musical prodigy, someone arranged for me to play for Toscanini, and I offered up Chopin's C-sharp Minor Scherzo on an old upright piano. He was singularly unimpressed. He was not there to hear some kid play a Chopin scherzo; he was there to visit his grandson. That was OK with me, because I wasn't there to make music either, although I did provide the accompaniment for the camp musicals. One summer I banged out all of *Hansel and Gretel* on that old upright.

But after a couple of years I started going up to Monteux's school in the summer instead. I went up every year until I was in my late teens. The main building was a beautiful old Down East farmhouse, spare in its furnishings. Doris, Monteux's wife, who was as short and tubby as her husband, used to brag that she and Pierre always slept there in a single bed, back to back, with their tummies hanging over the sides. Doris's brother was a local farmer; one summer he bet me that he could teach a horse to urinate in a bucket faster than I could learn the Liszt sonata, and I think he won. At least he got the horse to go in the bucket, which is some kind of achievement. Our own toilet facilities were only marginally less primitive: there was an indoor out-house. The paper products in that small room included *Reader's Digest* and the Sears catalogue, both literary materials virtually unknown to me at home, and I used to sequester myself for up to an hour at a time poring over them, focusing particularly on the feminine under-wear section of the Sears catalogue. My habit was so pronounced that whenever Monteux had to make *pipi*, as he termed it, he would excuse himself by saying, "*Je vais chercher Leon,*" I'm going to look for Leon.

The other object of my attentions in Hancock was Vera. She was my first great love. Despite my best efforts, however, the affection remained entirely one-sided. Two years older than I, she had already made successful debuts in Paris and Milan, and she was making the occasional appearance at places like Carnegie Hall. She was also Italian Catholic and was not about to be experimented on by a Jewish lad. She later appeared frequently with Monteux, married twice (the second time to an Italian tenor), and died, tragically, at forty.

Monteux gradually built up his school—which is still going strong—by instituting a requirement that prospective conductors had to play an instrument; this meant that the school gradually developed a real orchestra as well, since each student played when it wasn't his turn to conduct. It also meant there were some wonderful musicians around in the summer, like Anshel Brusilow, a huge violin talent who was the youngest conducting student Monteux ever accepted. He went on to be concertmaster of the Philadelphia Orchestra, and then left playing and turned entirely to conducting as head of the Dallas Symphony Orchestra for several seasons. Anshel, like all the other conducting students, had to play in the orchestra, which was very smart: like Schnabel's group lessons, it meant students had a chance to learn even when they weren't on the spot themselves. When I was seventeen or eighteen, my last summer there, I tried to join in the participatory nature of the program by asking Monteux if I could try my own hand at conducting. Unfortunately, his answer was an emphatic no. He thought the experience would ruin me for piano playing. "Once you get the stick in your hand," he said, "that will be that. You won't want to play the piano anymore. You won't want to practice."

Monteux had other ideas about where my career was headed. He didn't give up in his efforts to bring me out to perform with the San Francisco Symphony. He just took a different tack. When I was fourteen, he told Schnabel he'd like me to play with him and asked him what piece would be suitable. I was working on the Liszt A Major concerto at that point, his second concerto, so that's what we performed.

Today, people don't remember what a fine Liszt player Schnabel was, but in his youth, Liszt was one of his calling cards. Some people have tended to dismiss Liszt as no more than a virtuosic showman as a performer and an eccentric as a composer. But Liszt was an incredibly complex man. Some of the works have a kind of full religiosity or piety that really doesn't speak to me; but some of them are pure genius. And then there is this extraordinary virtuosity that really is intimidating. His two piano concertos are visionary outpourings, played in one go without a break between movements. They certainly don't accord with the forms or norms of their day. But Liszt was one of the most brilliant musicians who ever lived, and Schnabel never treated him with the least bit of condescension. He loved the music and gave it great respect. I had worked on the A Major concerto with both him and Ruli, and Ruli arranged some kind of reading for me with Leon Barzin and the National Orchestral Association, a training orchestra in New York, so I had had experience playing it for an audience.

I was ready for my grand return to the stage. I was very excited. I knew the music well, and it expressed things I felt very comfortable with. The A Major is a better and more beautiful piece than Liszt's first concerto, in E-flat Major. In the slow movement, there's a wonderful second theme to which Liszt gives the instruction *con abbandono*, with abandon. That really spoke to me. I gave it all the abandon I had. It's a hell of a piece—noble, militant, passionate, bittersweet, with a sense of relinquishment and, for me, a big fiery piano part. I certainly wasn't starting at the shallow end of the pool.

The audience approved. The critics approved. Monteux approved. And he and Schnabel decided I was ready to tackle the Brahms D Minor, which I performed in San Francisco the following year, when I was fifteen.

My relationship with Monteux was to be one of the most enduring artistic connections I had. Virtually every two-handed concerto I ever played I performed with him for the first time—except, I believe, for Beethoven's Third Concerto in C Minor and the Rachmaninoff Second Concerto. All the others, though, I debuted with him, and I performed with him for the rest of his life.

But the biggest one happened in 1944. Monteux was coming to Carnegie Hall to lead the New York Philharmonic. Pleased with my performance in San Francisco of the Brahms D Minor, he arranged for me to make my New York debut with the same piece—one of the biggest pieces in the repertory, with one of the best orchestras in the world.

I was sixteen years old—tall, gangly, and ready to take on anything. At last, it seemed, the career I had been preparing for for so many years was actually going to begin.

I had my first tails made for the occasion. Mrs. Zellerbach took me to Saks or some other high-end store on Fifth Avenue to order the suit: tails and a white vest. I learned the proper way the jacket comes down below the line of the white vest. I learned to tie a bow tie. I learned how to put on a cummerbund, with the creases turned up, to catch the crumbs. There's a right and a wrong way to do these things. I spent a considerable amount of time practicing sitting at the piano and flipping my tails casually over the seat, as I had seen so many pianists do it over the years. The question that occupied me was whether to flip the tails before or after you pull up your pants at the knees; the answer, for the record, is that the tails come first.

Management was procured for me. Someone—it may have been Monteux himself—advised my family that it would be a good idea to have someone representing me, to prepare me for all the benefits that would presumably follow on the heels of a successful New York Philharmonic appearance. (And how could my appearance be anything but a success?) The behemoth in the classical music world was Columbia Artists Management, under Arthur Judson, the larger-than-life patriarch who founded it and ruled it for decades. My management was not quite so blue chip: I was taken on by Marks Levine at the National Concert Artists Corporation, NCAC, a kind of poor-cousin competitor to Judson and Co.

I even had to audition for the musicians' union, Local 802. James

C. Petrillo, the union's old-time, hard-nosed boss, who led it with an iron and uncompromising fist for eighteen years, was cracking down on the union orchestras' use of nonunion performers (though he did relent so far as to allow Koussevitzky to conduct the New York Philharmonic in 1942). I therefore had to get a labor permit. I went to the head office of the local, sat down at an upright piano they had in one corner, and began playing the familiar entrance of the Brahms D Minor concerto while Petrillo, a quintessential Tony Soprano type, sat impassively on a swivel chair. After a few bars, he removed the cigar from the corner of his mouth and said, "OK, OK, kid." I was in.

It was hugely exciting, and yet in a way it was the most natural thing in the world. Carnegie Hall already felt like home. Standing in the wings on the night of the concert, looking out at the bright lights and dark suits of the players on stage, my heart pounded, but with adrenaline and excitement, not with terror. I wove my way out through the string section—it's not a straight line—and John Corigliano, the concertmaster (whose son and namesake would grow up to be one of the most highly regarded classical composers in America), watched me with a scowl. He wasn't very inviting. The Philharmonic players were generally a surly bunch in those days. All those string players had set out to be Heifetzes themselves; now, what the hell, a sixteen-year-old pianist. Back then, not many kids had played with the New York Philharmonic.

Monteux's tubby figure passed me and ascended the podium, and then I got to sit and listen to my favorite part of the whole concerto, that massed, defiant orchestra, rising up all around me. It seemed to go fast. It did go fast. Monteux raced through that opening tutti. I can't believe I was able to follow his tempo, but I didn't have any problem. The adrenaline was coursing through my veins like Niagara Falls.

Afterwards, there were flowers and congratulations and a crowd of people in the dressing room—including Artur Schnabel. For me, the fact that Schnabel was there was the most thrilling part of the whole night.

My mother may have been most pleased with the review in the *New York Times* the next morning, which hailed me as "one of the most remarkably gifted of the younger generation of American keyboard artists."

I was on my way. What could stop me now?

JOHANNES BRAHMS: PIANO CONCERTO NO. 1
IN D MINOR, OP. 15 (1861)

Brahms has always spoken to me in a special way. There's the warmth, the richness in the music. There's the sheer brilliance of the way he writes for the piano. There are the little references to other works, to other composers, buried in the score, winking out at you like in-jokes, or favorite combinations of notes that he returns to and uses over and over again, like old friends. Nothing he does is unconsidered. The more you look, the more you find.

Take his first piano concerto, the D Minor, my lifelong companion. The first movement begins with the sound of a fist defiantly thrust up at the heavens. The second movement, the Adagio, or slow movement, is a prayer, gentle and soft.

But go to the printed music and look at the beginning of that Adagio. The violins and violas open the movement by playing a melody, in unison, that's notated in half notes and quarter notes. (Half notes are held longer than quarter notes: on the page, they appear white, little circles with stems, as opposed to the black dots of the quarter notes.) If you look only at the white notes and disregard the black ones, you suddenly see the fierce opening theme of the first movement staring out at you, like a secret sign. I couldn't sleep for a week after I found that out.

Maybe the D Minor is a young man's concerto. It certainly seized my imagination when I was young with its bigness, its huge ambition, its nobility—and its immediate impact. If you're in a performance and this music doesn't rouse you within the first forty-five seconds, you might as well just walk off stage and call it a night. It tries to hit you in the face.

Brahms was a young man when he wrote it, and it shows. Part of the piece's appeal lies in its imperfections, its craggy awkwardnesses, its humanity. Brahms was trying something here on an unprecedented scale. His first piano concerto breaks open the whole notion of what a classical concerto had been for the previous seventy or eighty years. The first movement alone lasts for twenty minutes—longer than some entire Mozart concertos. It traverses everything: defiance, anguish, beauty, majesty. It's like a symphony, and in fact it was originally conceived as a symphony; there's certainly something symphonic in the way Brahms uses the piano, which makes huge blocks of sound rather than single virtuosic lines. The first movement is somewhat sectionalized, and it can fall into chasms, or pits, so that one of the things the soloist has to concentrate on is continuity, keeping it of a piece and understanding that it's one work. It's a huge role for the pianist: an epic, Shakespearean role, like Hamlet, like Othello.

There's a certain degree of autobiography in the D Minor concerto. The first movement was written soon after Robert Schumann, Brahms's close friend and mentor, threw himself into the river Rhine in a failed suicide attempt; though he lived, he was confined to an asylum for the rest of his life. A lot of commentators hear the D Minor concerto's brooding opening—not unlike the darkness of other masterworks in the key of D Minor, like Mozart's *Don Giovanni* overture or Beethoven's Ninth Symphony—as a response to that leap: agitated, full of terror, with sinister dissonances subverting the heroic cry of the strings.

I don't hear it that way, though. To me, the opening speaks of courage and daring. The composer marks it "maestoso," majestic. It's shaking your fist at the heavens, bravely going out to conquer. It's about the injustice of life, or the defiance of fate. You can make up your own story.

That first movement is so powerful in its sweep that it doesn't have a cadenza, the usual insert near the end of the movement where the orchestra stops dead and the soloist gets to show his stuff. There's no need to single out the piano here; it's part of something much bigger than mere virtuosity. Brahms does follow Classical sonata form—exposition of the basic musical material, development of that material, and recapitulation (or, as we say in the business, "exhibition, development, and rehabilitation"). But that form takes second place to the emotional force of what's happening in the music. A cadenza would only interrupt.

Yet Brahms was young and a little unsure of himself. He was still learning about orchestration—about how to use the instruments of the orchestra in an effective way to get his musical ideas across—and the concerto has its share of balance problems, which is to say places where some groups of instruments tend to dominate others. Sometimes the wind instruments drown out the lower strings, the violas and cellos. The awkwardness of the orchestration and the hugeness of the scale were hard for some people in Brahms's time to swallow. The concerto was criticized pretty harshly after its first performances, and I think its reception hurt Brahms deeply. In my opinion, he never quite touched the same heights as he did in the opening of the D Minor concerto. He got to something there that he wasn't able to access again.

The second movement comes as a huge relief. After all of that heroism and defying of destiny, you get to accept destiny. For me, it's a prayer. In the manuscript, Brahms inscribed it with the heading *"Benedictus qui venit in nomine Domini,"* blessed is he who comes in the name of the Lord: you can't be any more explicit than that. (The line is also said to be a coded homage, since Brahms sometimes addressed Schumann as "Mynheer Domine," lord or master, in their correspondence.) The music is soft, embracing, ethereal, and at times almost unbearably tender. It's sometimes seen as a portrait of Clara Schumann, whom Brahms loved tremendously, in some form or other, for their whole lives.

The details can always surprise you in Brahms. When the piano first enters with the theme, in the second movement, the indication is *molto dolce espressivo,* very sweet and expressive. When the theme returns in the recapitulation, the indication is *molto espressivo dolce*—the same emotions but with a slightly different emphasis. Those are the kind of small indications that can help you unlock a piece for yourself.

That recap is genius too. Shortly after the piano comes in, the basses and cellos hold out this long note on D—what's known as a pedal point, meaning that the held note sustains the harmony while all kinds of other things are going on above it. In this case the piano, thundering out over that dark long note, ascends to heaven, rising up, triumphant. Then the winds come in while the piano embarks on a cascade of big arpeggiated chords. It's very tempting to turn those chords into tidal waves, but you have to be careful not to drown out the lone flute up at the top of the chord, so there are balance challenges and questions of restraint even at a moment of abandon.

Then there's the second-movement cadenza, which is pure inspiration, with its arpeggios and ascending trills. The rate at which it unfolds has nothing to do with the rate at which our lives move today. It takes on a different, otherworldly dimension. The trill begins in one hand and the other hand takes over as a tritone. And then the same thing happens an octave higher. And again. The fourth time you get up there, the trill still shimmering, it's as if you've reached an apex and the sun comes out. Some people interrupt the trill a little bit each time a new hand comes in, but I think that's all wrong; the idea is that each trill is joined by the next, rather than each entering as a new event. I also keep all of that ascending trill in one pedal, because you need the resonance of the A in the bass. Many people change the pedal when they get up to the top, because they don't like that resonance, but that resonance is the shimmering of the universe and I think you have to hold it out, with the pedal, until the next A comes in. And then you're left absolutely drained, while the orchestra finishes out the movement, the last notes falling like felt on the muffled heartbeat of the timpani before one final, golden chord.

After this, Brahms had a problem: how can you find an appropriate

finish after so much power and beauty? How do you reconcile the traditional lighthearted ending of the Classical concerto with the weighty
statements that Brahms was striving for?

He had a very similar problem in his other piano concerto, the
one in B-flat. The B-flat is a contrast to the D Minor in that it represents a kind of polished technical mastery while the D Minor shows,
if you will, the artist still hewing away at the stone. The D Minor has
rough moments; the B-flat is supremely secure. It's even longer than
the D Minor—it lasts fifty minutes to the D Minor's forty-five—and no
less symphonic; it even has four movements (like a symphony) instead
of a concerto's usual three. The B-flat also opens with an Olympian
first movement; this is followed by a revolutionary "wisp" (as Brahms
called it, tongue in cheek) of a scherzo, wild and impassioned and
syncopated, and then there's a sublime third movement, starting with
a gorgeous solo for cello, which is extremely unusual in a concerto
that's supposed to focus on another solo instrument. What can a composer possibly do for a final movement after that?

The answer, in both concertos, is simple. He resorts to the dance.
Brahms was a frustrated Hungarian at heart, and he wrote Hungarian
dance after Hungarian dance. He wrote them as stand-alone pieces; he
wove them into his larger works. And he used them to cap both of his
piano concertos. In the D Minor, actually, he cribbed a bit. He went
back to the last movement of Beethoven's third piano concerto and
faithfully echoed its structure, if not its exact notes. If it worked for
Beethoven, he would make it work for him as well. (It wasn't uncom-
mon for Brahms to turn to Beethoven, most obviously in the theme
of the final movement of his first symphony, which bears a striking
similarity to the "Ode to Joy," the famous final theme of Beethoven's
Ninth.) It's more an act of homage than an act of copying. Plenty of
other composers have engaged in similar borrowings—or whatever
you want to call them. Igor Stravinsky summed it up nicely when he
said, "Good composers borrow. Great composers steal."

Some people find the D Minor concerto's final movement oddly lightweight after the power of the first two movements. I think it's genius. Brahms starts with one of his favorite melodic progressions, a fourth followed by a whole step followed by a whole step (or a half step, if it's in a minor key)—or, to put it in more prosaic terms, the start of the song "How Dry I Am." He uses that progression in so many pieces: the waltzes, the piano quintet, the trio of the second piano sonata. Here, it kicks off this rousing Gypsy dance. The movement is a rondo, meaning that the main theme keeps returning, like a chorus in a song that comes back over and over again, each time after a different musical episode. There's a particularly nice moment toward the end where the theme is varied to sound like Scottish bagpipes, with the oboes and bassoons coming in over a pedal point, and George Szell always brought that out in performance. The second theme of that movement is filled with fervor—and triplets, skipping little groups of three-to-a-beat notes. Whenever composers write triplets, I find it particularly affecting. All my life, that theme has made the hair stand up on my arms and at the back of my neck.

The Brahms D Minor concerto has accompanied me throughout my life. It's never lost its freshness. And in ways it's grown with me—or I with it.

There are certainly plenty of technical challenges. There are clusters of octave trills in the first movement that are supposed to be particularly difficult. I don't have a real problem with those, though. It's a question of how to approach them. Pianists tend to take the literature terribly literally: they see a hurdle in the score and think they have to practice for hours to get it note-perfect, exactly as written. I'm all for fidelity to the score, but the real point is to see the music in terms of the gesture that the composer intended. What you want is to figure out the intention of the music and how you're going to get it across. It's not that you want to play it incorrectly; you just want to avoid being so hypercorrect that you lose the integrity of the gesture in what amounts to inessential details. So I go for the gesture rather than working for hours and hours to perfect some detail that, even when you get it, is not really worth all the effort you put in. Those octave trills are an integrated part of the work, and the whole work is, to me, a single, unified piece of heaven—or a cosmos of its own.

CHAPTER 3

OUTSTANDING
YOUNG
AMERICAN
PIANIST

A publicity shot from the 1940s. (Author's collection)

That's what the press called us. OYAP, for short. There was a whole group of us young piano talents: me, Eugene Istomin, Gary Graffman, Jacob Lateiner, Claude Frank. There was also William Kapell, but he was a little older than the pack and was hitting the big time while we were still playing the Tchaikovsky concerto for one another in our parents' living rooms. For a while, four of us were known under the conglomerate moniker of "Leogene Graffteiner." We banded together and arranged to have Steinway ship our favorite piano—affectionately known by its assigned number, CD 199—out to where the four of us were on tours at the same time, crisscrossing California and arguing about whether a solo recital in Pasadena should take precedence over an orchestral appearance in San Francisco when two of us happened to be scheduled to perform on the same night.

We played for one another constantly. We were in and out of one another's houses, trying out new repertory on one another, listening, playing, talking. We frequented the basement of Steinway Hall, where the concert grands used to sit waiting, silent, to be set off by a touch from a touring soloist stopping off to select an instrument for an appearance at Carnegie or Town Hall. (Lincoln Center hadn't been built yet.) We used to hang out down there and goggle at the instruments reserved for Horowitz or Rubinstein, and play them whenever we could—they were usually kept under lock and key, but sometimes, if we were lucky, someone would forget. Later, when we all became better known, we would each reserve the basement for two-hour practice slots. I would take it for a couple of hours, and then Gary, and then Eugene, and then Jake or Claude, and sometimes our friend Piero Weiss, and if we planned it right, we could tie up the room all night long. When we weren't practicing, we went to concerts across the street at Carnegie Hall and afterwards went around to the Carnegie Deli to eat pastrami sandwiches and deconstruct what we'd heard. We had a remarkable camaraderie. If we were competitive, it was healthy competition. We each had our own approach to the instrument, and making music for one another was the way we discussed it.

Of course, coming from Schnabel, I felt I had a privileged viewpoint. I had had my Word straight from the master. The others had formidable techniques, brilliant talents. But the ability to get to the heart of a piece, that was mine.

But the others probably felt more or less the same way about themselves.

We all looked up to Kapell. You couldn't not look up to Kapell. He was a compact mass of raw, breathtaking talent. He was probably the greatest American pianist who ever lived. Listen to his recording of Liszt's "Mephisto Waltz" to see what I mean: he makes this formidable piece sound almost easy, taking time to bring out details where many pianists are just struggling to get through it, while at the same time delivering something that crackles with virtuosity. He was all of twenty-two when he recorded it. Schnabel had tremendous regard for him. He was once listening to the radio and heard a recording of the Beethoven B-flat concerto and thought it was his own, but then found out that it was Willy's. That story cut me to the quick with a stab of pure jealousy.

Willy was a cocky little guy. He walked with his palms facing backward, rather than parallel to his body. I eventually realized that all pianists walk that way—we spend so much time with our hands in that position at the keyboard—but Willy was the first person in whom I noticed it. When he was starting out, he made a huge splash with pieces like the Khachaturian Concerto. It's a showy, virtuosic, and really pretty cruddy piece, but Willy played it with such panache it sounded like Ben-Hur: huge, epic, over-the-top. He continued to push himself and develop and explore so that by the end of his career—which was cruelly curtailed by a plane crash when he was thirty-one—he was playing Schubert sonatas, pieces of great nobility and subtlety that weren't showy at all. It was just the opposite of my own trajectory, since I started with the Viennese greats under Schnabel, and it took me a while to open up to the likes of Ravel or the perhaps too popular Tchaikovsky.

Willy was good-looking and pockmarked and forcefully opinionated. He didn't hold back. He could be devastating. When I was going through a period of being very free with my arms and in my motions when I played, he'd say, There you go, looking like a fat-assed bird. He went up to Gary once after a concert and told him he had played like a pig, and walked away. But he could be equally vehement in his warmth when he liked something you did. And he really tried to help us. Not only by giving us advice or having us listen to recordings of Artur Rubinstein playing Chopin—though he did do those things—but also by taking an active interest in our careers. He had a high regard for Eugene Istomin and thought he was underrated, and he used to push people to hire him. In fact, he bugged Eugene Ormandy about it so much that Ormandy finally said to him, "Look, if you mention him to me again I won't engage *you* next year, either." But eventually Ormandy did perform quite a lot with Eugene, so Willy's machinations may have had some effect.

Eugene Istomin was a couple of years older than me and Gary, who were born only three months apart. His parents and Gary's parents were immigrants from Russia, fellow musicians, and good friends, so Eugene and Gary had known each other since early childhood and both spoke fluent Russian—something they weren't particularly shy about showing off, leaving the rest of us at a loss while they prattled away together. Eugene treated Gary with the affectionate bossiness of a big brother. Actually, he treated everyone with the affectionate bossiness of a big brother. He would have treated Willy that way, too, except that Willy was enough older to keep a little bit out of it; but he spoke about Willy with a slightly derogatory air when Willy wasn't around. And we younger pianists didn't have a chance; we got a lot of advice, whether we wanted it or not. Eugene styled himself as something of a mentor to me, and I more or less humored him. I knew the truth.

Eugene had studied at the Curtis Institute of Music in Philadelphia with Rudolf Serkin, who was both one of the leading soloists of his day and a revered teacher to generations of students, both at Curtis and at the Marlboro Music School and Festival in Vermont, the famous summer program that he cofounded in 1951. Serkin's approach was very different from Schnabel's genial twinkle. It involved a certain amount of torment. He struggled mightily, and his music making sounded it. His performances were as jerky and intense and driven as Schnabel's were serene and ethereal; he attacked the piano to get it to do what he wanted. My image of him was always of Prometheus, shackled to the piano with a roc pecking at his liver. He made huge demands of himself, and he was no less demanding of his students. He was the originator of pianist guilt. If he practiced nine hours a day, his students had better be practicing nine and a half. Again, this was certainly a far cry from Schnabel, who thought that practicing more than three or four hours a day was a waste of time. Schnabel, when he spoke of Serkin, conveyed the idea that he was a young man of great promise who unfortunately had not fulfilled that promise, and I couldn't help carrying that attitude with me a bit, in the back of my mind, though he was always very kind to me.

As a child, Eugene was viewed as the next great thing in piano. I believe he toured with some kind of chamber ensemble arranged by the great violinist Adolf Busch, Serkin's father-in-law and cofounder of Marlboro, playing Bach Brandenburgs and Mozart concerti—a serious musical diet, in other words, rather than mere wunderkind fare. He went to Curtis at the same time as people like Leonard Bernstein

and Samuel Barber, but it was Eugene who everyone thought was the
most incredible talent they'd ever heard. Bernstein once said that if he
imagined himself playing the piano as well as he could possibly play
it, it would sound like Eugene. So his air of superiority came from
that. It probably got complicated for him when he met us, since, of
course, all of us had been prodigies as well.

Gary Graffman was also a big practicer, but he was altogether
more relaxed about it. He, like Eugene, studied at Curtis, America's
leading conservatory, which only accepts students of truly exceptional
ability and then teaches them for free. He worked, however, not with
Serkin but with Isabelle Vengerova, one of the school's first teachers, a
grande dame from the Russian school. Like Schnabel, she had studied
with Leschetizky, which only goes to show that Leschetizky didn't
straitjacket his students into a single fixed method, since Vengerova's
approach and repertory were as Russian as Schnabel's were Germanic.
There was a lot of emoting and, as Gary reports it, even chair throwing in lessons. Gary had known Vengerova since his birth—she was
also a friend of his parents—so he regarded this with equanimity. Gary
was, and remains, pretty unflappable, which stood him in good stead
when he eventually became the director of Curtis himself.

Coming from a musical family definitely had its advantages. The
Graffman household was the only one in our circle that had not one
piano but two in the living room. Consequently, we all tended to
gravitate there, since it gave us a chance to play for one another—or
accompany one another. I spent a lot of the summer of 1949 in the
Graffman apartment on West Ninety-seventh Street at the second
piano, playing the Brahms D Minor concerto—but taking the role of
the orchestra, while Gary played the solo line of it and several other
concerti he was preparing for the prestigious Leventritt Competition.
For my pains, I was dubbed "the Phleisher Filharmonic." It turned
out to be rather a memorable competition in that there were no other
finalists: Gary impressed the judges at the first round so much that he
appeared alone in the finals, played for a while, and then got the prize.

I didn't play so badly myself; the story goes that George Szell, who was on the jury, suggested awarding me the prize instead.

But in general, I wasn't getting much of that kind of encouragement. And playing for my friends was rapidly becoming the only opportunity I had to perform. True, I had made a huge leap into the big time with my New York Philharmonic debut in 1944. But within a few years—by 1948 or 1949—my professional engagements had first slowed to a trickle and then dried up altogether.

It had been such a promising beginning. My New York Philharmonic debut had made just the kind of splash it was supposed to. One consequence was that I was promptly engaged to play with the Chicago Symphony at their summer home, the Ravinia Festival, in the summer of 1945. In those days, artist bookings weren't made as far in advance as they are now, so you could get onto a presenter's calendar fairly quickly. Ravinia is a bucolic swathe of green lawn, dotted with plantings and a building or two, in the suburbs north of Chicago. It started life as an amusement park at the beginning of the twentieth century, and there's still a feeling of old-time entertainment as the crowds, armed with blankets and picnic baskets, swarm across the lawn to hear music from the open-air pavilion where the symphony gives its concerts. This populist atmosphere, combined with the minimal rehearsal time that's an unfortunate feature of most summer festivals, is not to everyone's taste. Schnabel played four concertos in four concerts at Ravinia in 1942, "in defiance of bugs and beetles," and swore never to do anything like that again.

But for a seventeen-year-old pianist, it was just fine to play with the Chicago Symphony and a young American conductor named Leonard Bernstein, in his second Ravinia appearance, in front of ten thousand or so people. I did my standbys: the Liszt A Major one night, the Brahms D Minor the next. In those days, the pavilion was a kind of tent, with a canvas top and canvas sides that were tied back, like curtains, during a concert. As if on cue, the brooding thunder at the start of the Brahms D Minor drew forth from the heavens a full-fledged thunderstorm. Bernstein, dark and handsome, ten years my senior, strove to make the orchestra heard through the thunder and the drumming of rain on the tent roof and the loud flapping of the canvas sides, while the listeners, soaked to the skin, huddled into the tent for shelter and I answered the lightning with great flashes of sound from the keyboard. It was terribly exciting.

Ravinia's presenters must have liked it, too, since they reengaged me for the following summer, 1946, to play four concertos with two different conductors. With William Steinberg—the German-born conductor who had fled the Nazis and was, at the time, conducting the Buffalo Philharmonic before moving on to make an enduring mark and attain his greatest fame as music director of the Pittsburgh Symphony Orchestra—I played my old childhood staple, Beethoven's B-flat (finally including the slow movement), and the Rachmaninoff Second, much, no doubt, to my teacher's discomfort. But best of all, I played the Schumann concerto and my trademark, the Brahms D Minor, with George Szell.

My first meeting with the legendary George Szell had actually taken place a few years earlier, at a concert at Town Hall. In an effort to bring music to a wider audience, Schnabel had helped organize a concert series called New Friends of Music, based on the idea of presenting quality music (rather than merely popular pieces) at low prices. The idea wasn't limited to New York—he was or had been involved with similar series in Pittsburgh and London and Los Angeles—but New York was, of course, the series I was involved with, because Schnabel insisted that we take season tickets as part of our musical education. My seat was back in the balcony and Schnabel's box was down at the front, and one winter afternoon when I was about fourteen, during intermission, I saw a great figure of a man, in a black overcoat and black homburg hat, striding down the aisle toward my teacher. Schnabel motioned to me to come down and I obeyed, nervous, excited. The man turned his gaze on me: ice blue eyes, magnified by glasses with lenses as thick as Coke bottles. This was George

Szell, who had conducted the recording of Brahms's first concerto that I had absorbed into my inmost soul.

And now, only a few years later, I was sitting under the canvas tent at Ravinia, playing the piece with him myself, hearing the same biting, thunderous opening from the orchestra as I sat rapt, vibrating in front of the piano, my heart pounding with excitement and adrenaline. Szell was a conductor who struck terror into the hearts of musicians. He was a forbidding perfectionist, and he thought nothing of cutting even his big-name soloists down to size. He must have liked what he heard from me that first summer, though. When we played at Ravinia, he was just about to take over the Cleveland Orchestra, which he would transform from a promising regional ensemble into the leading symphony orchestra in America. And he engaged me with that orchestra as one of his very first soloists. Playing with him was wondrous, and scary, no matter how many times I did it.

I performed quite a lot around the country for a couple of years. It was all very exciting. I remember playing at a women's college in North Carolina and being mobbed by a horde of bobby-soxers, so that a police escort had to come help me out—adulation I didn't mind a bit. Traveling alone was a new experience. After one Ravinia concert, I had to go on from Chicago to Denver by plane. Flying itself was totally new to me. We boarded that little two-engine DC-3 and embarked on an overnight flight, all the way to Denver. Today, of course, it would take no more than a couple of hours.

The logical next step was a Carnegie Hall recital; I made my solo debut there in 1946. My agent thought it was time to capitalize on all of my success. Renting the hall out wasn't as expensive as you might think, though naturally without the Zellerbachs we couldn't even have dreamed of it. Together with Schnabel and Ruli, I planned out a program that I hoped would demonstrate a breadth of interest and understanding: from a Bach toccata and Mozart's K. 332 sonata through Beethoven to Chopin and Liszt's epic, virtuosic sonata in B Minor.

I even included a contemporary work: three small pieces by Roger

Sessions. The composer had sent Schnabel a manuscript copy of his four-movement work "From My Diary," and Schnabel gave it to me at a lesson and said, "You must learn these; they're very good." What was striking was that when I brought them in to my next lesson, Schnabel virtually sight-read them but made far greater sense of the work than I had managed to do. Since I had worked with Sessions myself in those abortive music theory lessons at eleven, there seemed to me a certain justice—like closing a circle—in putting a piece of his on my debut program, though I didn't manage to learn the whole piece to my satisfaction by the time the concert rolled around; I played three of its four sections. The Three Pieces went down without objection. And the reviews of my Carnegie Hall debut were encouraging—though perhaps more in spite of the Sessions than because of it.

At first, with the help of my agent and my good reviews, the engagements kept on coming. I made my Philadelphia Orchestra debut in 1946 with Eugene Ormandy, playing the Rachmaninoff Second Concerto, a most un-Schnabelian piece that was a particular specialty of the Philadelphians. While we were rehearsing the second movement, I made a fundamental mistake. There's a passage in the second movement where the soloist holds a long trill, getting more and more quiet, and then two flutes come in; after we played it I asked Ormandy—very politely, I thought—if he could hold back the flutes to give me a little more time. That night, when we got to the trill, I started playing more and more softly and looked up to see Ormandy apparently gazing off into the distance as if he'd forgotten about me. I kept playing the trill, my arms tightening up, my fingers feeling as if they were about to fall off, until finally he looked down with a little smile and brought the flutes in. Gary Graffman swears that the exact same thing happened to him, but perhaps it bothered Ormandy less in his case; I, however, was penalized. It was fifty years before I was invited to play with the Philadelphia Orchestra again.

I played with the New Orleans Symphony. I played in Denver. I played in St. Louis. I played with the Los Angeles Philharmonic and

Bruno Walter, doing the twenty-third Mozart concerto, K. 488, which I had never played before. Walter is remembered as a warm, Romantic conductor with a quality of gentleness to his throbbing, singing playing, but he was also extremely demanding. Coming from Schnabel, I thought I was very high-minded about Mozart, and I played it with, in my terms, a certain purity. Schnabel was in a way the antecedent of today's period-instrument approach to Classical music: he cleaned up a lot of the excesses that his contemporaries tended to indulge in. But Walter was an old-school Romantic, and he wanted a lot of Romantic stuff in the concerto. He sang full voice, with heavy Romantic tinges, to show me what he wanted. By the time the performance rolled around, I was in a state of considerable nervousness. I guess I wound up doing something that was somewhat to his liking.

I wasn't usually particularly nervous. But I did develop something of a phobia about memory slips, which was to dog me throughout my career, and K. 488 had a particularly bad association for me. The direct cause of this was a performance that my teacher gave of it with the New York Philharmonic in 1946, on a live national broadcast. In the last movement—which he had, of course, played countless times—Schnabel lost his way. He wasn't able to get back on track at all, and right there, on live radio, the entire New York Philharmonic ground to a halt. My heart fell to the soles of my feet and my blood ran cold in horror as Schnabel got up from his bench, went up to Artur Rodzinski on the podium, and conferred with him while consulting his score. They must have agreed on a place to start again; Schnabel sat back down, the music continued, and they finished without further incident. After the piece was over and they had taken their bows, by mutual agreement Schnabel returned to the piano and Rodzinski got back on the podium and they played the whole movement again without a single flaw. By that time, of course, the broadcast had ended, so the national audience didn't get to hear it done right.

Schnabel didn't seem too fazed by the incident. But for me, it was downright traumatic, and the thought of a comparable memory slip remained a nightmare fear, able to summon a cold sweat, for the rest of my life.

A year after my debut, in 1947, I returned to Carnegie Hall for a second solo recital: Beethoven, Chopin, Schubert, and Brahms. That was probably a mistake. It was nowhere near as good as my first recital. And the reviews reflected that.

For something wasn't quite working. The reengagements stopped coming. By 1949, I had no performances coming up at all. In fact, I was a has-been. When Gary mentioned my name to his manager, Arthur Judson, the most important artists' manager in America, Judson said he wouldn't touch me with a ten-foot pole.

I know why it happened. I wasn't focusing. Always susceptible to the opposite sex, I had fallen altogether under its sway. I was more interested in girls than I was in practicing.

Girls. Women. Skirts. Sometimes it seemed I could hardly think of anything else. I hadn't really had a childhood, and I had been cut off from people. I had had a crush on our upstairs neighbor Alice when I was thirteen or fourteen, and my mother saw us together and forbade me ever to see her again. Well, no one was going to forbid me now.

It was girls in general. And one girl in particular.

Marjorie Weitzner's father, Julius, was a prominent New York art dealer who traded in old masters. Her mother, Ruth Klug, was a student of Schnabel's who occasionally sat in on a lesson. In our lessons, Ruth got to know me a little bit, and eventually she invited me to dinner. The Weitzners lived on Park Avenue, in a building modeled on an Italian palazzo: a real wow of an apartment, with museum-quality paintings in rotation on the dark walls. And there, at dinner, sat Marjorie, one of the most beautiful girls I had ever seen, with creamy white skin and spit curls framing her face.

I was lost.

Marjorie was a painter. She had studied with Raphael Soyer at the Art Students League. She was actually a very talented painter, and over the years she would paint all our portraits—Gary Graffman's, Claude Frank's, mine.

She also loved music. There was, in fact, a great deal of music in the Weitzner household. Julius Weitzner was an amateur violinist of some ability, although he often smoked cigars while playing and his violins tended to be strewn with ashes. And Marjorie's mother, of course, was passionate about piano; she went so far as to give a recital at Town Hall a few years after my Philharmonic debut. So Marjorie had music in her as well.

Did I mention that she was gorgeous? She dressed impeccably, and always those tight spit curls around her face. With my proclivity to develop lasting crushes on every woman I met, I didn't stand a chance.

I immediately asked her out. Shortly after my Philharmonic debut, the National Concert Artists Corporation was giving a ball. Today, they might hold a conference for their managers, but in those days it was a ball, a formal affair that included their artists as well as their employees. As one of their rising stars, I was included, and I asked Marjorie to come with me and she did, spit curls and all. I was in my working clothes—that is, formal wear—and Marjorie was in an amazing gown, and I was on top of the world. It was my first real date.

Marjorie and I went out, on and off, for several years. I was besotted with her. We would meet, and go to the movies, or sit and talk, or make music. Marjorie greatly fancied German lieder, which she would sing in a sweet reedy little voice, while I accompanied her. And of course we went to concerts together. I loved being seen with her and tried to dress to meet her standards. I became a model of sartorial elegance. I never appeared without a tie; I even acquired a homburg hat, which I wore with some regularity. Marjorie, of course, always outshone me in her satin gowns. It didn't hurt that she didn't always wear a bra. When Marjorie and I went to Carnegie Hall, Gary Graffman always wanted to sit nearby, just so he could look at her.

Marjorie also fancied pianists. Perhaps she fancied us a little too much. She had another boyfriend, my friend and fellow Schnabel student Claude Frank. Claude was a couple of years older than I was. I admired him enormously. I thought he was a wonderful musician and pianist. But he was also my rival for the thing I wanted most in the world. Sometimes it seemed he had an edge on me. Since he was born in Germany, the lieder repertory that Marjorie liked so much was to him like mother's milk. I felt myself at a gross disadvantage. Claude and I did our best to keep it under wraps, but the feeling of competition was always there. Marjorie juggled us both for a long time, and I suffered, and moped, and neglected my practicing.

Then my lessons with Schnabel ended.

After ten years of working with Schnabel, I had become a little lazy. When I approached a piece for the first time, I would get it into my mind and fingers, but I didn't always work on unlocking its deeper mysteries and challenges for myself. I knew I would get the word from on high in a couple of weeks when I played the piece for my teacher. There seemed little point to exerting too much thought when I had direct access to someone who would, in a few crisp sentences, reveal all manner of things I had never thought of before.

Schnabel knew this, of course. By 1949, after a decade of teaching me, he probably knew my playing better than anybody in the world. He wasn't very concerned about the decline in my career; I'm not sure he even noticed. He really didn't care about that side of things at all. But he also knew all about the risks of students becoming too dependent on him. It's true that some of his students kept sitting in on lessons occasionally through most of their professional careers. But with other students, he would cut the cord and tell them it was time to go out on their own.

One day, at the end of a lesson, he asked me to stay so that we could have a little talk. In his avuncular manner, which had become so familiar over the years, he said that he thought that I had now learned how to learn. I knew—even if I didn't think I did—how to approach a piece of music and find the answers for myself, and it was time that I did so. I had to make my own choices, decisions, mistakes. I had to, as it were, become a man.

Objectively speaking, it made perfect sense. To a teenager whose career was slipping through his fingers, it felt like the end of the world. I was almost too numb to speak. I walked out with the blood filling my cheeks, in a kind of silent anguish, and sat dumbly in the subway train all the way home, my mind a blank as I tried to hide from the unimaginable disaster that had just befallen me.

I had been thrown out, expelled. I felt I hadn't measured up. And I was terribly concerned, and guilt-ridden, that I hadn't paid attention as much as I could have. As I said, we didn't have tape recorders or any way to document our lessons, and he would tease us when we took notes on what he said. Now, I was sure that 90 percent of what he'd taught me had been lost.

When I was nineteen, I moved out of the family apartment in Washington Heights into a little apartment on Seventy-seventh Street and Third Avenue, under the El, the elevated subway train that in those years still ran on iron girders down Manhattan's East Side, casting the street below in a sooty shade striped with bits of sun filtered down through the tracks. I had a piano, and I practiced to a certain extent, but I was aware I was neglecting it. I enrolled at New York University for a couple of semesters, but my second attempt at formal education was not much more successful than my first, in kindergarten. I didn't really fit in. Furthermore, I needed to concentrate on finding some piano students myself to earn some money, since my savings from my short-lived concert career weren't going to last forever. A couple of times a week my mother would show up at my door, laden with groceries and ready to take my laundry. She was concerned, but she knew that I had to spread my wings, even if I didn't seem to be embarked on any kind of sustained flight. More a sequence of short hops.

I saw Marjorie as often as I could. I hung out with Gary and Eugene and my other pianist friends, including Piero Weiss, who was close friends with the Toscanini family and a favorite of the great maestro Arturo. And I sampled a lot of forbidden fruit. Musically, that is. I would have been happy to sample other kinds of forbidden fruit as well, but I wasn't quite sure how to go about it.

So I was left to transgress in the musical arena. It was at this time that Eugene really tried to move into a role as my mentor and started broadening my musical horizons with all kinds of music I'd never heard before. He introduced me to Ravel and to Couperin's "Leçons de ténèbres," Lessons of Darkness, a set of late Baroque church motets, chromatic and brooding and otherworldly with sexless-sounding singers channeling an unadorned sound that seemed itself centuries old, unlike anything I knew. And I allowed myself to be taken by Tchaikovsky and Rachmaninoff, composers I had learned to turn up my nose at in my years with Schnabel. I was exploring a different side of music, feeling its sensuality, its perversity, its rich, dark underbelly. Sometimes I feel students today don't understand that aspect of music at all.

Take the playing of Vladimir Horowitz. Horowitz was, of course, one of the greatest virtuosos of all time. He was brilliant, eccentric, and neurasthenic. He could draw an unbelievable range of colors from the keyboard; he could thunder Tchaikovsky's octaves from the piano with Romantic gusto but then take delight in a Scarlatti sonata, the epitome of Classicism. But oh, he was perverse. Beset by inner demons, he would go into protracted periods of retirement from the stage, only to return with renewed vigor a few years later; he had done this in the late 1930s, and he would do it three more times in the years after I met him. It wasn't only his behavior: his playing could be terribly perverse as well. He would play something that would lead your ear to expect a clear consequence, and then he would turn around and give you something completely different from what you expected. It was a variant of the old sadomasochist story: he kept you

hanging, begging for something he deliberately withheld. Those ruba-
tos of Horowitz's were positively erotic.

I believe it was through Eugene that I met Horowitz. He followed,
of course, everything that was going on among younger pianists, and
he was interested in meeting us. Gary later studied with him for a
couple of years. I never actually did what you could call study with
him. I met him only about three times. Meetings with Horowitz had
a certain fixed pattern. I would call on the phone, and a deep, sepulchral voice would answer with a guttural "Hyello?"

Hello, I'd say, this is Leon Fleisher—

"Oh, hyello! Hyello! How are you?!" the voice would say, moving about two octaves up the scale to the high-pitched, wavery tenor
that was Horowitz's normal range. He just didn't want to answer to
anybody.

I would go to Horowitz's house and play my piece, whatever it
happened to be at the moment. I know I played Beethoven's Op. 10,
No. 3, for him once. And he would listen, and nod, and say, "Very
nice, very nice, very nice." Then he would push me off the piano
bench and play, for several hours, whatever was holding his imagination. I once got three hours of Clementi sonatas.

It was fascinating to sit so close to such a brilliant musician. I
was struck by Horowitz's fingers, which were always held very flat.
Schnabel's hand was slightly higher, slightly more relaxed above the
keys, but Horowitz's was almost completely horizontal. That gives rise
to a certain kind of sound: a certain stroke, a certain way of depressing
the key, a caress that takes a sensual pleasure in the sensation of finger
on ivory. I later incorporated this into my own playing when it suited
my goals—when I wanted a particular kind of sensuousness. Horowitz
revealed a whole new world of color to me, and he played with a
rhythmic instability that was, in a way, intoxicating. When he played a
certain repertoire—like sonatas by the anarchic, singular Russian composer Alexander Scriabin—he was unmatched. But his Schubert B-flat
sonata (D. 960) was an embarrassment. It represented, I think, a total

misapprehension of what the piece was about. He didn't have any idea what the hell he was doing.

As I said, I didn't meet Horowitz often. But I believe word of our encounters got back to Schnabel. I don't know if that played any role in his expelling me or not. He didn't mention it to me. But some time later, I heard from a third party that Schnabel had said to him, "Fleisher's gone to study with Horowitz." I never had a chance to set the record straight, because Schnabel died in the fall of 1951. It has always haunted me that he might have misunderstood.

CHAPTER 4

THE
BOHEMIAN

Rehearsing with Pablo Casals at the Prades Festival, 1953.
Paul Moor/Magnum Photos (Author's collection)

It was Eugene who had the idea of going to Paris. He had been invited to take part in the first Casals festival, in the south of France. After Generalissimo Francisco Franco's rise to power in Spain, the Spanish cellist Pablo Casals had moved out of the country to the small village of Prades, just north of the Spanish border, and eventually, after World War II, declared he would not play publicly in any country that recognized the dictatorial, right-wing Franco government, which effectively meant a number of years without any public playing at all. In 1950—due largely to the very active instigation of Alexander ("Sasha") Schneider, the violinist and conductor—Casals relented, lifting his veil of silence on the occasion of the two hundredth anniversary of the death of Johann Sebastian Bach. The festival that June marked his first performance for several years, and major artists from around the world flocked to Prades to perform with him. Schneider was a big fan of Eugene's and wanted Eugene to be one of the pianists at the festival, and he arranged for him to audition for Casals.

Eugene, so anxious to be a leader himself, had steadfastly resisted falling into any form of hero worship of his own teachers. For all his affection for Serkin, he saw Serkin's human weaknesses quite clearly, and he used to make gentle fun of Schnabel for his tendency to rush and to play clinkers. He never really allowed himself to have a role model until he met Casals. Then it hit him like a ton of bricks. Prades was, for him, the beginning of an extraordinary relationship.

Eugene had an ulterior motive for wanting to go to Paris on his way to Prades. Her name, at the time, was Xenia. Her real name was Shirley Gabis, and she was an old friend of Eugene's from Curtis days; in fact, he had helped coach her for her own Curtis audition. She was also a good friend—and sometime paramour—of Leonard Bernstein, whom, of course, everybody loved. In 1950 Shirley, having failed with Lenny and having married and divorced a cellist (and later composer) named Seymour Barab, was living in Paris in an apartment she was occasionally sharing with another old friend of hers from Curtis, the composer Ned Rorem, who would become an enduring figure in American composition but who then was still young and little known and had not yet published the first of the diaries that were to help cement his fame and his skills as a raconteur. They were cohabiting purely platonically, of course, since Ned was gay.

Eugene thought that Paris would be a good thing for me. My own decision was also influenced by a woman. Marjorie had finally thrown over both me and Claude, and gone off to Paris herself. I knew that things between us were really over, but at the same time there was something comforting in the idea of being in the same city as she was. And I honestly had nothing better to do. I wanted to get away from my parents, and away from New York, and away from all the bad memories and the sense of unworthiness and aimlessness that had seized me. So Eugene and I went to Paris in the spring of 1950, and went straight to Shirley's apartment at 53, rue de la Harpe.

53, rue de la Harpe had been a brothel before the war. The brothel had been something of a landmark in its day. It even makes an appearance in French literature, with a mention in a short story by Guy de Maupassant. After the war, the French government cracked down on prostitution; although this didn't actually have much effect on the world's oldest profession, the owner of this particular establishment evidently decided that it would be easier to go along with the prohibition and turned the building into a rooming house. Not everyone was aware of the change. On a couple of occasions, we were awakened by pounding at the door: French servicemen returned from abroad were seeking out the site of their former diversions.

When I got there, though, the ground floor had been transformed into a nightclub called La Rose Rouge, frequented by Senegalese men and young French women who went there to meet them. The African men would sit on the floor and beat drums, and on weekends the sound of drumming would vibrate through the floor into the wee hours of the morning. Above the nightclub was an apartment inhabited by the principal male dancer of the Folies Bergére, who had enclosed half his living room with chicken wire and filled it with hundreds of canaries and parakeets. The top floor was a back apartment occupied by a tailor by day and an abortionist by night. And above the dancer, and below the tailor, was Shirley and Ned's apartment.

The apartment had two bedrooms separated by a single room that did triple duty as living room, kitchen, and bathroom. It had a steady stream of visitors. Ned was in and out, traveling around to Morocco and the south of France. Shirley had taken up with a *petit ami*, a poet named Jean. Eventually Shirley left and turned the apartment over to me. For a while, I shared it with a clarinet player named Ernest Bright, with whom I enjoyed the nightlife. That is, we stayed up playing gin rummy until all hours. I wasn't exactly plunging right into the beau monde.

For all of the bohemian setting of my dwelling and for all of my romantic imaginings of Paris, I found that the city, outside of the summer months, was really rather dismal and dreary, and damp. I spent a lot of time wandering the streets those first weeks, feeling utterly lost and dejected. When I was with a friend, we would go and sit in cafés. We weren't entirely sure what to do with ourselves. We went out to cat, which you could do cheaply and well in those days. But it didn't feel quite like real life.

Not that I was entirely without occupation. Shirley and I quickly hit it off. One of the icebreakers in our relationship was a recital she was supposed to give at the American Embassy, where she was to perform the world premiere of two pieces of Ned's, his second piano sonata and the Barcarolles, which he had just completed on a trip to Morocco. Shirley, however, didn't feel she had Ned's works ready to her satisfaction—she may have been somewhat distracted by Jean—so she asked me if I would play them instead. I was a quick learner and I had no reason to say no, and I thus found myself giving a concert within three weeks of my arrival in Paris. It went off well enough. Ned's music was pleasant—very Frenchy, charming, and facile. Ned, certainly, was so pleased with the performance that he dedicated the sonata to me. I was disabused not long afterwards. Ned was close friends with the brilliant American pianist Julius Katchen, who also lived in Paris. The sonata had only had three movements, and Ned wrote another movement for Julius and then rededicated the whole piece to him instead.

The embassy recital didn't exactly take the world by storm, but it did help me meet a few people. One was a bass-baritone named Doda Conrad. Doda was a colorful figure. Tall, patrician, and with strong features, born in Poland, an American citizen living in Paris, he was multilingual and extraordinarily knowledgeable. After the war, he had worked in the Monuments, Fine Arts, and Archives program of the Allied armies—he was a lieutenant in the U.S. Army—to recover and protect art looted by the Nazis or damaged in the bombings. He also had an illustrious musical heritage. His mother was Marya Freund, a soprano who gave the first performances of several works by Arnold Schoenberg, including the Paris premiere of his chamber piece "Pierrot lunaire," a set of songs performed in *Sprechgesang*, midway between singing and talking.

Doda's voice, admittedly, was rather modest and had deteriorated considerably by the time I met him. Still, he was a terrific musician—he had studied with Therese Schnabel and had some of her keen understanding of the song literature—as well as an extraordinary mensch. Other musicians loved and appreciated him. He was part of the circle of Nadia Boulanger, who is remembered today mainly as a legendary teacher to several generations of American and French composers but who was also an early-music pioneer. Her groundbreaking 1937 recording of Monteverdi madrigals, which introduced a whole generation to the music of that major early composer, includes Doda, along with the great tenor Hugues Cuénod, as part of the vocal quartet. And Doda was the only vocalist Casals invited to perform in Prades at that first festival in 1950. Somehow, I made music in a way that meant something to Doda. So he invited me to perform with him in a series of recitals.

Doda was scheduled to give a tour in Germany of the Amerika Hauses, facilities of the U.S. Information Service designed to promote American culture to a country whose cultural experience had been rather limited during the twelve years of Hitler's "thousand-year Reich." Whole worlds of achievement—any art that smacked of the avant-garde, the "degenerate," or, of course, the Jewish—had been effectively kept out of Germany for that period. If the Amerika Hauses didn't explicitly set out to redress the deficit, they at least attempted to bolster the image of American culture, and they were eagerly frequented in the postwar years as Germany worked to get its own cultural institutions up and running again. The point wasn't so much that Doda and I were going to present American music but simply that we were Americans. In fact, our programs were pretty much all German (or Viennese). We did Schubert's song cycles "Winterreise" and "Schwanengesang." We worked out one program of Schumann and Brahms—with Brahms's "Vier ernste Gesänge" (Four Serious Songs) and Variations on a Theme by Händel, and Schumann's "Papillons" and Opus 39 Heine songs—balancing solo piano works with vocal sets. And we performed this program all over Germany.

I was curious to see Germany, a world whose culture I had been so steeped in for so many years. Of course, my curiosity was mingled with ambivalence about Germany's recent political past— with the unanswerable question of how a people with such a great heritage could have let such horrors happen. Doda was less nuanced in his views, not least as a result of his experiences serving in the U.S. Army. He was a rabid anti-German. As our train pulled into a station, he would lean out the window, imperious, and call "*Gepäcktrrrräger!*" (Porter!) in a tone of regal disdain, to summon a minion to convey our luggage to the nearest taxi.

Back in Paris, Doda also opened a door for me into the heady, elegant, drug-ridden world of the French salons. I never got very far inside. Sundays belonged to the Countess Marie-Blanche de Polignac, who was also a singer and had appeared with Doda on that Boulanger Monteverdi recording. Marie-Blanche was the daughter of the fashion designer Jeanne Lanvin; she trained as an opera singer, married a count, took over the Lanvin fashion house after her mother died, and held court on Sundays, assembling at her home a whole host of splendid names, aristocrats and cultural figures alike. Among these were composers like Jean Françaix, Henri Sauguet, and even Francis Poulenc, the most illustrious of the group, a large man who wore his dark hair in a kind of long crew cut. I attended some of these salons and performed at them a few times, but apart from weekends I never saw these people anywhere else. There wasn't a lot of common ground. They weren't too interested in Schubert sonatas. I got a lot of "O, moi, j'adore ça," an affected protestation of how they just *loved* this *unusual* fare, before they moved on to the next topic.

I wasn't too interested in what they had to offer, either. Doda was very plugged into the circle of French composers, and he introduced quite a bit of their music to New York at his Carnegie Hall recitals over the years. But my tastes still sat firmly in the Germanic camp. I thought Poulenc's music was utterly third-rate. All, that is, except that wonderful song "C," which Eugene introduced me to and which is about the joys of cannabis—of smoking pot. The text is by Louis Aragon, written while the poet was a part of the French Resistance to the Nazis in the 1940s, and it can be read as a protest against the Occupation. But as Eugene explained to me, it also evokes the dreamy haze of a drug trip, starting with the opening line, "I have crossed the bridges of C," and describing the beautiful things that are found on the other side. What a song that is. Later in my life I had to concede that Poulenc's piano concertos were very effective writing. And when I met the composer, he hadn't yet written the operas he's best known for today, *Dialogues of the Carmelites* and the soprano monologue *La voix humaine*. But at the time I wasn't very impressed.

Another host was Julius Katchen. Julius, a couple of years older than me, was the first of us to arrive in Paris after the war; he got there around 1947, and he never left. The French were extraordinarily grateful to him for that. He had a terrific talent and a large repertoire, and he played, and played, and played, and played—and it was damn good playing. He recorded Brahms's complete solo piano works for Decca, and this set remains just about unmatched: his approach has a gravitas, a massiveness to it that feels to me absolutely appropriate. He was also brilliant. He had gotten a degree in philosophy from Haverford College in only three years and been elected to Phi Beta Kappa, all on his way to a serious solo piano career. He was the reigning expat in our circle in Paris, and one of the first people we went to see when we arrived. He, along with his future wife, Arlette, enjoyed knowing his way around and was extremely generous about showing their friends the ropes. The Katchens had an extraordinary duplex apartment on the Left Bank, and they threw wonderful parties, and we all came.

It was at one of Julius's parties, soon after I arrived, that I met the composer Alexandre Tansman, who was very much a part of the French composers' circle. Tansman, Polish born, had been a gifted pianist and a fast-rising composer before the war but had fled to the United States in 1941, composed a couple of scores for Hollywood, and never quite regained his former footing when he returned to Paris after the war was over. A small man with a sharply etched face and a perpetual air of sardonic humor, Tansman nodded at me and then asked point-blank if I was homosexual. I was speechless. I had nothing against homosexuality; it was simply something that I had never encountered. No, I managed to answer, I wasn't. "What a pity," Tansman said, "because it would open for you all the doors in Paris."

I left that to Ned. He had learned a similar lesson himself, in a rather different way. He was eager to meet the celebrated writer and Nobel Prize winner André Gide, who was by then quite elderly. Ned kept writing to Gide, sending him message after message through the network of pneumatic tubes that were the primary means of correspondence within Paris, but never getting any response. Finally, Ned went up onto the roof of the building at rue de la Harpe, took off all his clothes, and had a friend take a photograph of him. He sent the photograph to Gide, and the next day he got a card inviting him to lunch.

At the same time I went to Paris, Gary Graffman had gotten a Fulbright and gone to Rome. In practical terms, this meant he had a steady source of income and some free time. He had even more free time when he accidentally slammed his hand in a car door. Fortunately, nothing was broken, but he certainly couldn't practice. He decided to take the opportunity to travel. Accordingly, he joined us in Paris and took up tenancy in the spare bedroom on rue de la Harpe for a while.

The Prades festival, which was part of the reason for our all congregating in Paris to begin with, finally rolled around in a blaze of hot southern sun. We made the pilgrimage together, though Gary and I were only really there in the role of Eugene's supporters. Casals called us "the Egyptians," presumably because we rapidly developed dark tans in the Mediterranean warmth. Eugene was actually a bit nervous about the whole thing, being one of the youngest performers invited to participate.

Rudi Serkin was there as well. He was, however, late arriving—his plane was delayed—leaving Casals and the orchestra sitting there at rehearsal with no soloist to play the Beethoven B-flat concerto. Eugene—who was, for all of his mentoring air, a very generous colleague—said, "Leon plays that piece." So I got to rehearse, with

Casals, the concerto I had been playing since I was a little boy. This time I remembered where my hands were supposed to go in the third movement. Casals was a wonderfully sweet man. Later that week, at a party at his house, he and I attempted to play Debussy's wonderful arrangements of Schumann étude-canons, written for two pianos. We had only one piano, though, so we tried it out as a four-hand work, sitting side by side on the same piano bench. Four-hand works, however, are composed in such a way that the players don't get in each other's way, while two-piano works take advantage of the full range of two separate keyboards. Predictably, the attempt ended in a hopeless tangle of arms and lots of laughter.

So I was certainly playing. I may not have had any concerts on the level that I had been accustomed to before I went to Paris. But all the performing I was doing was a good sign. I was beginning to find my own way back to the piano.

I don't know why I decided, one day, to look at the Schubert B-flat sonata (D. 960). I had never played it, though I had heard some of Schnabel's other students play it during our lessons. It poses considerable challenges. How do you create a sound that communicates bliss, or transcendence? How do you make sure the notes are falling at just the right moments? As I was playing through it and thinking about it, I reached a place that I wasn't quite sure what to do with. I thought about that place and went back to it and probed it until suddenly a little bubble rose through my mind and burst over my head. It was like the old commercial images of the Maxwell House coffee percolators, with the coffee rising and appearing through the little clear knob at the top. It came to me that I knew what Schnabel would have said. I didn't remember what he'd actually said, but this was the kind of thing that he said this kind of thing about. The experience gave me a tremendous sense of comfort—and, subsequently, of encouragement. Maybe I hadn't forgotten everything after all. Gradually, the more I played, the more I came to realize that I really did have everything he said in my head. I just had to clear away all the crap that was encrusted on top of it and let it percolate forth.

So I was encouraged and energized to start working seriously again. I began to regurgitate, bit by bit, everything that I had stored up over those ten years of study. I had, of course, all the repertoire I had played before I came to Europe, but now I suddenly felt ready to learn new things, and to relish the challenge.

I took another big step one day when I put on a recording of Schnabel playing Beethoven's B-flat Major sonata, Op. 22, the tenth sonata of Beethoven's thirty-two. The sound of Schnabel's playing, his touch, was so familiar that I was enraptured, and I listened with a great deal of love and appreciation. That was great, I said to myself, when it was over. But I realized that there were certain passages I might not have played the way he did. I might have chosen to play them differently. And this sign of freedom, of independent thinking, hit me like a lightning bolt. Maybe I did have my own opinions about music after all. In fact, when I practiced now, I started thinking about what Schnabel might have done, and then experimented by trying the opposite. It was surprising how often that seemed to work.

As a boy, I had been rather literal-minded. I had focused on the details, on mastering the myriad challenges and questions and quirks each piece presented to a player. It took a certain amount of distance for me to start looking beyond the individual details of a piece and understanding the overall principles, the overall approach to music that Schnabel's instruction had been all about. Each piece of music contains within itself the tools for approaching every other piece of music. I was moving from being a student who does what he is told to being able to look at a piece and, if not making my own choices right away, at least determining what the choices were before selecting an option. It's a pivotal moment for every artist. It marks the moment when you are no longer your teacher's student but your own student.

And then, to improve matters still further, another beautiful woman walked into my life.

Her name was Dorothy Druzinsky. Everyone called her Dot. She came from a musical family. Her parents played in the St. Louis Symphony, her father the violin and her mother the harp. Nettie Druzinsky was a petite woman who had played piano when she met Dot's father, but he put her right on harp because, he said, there were fewer harpists around and that's where she would find the most steady jobs. Nettie was all of fifteen when they met. She must have been an amazing musician. She was essentially self-taught on harp, but she worked pretty much nonstop after she learned it. The couple eventually moved to New York, where Louis was in charge of auditioning players for St. Louis to help build up the orchestra and where Nettie played in Broadway shows, in jazz clubs with the likes of Charlie Parker and Charles Mingus, and as an accompanist to the burlesque dancer Sally Rand, famous for her interpretation of the ostrich-feather fan dance. She toured with the Ballets Russes and *The Sound of Music*. She was quite a character. The oldest son of this union, Eddie, was a harpist as well, and a brilliant one. He went to Curtis and studied with Carlos Salzedo, the leading harpist of the twentieth century. When he came home from school and heard his mother play, he'd say, "No, Mom," and show her what he had learned from Salzedo, and she picked that right up too. Eddie went on to be the first harp with the Pittsburgh Symphony, and then the Detroit Symphony, and then the Chicago Symphony, one of the top orchestras in America, where he stayed for decades. You can't get much higher in the harp hierarchy than that.

Dot wasn't a musician at all. She had left all of this, doubtless to save her soul, and was taking a bicycling tour through France. We had something in common right away. We had both come to Europe to get away from our families.

I met Dot through a bass player named June Rotenburg, a compact woman who looked something like her instrument, only shorter.

June knew Dot from St. Louis—she had played with Dot's parents in the orchestra—and she had met me through all of my friends at the Casals festival in Prades, which she had taken part in as well. June thought we might like each other. We met at a café, and they were late. In walked June, accompanied by this girl with a gorgeous head of red-gold hair shining around her face. I could think of nothing better to say than, "Well, it's about time."

And it was. We understood each other right away. We came from similar backgrounds and had similar urges to free ourselves from them. And we were both in Paris. The world was our oyster. Dot was not without other suitors. Leonard Bernstein was interested, at least briefly; I believe he asked her out on a date. Shirley and Ned, Lenny's old friends from Curtis, threw a party for him at the rue de la Harpe apartment; Lukas Foss, another wunderkind from Curtis, came as well, and he also took a shine to Dot. Lukas was on a fellowship at the American Academy in Rome at that point; he had already been the youngest-ever composer to receive a Guggenheim fellowship, and he also had a Fulbright. He was one of those composer-conductor-pianist prodigies (when his second piano concerto was premiered that year in Venice, he played the solo part himself), and he was a very big deal in those days. When he met Dot, he invited her to go with him the following weekend to Brussels, where he was meeting a concert promoter to talk about putting on some of his work. Dot said she would go only if her friend could come along. Her friend was me, and the three of us drove up to Brussels in a Volkswagen Beetle, with Lukas sitting in the back like the proverbial third wheel. Evidently Lukas didn't hold it against me, since many years later we became close friends.

As for Dot, within a few months, we had moved in together, and soon thereafter we decided to get married. Everything just felt right. She was beautiful, she was fun, and she understood the ins and outs of a musical life from her own family, which seemed to be a big advantage. It was certainly the first physical relationship either of us had ever had: in those days such things took a lot longer to come about. And I was filled with a sense that my mother would approve. At last I was doing something that met her standards of what I should be doing with my life. In short: I was still very much a kid. Marjorie was quite eclipsed in my mind—not that she noticed. She ended up staying in Europe and marrying an Italian count named Ferruccio. You really can't blame her.

Dot and I were faced with the problem that we didn't have any money, because I still didn't have any real source of income from my concerts. Dot, therefore, went back to the States and took a temp job as a typist for Esso Standard Oil, just to have some source of income. Company policy at Standard Oil was that every employee had to have a mandatory physical exam, and as fate would have it they discovered a spot of tuberculosis on one of her lungs. So Dot, in the summer of 1951, found herself at a sanatorium in the Adirondacks—only a few years before the advent of antibiotics obviated the need for such facilities and the sanatorium was closed for good. It was a lovely place, the Trudeau Sanatorium; in fact, it was the oldest sanatorium in the United States. Dot made the best of her situation, starting with reading Thomas Mann's *Magic Mountain*, perhaps the most famous literary treatment of life in a TB sanatorium.

I, of course, came home to visit her. I even gave a recital at the sanatorium during her stay, thanks to a man named Elliott Galkin, a brilliant musicologist who happened to be a patient at the same time as Dot and was serving as the facility's social director. The whole time I lived in Europe, I would come back to the States regularly, once or twice a year. I found it curious that, although I missed my family terribly when I was away from them, as soon as I got home I couldn't wait to leave again. Now that Dot was in the picture, there was another family to meet. Because she was in the sanatorium, she couldn't even be present at my meeting with her parents. Her parents, however, were fairly straightforward. They knew what they needed to know about me. The first thing I had to do was audition for them. Being musicians themselves, they had high standards, and if their daughter was going to marry a virtually unknown pianist, he had at least better be good. Fortunately, they liked my playing. Indeed, once I had passed the test, Dot's father welcomed me into the family with open arms. He was delighted to have a fresh ear into which he could pour his copious stream of advice, to which his immediate family members, oddly enough, had grown increasingly deaf over the years.

My mother was straightforward, too. My idea that she would approve of my marriage seemed to have some basis in reality, but of course she also had her own ideas about what would be required of her son's wife. She seemed to like Dot well enough and was reasonably pleasant to her. "Oh," she said, on hearing that Dot made her own clothes, "you're Hattie Carnegie!" But once it was clear that we really were going to get married, and Dot was out of the sanatorium, my parents went to visit her parents and she was sent out of the room while my mother explained to them all the things that Leon's wife would need to be. Finally Nettie said, "Mrs. Fleisher, do you believe there's a girl alive in the world today who could meet all of these qualifications?" My mother, to her credit, burst out laughing.

Dot and I were married in a simple Jewish wedding, to please my mother, at the end of 1951. My mother had lined up the rabbi. The rabbi came from San Francisco, and my mother kept informing us that he was a big fan of mine and had been following my career since I was a boy. He threw a slight fly into the ointment when, as we were assembling before the wedding, he turned to my mother and said, "Now, Mrs. Fleisher, what instrument does your son play?" My mother was unfazed at this demonstration of her occasional talent for, shall we say, elaboration. Dot and I were married, I broke the glass under my heel, and we said good-bye to our families and sailed back to Paris with a combination of elation at starting a new life and a not inconsiderable feeling of relief.

Meanwhile, in a rather unprecedented development, the State Department had started taking an interest in classical music.

Queen Elisabeth was the queen mother of Belgium. She was also fairly serious about music—not wildly talented, but serious. She played the violin; she had studied with the great Eugène Ysaÿe, and Joseph Joachim, Brahms's sometime friend and longtime colleague, had helped her work out her fingerings. Royalty is a great help in establishing musical connections. The queen was very loyal to her friends, though. Ysaÿe had long wanted to create a competition for young musicians, and after he died she set one up in his name, starting in 1937.

The competition alternated from the very beginning: one year it was for violinists and the next year for pianists. In 1937, it was for violinists and the Soviet soloist David Oistrakh won. In 1938, it was for pianists and the Soviet soloist Emil Gilels won. There followed a long hiatus due to the war and postwar reconstruction, and the competition didn't resume until 1951, when it was for violinists again and the Soviet soloist Leonid Kogan won. It was at this point that the State Department began to wonder if the Soviets weren't a little too dominant.

Oistrakh, Gilels, and Kogan were among the greatest soloists of the twentieth century. It was clear that it was going to take some high-class talent to compete on this level. Accordingly, the State Department's division of cultural affairs convened a panel of some of the leading artists in the world—Vladimir Horowitz, George Szell, and their ilk—to come up with a list of America's top young pianists to compete in Brussels. And the State Department began contacting people on their list—Willy Kapell and Byron Janis and Gary and Eugene and a few others—to ask if they would like the department to pay their way to the competition.

This was all very flattering, but no one was very keen on going. All of these young players were already tending burgeoning careers. Winning a competition is great, but there is also the risk of not winning it, which might have a detrimental effect on one's future ability to get concerts. And there was certainly no advantage to being part of any kind of American team, since only one pianist could actually win. So nobody was very interested, even when the State Department offered to pay the way. Some of the pianists who were approached got together and wrote a letter explaining why they didn't want to compete.

But I had nothing to lose.

It was Willy, actually, who thought of me and told me about the scenario, after he'd been approached and before I was. He knew I was probably good enough to win. And he knew I didn't have any notable engagements coming up on my schedule or much of a public reputation, at that point, to damage. When I was in New York he encouraged me: You should really try this.

I have mixed feelings about competitions. I've never been sure what they really achieve. They're so antimusical. They tend to reflect the opinions of the jury rather than any kind of objective criteria. If you have a jury whose members communicate well and think alike, that's one thing, but what's depressing today is that you find the panels made up of people from all different schools of thought and walks of life, and the competitor who winds up winning is the one who least offends the greatest number of jurors. It's hard for anybody with a quirky or distinctive point of view to get by; instead, you end up with the lowest common denominator. The jurors hate to be embarrassed, so they pick the performer who's the closest to machine-perfect. And very often you find virtually the same jury at different competitions all over the world. The same canapé-eating people, sitting in judgment, over and over.

My limited personal exposure to competitions had not been calculated to instill confidence. My only other competition had been one I entered in San Francisco when I was eight years old. There were three finalists: a violinist, a cellist, and myself. The judges couldn't decide among us, so they ended up putting our names in a hat and choosing that way. The cellist was a little boy named Jimmy Arkatov, who ended up as principal cellist of the Pittsburgh Symphony. The pianist was me, and I haven't done so badly. But the winner was the violinist, and

I'm not sure anything became of her at all. I was left with a lingering sense of mistrust.

Still, a competition can kick-start a career, if the cards fall right. Doda was all for my entering. He had already wanted me to enter another competition, the Marguerite Long Competition, in the Salle Gaveau in Paris. I considered the idea, but I was reluctant. The competition had a reputation for not being entirely serious, in part because Mme. Long herself—a pianist of not inconsiderable stature, who premiered Ravel's piano concerto in G—would preside and play a decisive role in influencing the outcome. One year when Artur Rubinstein was on the jury, a winner was selected who was not to Madame's liking. The elderly lady got up on one of the chairs at the front of the auditorium and, turning around to her unsatisfactory colleagues, called out, in a hooty falsetto, "Voilà mon jury des incompétents!"

Another factor in my reluctance was, of course, fear of losing. I might not have had much of a career to jeopardize, but still, I had given some impressive performances and there was some degree of name recognition. Doda had a solution for this, too: why didn't I just reverse the letters of my name and compete as "Noel Rehsielf"? I actually filled out an application to enter the Long competition under this rather awkward appellation, but I got cold feet and backed out. My excuse was that the competition required everyone to play on a Gaveau piano, and since my Philharmonic debut—to say nothing of the hours I had spent in the Steinway basement—I was a Steinway artist. Steinway establishes relationships with many professional concert pianists who agree that they will perform only on Steinway instruments: it's a good association for both the artist and the company. Of course, Steinway is willing to look the other way if certain situations come up that oblige one to use some other piano. But in this case the association was a useful excuse.

I applied for the Queen Elisabeth Competition as Noel Rehsielf, as well. A month later, I got a letter back asking whether I wanted to register as Leon Fleisher or Noel Rehsielf. So I guess my alias wasn't as clever as I thought. Anyway, I had taken the plunge.

Dot and I had taken over a friend's apartment on the rue de Verneuil, a wonderful place. By now, Paris was feeling like home. And I immersed myself totally in practicing for the competition.

The Queen Elisabeth Competition was held in May 1952 in Brussels and lasted for a month. The month was divided into several stages. In the first round, everyone had to play the Mozart K. 282 sonata in E-flat, one of the infrequently played earlier ones, as well as a piece of their choice by Bach. That winnowed out fifty of the seventy-five contestants (and my performance was so well received that the jury had to ring a bell to restore order in the room, which certainly helped my confidence). Those who made it to the next round had to play a sonatina written expressly for the event by Francis de Bourguignon, a Belgian composer who was wounded in World War I and subsequently accompanied the soprano Dame Nellie Melba in concerts for the troops. We also played another piece of our own choosing, and then the jury asked for works they wanted to hear from our repertory lists. I felt pretty secure. Most of the works I was bringing to Brussels were pieces I had performed in my first career as a sixteen- or seventeen-year old: the Liszt Hungarian Rhapsody No. 6 (the one that features an extended section in which the right hand plays entirely in octaves), the Liszt sonata, the Stravinsky Serenade in A, the Schubert B-flat sonata. I had them under my belt.

Those first two rounds took two weeks. At the end of that period there were twelve of us left standing, and we were all taken off to one of Queen Elisabeth's chateaux for a week—in, of all places, the suburb of Waterloo—so we could learn a brand-new concerto written by another Belgian composer none of us had ever heard of, Raymond Chevreuille, for the finals, as well as working on a concerto of our choice. For this, we were on our own. We were expressly cut off from any communication with the outside world, by phone or mail or anything else, so that we wouldn't get any help on the new piece. It was a pretty stupid rule, since of course we were constantly playing the piece for one another in the chateau, something that had a lot more influence on our performances than anything that most of our families and friends could have offered. Dot, meanwhile, was left to her own devices in Brussels for a week, though one evening she snuck over and we were able to exchange a few words through a hedge or door on the chateau grounds in a kind of *Romeo and Juliet* moment.

The competitors developed quite a camaraderie during those seven days. We each had a little apartment with a piano in it, but all our meals were communal and we quickly got to know one another and one another's characteristics as players. We also devised whatever form of recreation we could when we needed to get away from our keyboards. We developed a game with a Ping-Pong table that involved taking the net off the table and, in teams of four or five, trying to blow the ball off the opponents' side. This led to a considerable amount of hyperventilation. There were only two women in the finals, a little brunette Belgian girl named Janine Kinet and Maria Tipo, the Italian virtuoso, who was just an angel, a blond angel, and was already embarked on an enduring solo career. The chateau had a central courtyard with a fountain that featured a nymph spraying water, and on the third morning of our exile, when we awoke and looked out our windows, the nymph was wearing a brassiere. The big question was, Whose? Nobody was talking.

We also rapidly reached a consensus about the Chevreuille concerto. It was quite tricky and not a very good piece at all, and we decided that we didn't want to play the whole thing; it should be enough to play just two movements. That is, eleven of us decided this. There was one holdout, Philippe Entremont, who was only a seventeen-year-old kid (and is now a distinguished soloist and conductor). Not only did he learn the whole concerto, but he played it from memory. The little twerp. The rest of us weren't about to let him make us look bad. One night a finalist named Yuri Boukoff and I got together and backed Philippe into a corner. Yuri, who came from Bulgaria, had been a boxer in a former life, and he towered over Philippe, who sat under us slightly goggle-eyed as we informed him in our best simulation of a gang-member tone that if he didn't at least pretend to read the music from the printed page during the final like the rest of us, bad things were going to happen. Philippe, though, had the last laugh. He did put the score up on the music rack during the final, but he didn't turn a page through his whole performance, so it was obvious to everybody that he wasn't actually referring to it.

There was a certain consensus about the concerto that we got to choose, as well. Four of us—including one of the other American finalists, Lamar Crowson—picked the Brahms D Minor. I wasn't worried. It was, after all, my piece, and though my heart was racing eagerly as I sat down to play in the final round, I was soon swept up in the storm of the opening tutti, and then I was off and running myself. And then—two of the piano's strings snapped. It happens sometimes. An anxious buzz rose from the audience, but I silenced it by continuing playing. Piano notes are triple-strung, and in this case one string had broken on each of two different notes, so there were still two strings left to make a sound when I hit the keys in question. At the end of the first movement, a piano technician raced in from backstage to repair the damage.

The incident didn't shake my confidence. I felt I was in a groove. For the whole competition, I had sailed along feeling fairly sure I could win. Still, there was a sense of anticipation when the jurors called us back to the stage to make their final announcement. They read my name first, and three thousand people in the audience greeted it with a roar of approval.

Victory was sweet. Just how sweet it was wouldn't fully emerge until later. What I most remember about the night is a sense of anticlimax. It had in part to do with the bonding period we had been through at the chateau. We had gotten to know one another and one another's playing so well that to be summarily labeled best, second

best, third best, and so on left a very bad taste in the mouth. Karl
Engel, a Swiss pianist, came in second, and Maria, who had played
the Saint-Saëns Fifth Concerto, called the Egyptian concerto because
of all the exotic non-Western touches (and because Saint-Saëns wrote
it in Egypt), came in third. One of the contestants who had done very
well in the first rounds came in quite a bit lower than he expected
and burst into tears when his name was announced. We all went over
to comfort him.

And then there was a reception, where we all received the congratulations of the queen and celebrated the release of four weeks of
tension. And then there were the hugs good-bye and the leave-takings,
and Dot and I went back to our hotel, and the competition was over.

There were, of course, almost immediate repercussions. For one
thing, as the winner of the competition, I had a string of concerts
lined up, part of the automatic benefits waiting for whoever took the
prize.

For another, Willy Kapell, hearing I had won, went straight to
Arthur Judson, his manager, and said, Give him a contract. Which
Judson, conveniently having forgotten his previously stated unwilling-
ness to touch me with a ten-foot pole, promptly did.

For a third, I went over to the queen's for a private tête-à-tête
and accompanied her in a Vivaldi concerto, which greatly gratified
her. She was in her late seventies by then, and she was a sweet, wonderful old lady. It was discreetly pointed out to me that all of her
ladies-in-waiting were at least a few years older than she was. She may
have been elderly, but she had her vanity.

And, of course, the State Department had an American victory to
trumpet. It was slightly diminished by the fact that the Russians, in
1952, didn't send a team at all. That did take a wee bit of the shine out
of the win, for me. Nonetheless, the competition served me very well.

CHAPTER 5

THE
YOUNG LION

The keyboard: the center of my life.
UPI Roto Service/Corbis (Author's collection)

George Szell's ice blue eyes, through those thick, round Coke-bottle glasses, were piercing. They fixed you like a butterfly on a pin. When Szell looked at you, you felt he was seeing into your inner-most being. He seemed to penetrate the music in the same way. Very few conductors have that quality of getting to the very essence of the material while somehow being in control of it at the same time. Otto Klemperer was one. George Szell was another.

Szell had the greatest ears I have ever encountered. He had scars behind his ears—I believe they were from mastoid operations in his youth—that made him seem almost alien, as if he had been fitted out with an ability to hear beyond that of mere mortals. He heard everything. And his inner ear had a veritable need for a kind of aural transparency: he had to hear each element of the music standing out in relief from all the others. Balance. Timbre. The juxtaposition of two or three particular kinds of sound. The result, when he conducted, was music that sounded as clear and new as if you had just washed out your own ears. You heard the music freshly and became aware of things that you never heard, in the same piece, from anyone else.

Szell's high standards were legendary. He would dismiss musi-cians for making too many mistakes in rehearsals or criticize them if he happened to hear them warming up backstage in a way he didn't like. There was a huge turnover at the Cleveland Orchestra in the years after he was appointed music director. It paid off, though. He turned that orchestra into an ensemble capable of hair-trigger control, attuned to every nuance of what was happening in the music, playing at a level you usually find only in the highest-level string quartets. If you undertook to make music with George Szell, you were expected to share his standards. If not, you might find yourself at the receiving end of a fierce glare that inspired a jolt of pure terror. Those eyes never let you forget.

I had played with Szell before I won the Queen Elisabeth Competition. But the real beginning of our artistic collaboration came in 1954, after my victory, when I played with him at the New York Philharmonic. Over the next ten years, we forged an enduring relationship that proved to be one of the most rewarding artistic experiences of my life.

Playing the piano is a joy, but it can also be sheer terror. This was never more true than when you were about to perform with George Szell. Making music with him was thrilling, and exhilarating, and terrifying. On the one hand, it gave you wings. On the other, you never knew when he might cut you down. Every time I landed at the Cleveland airport, I could feel a knot of tension forming in my stomach—partly excitement, partly sheer panic. You had to rev yourself up to play with Szell. You reached this level of hyperawareness, of total focus, what athletes call being in the zone. It was scary, but it was also ecstatic because it was such damn good music making.

Szell was not generally intimidated by his soloists. He thought nothing of pushing the likes of Clifford Curzon or Rudi Serkin off the piano bench during a rehearsal to demonstrate how a certain passage should go. Szell was an impressive pianist himself, and he had also known Rudi since they were teenagers in Vienna, so he wasn't awed by him in any sense. Serkin used to make mistakes when he was playing with Szell that he would never make when he was playing with other conductors. It was a liability of Szell's that he used to make musicians, both orchestra players and soloists, so nervous that sometimes it interfered with their playing. He once emerged from listening to the playback of a Mozart recording and barked at the orchestra,

"Gentlemen, it just sounds tense! Relax!" Everyone burst out laughing. There was a wonderful irony in barking out a command to relax in a voice that was guaranteed to increase everyone's tension.

I was no less scared than anybody else, but my fear evidently spurred me on. Still, I don't quite understand why, of all the great pianists Szell worked with, it was I who became, in a sense, his musical son. Somehow, we had the same approach to making music. Szell adored Schnabel, and I was a student of Schnabel, and in many ways we had the same understanding of the challenges that some of the great composers represent. We thought about music in very similar ways. We were, perhaps, both self-driven in a relentless striving for the perfect realization of the music we were attacking. We never had a word of disagreement about interpretation or approach. One of Szell's weaknesses was that he sometimes got so hung up on perfection that what emerged was a coldly clinical display of the innards of the piece. I like to think that I helped him release some of the warmth that was occasionally lacking in his music making.

He often showed me a great deal of affection in rehearsals. He used to call me "Schnozzola." Then, if I did something rather subtle and refined that he particularly liked, he would call me "Schnozzolino." If I played something big, powerful, and meaty, I was "Schnozzolone." I don't know where he got that—maybe from Jimmy Durante. I suspect he just wanted to show off his knowledge of Italian.

And he could become almost embarrassingly sentimental at times. There's a picture of us together in which he appears to be about to chuck me under the chin. I am recoiling a bit. Even by the great George Szell, one did not want to be chucked.

Of course, I was sometimes—even frequently—intimidated by him. But because I sensed his regard for me, I was also sometimes pretty fearless about making suggestions to him. When we were recording the Beethoven B-flat concerto, my old standby, he couldn't get the orchestra to play the opening tutti to his satisfaction. He put his hand out to signal to me that I shouldn't play, and he did a couple of takes, but he still wasn't happy. I went up to him on the podium and said, "I think if they played it a little more debonair." He loved it. He immediately latched on to the word, turned to the orchestra, and said, "Gentlemen, more *debonair*." They, of course, obeyed. If you listen to that recording, you can hear that debonair quality, right at the start: like Charlie Chaplin walking down the Champs-Élysées.

I even had the nerve to play jokes on him. When we were rehearsing in the studio for our recording of the Schumann concerto, as we were about to start the second movement, he stopped. "We don't have to rehearse this," he said. "I've trained the orchestra so that whatever you do in those four opening chords, they will respond in kind. The inflection, the articulation, everything: they will follow you." So we didn't rehearse it in the studio. Then we went out on stage for the orchestral rehearsal and played through the first movement, and some dybbuk took hold of me. As he turned to prepare for the second movement, before he had even gotten his stick up to give the downbeat, I sprang into the opening, those four gentle little chords, like an eager puppy, playing them twice as fast as they would normally go. After all, he had told me that the orchestra would follow whatever I did. Szell, caught by surprise, just stood there frozen, holding his stick in midair, while the orchestra hopped in after me. They did follow me. They played exactly in my tempo, as if we'd been practicing it that way. Szell couldn't restrain a huge smile.

Another time, when we were on an American tour somewhere in the Southwest, I went up to him after a performance of the Tchaikovsky Fifth Symphony and suggested, half jokingly, that he hold out the last long chord until the audience started clapping. You can actually force the audience to start clapping if you maintain the chord with that kind of intensity. He loved that, too. I don't know if he always did it that way, but he certainly kept doing it for the remainder of that tour. For all of his purism, he had a performer's instincts. He was happy to get the audience to applaud for Tchaikovsky, and for him, when he had the chance and it was in keeping with the spirit of the music.

And our one-on-one dealings also had a certain zany quality. I often tell the story about Szell, in his hotel room in London, wanting me to run through with him one of the Beethoven concertos we were in the process of recording. The problem was that there was no piano in the room. Szell suggested that I simply play the piece on the coffee table; he knew the concerto so well, he said, that he would be able to tell if I slipped up. So I drummed out the notes soundlessly on the tabletop until the maestro stopped me. "You made a mistake," he said.

"Well, what do you expect?" I said. "I've never played this coffee table before."

When it became clear that Szell was turning Cleveland into one of the world's preeminent orchestras, the record labels started itching to record him. In those days, classical music recordings made big money, and big conductors were hot properties. Herbert von Karajan's recordings sold so well that they practically supported his label, Deutsche Grammophon. So Columbia Records had its eye on Szell. Columbia's problem was that it already had contracts with the Philadelphia Orchestra and Eugene Ormandy, and with the New York Philharmonic and Leonard Bernstein, and it didn't really have the ability to sign up another conductor. The company's solution was to take a small jazz label called Epic Records, turn it into a classical label, and have Szell record on that. It asked him to become Epic's house conductor and record the entire literature.

Szell accepted. Then he approached me and asked me to become, in effect, his house pianist: to record with him and the Clevelanders every major work ever written for piano and orchestra. It was the greatest opportunity a pianist could have dreamed of.

So help me, my first fleeting thought was, "Then I'll never be able to record with Lenny." I hesitated, for a split second.

Szell, who missed nothing, saw it. He roared, "You hesitate? To record the entire piano literature with me?"

I said hastily, "No, no, no, I'd love to, thank you."

Our first recording consisted of Rachmaninoff's "Rhapsody on a Theme of Paganini" and my one-time nemesis, Franck's *Symphonic Variations*, which Karl Ulrich Schnabel, all those years ago, had fortunately finally succeeded in getting me to learn. The Rachmaninoff was something of a challenge for George, since it really wasn't his music any more than it had been Schnabel's. Szell shared Schnabel's taste for music that contained a minimum of schmaltz. Rachmaninoff is rather heavy on the schmaltz factor. I can't quite believe my memory on this, but I could swear now that when we reached the eighteenth variation—the most famous section of the piece, a big, goopy crowd-pleasing tune that's appeared on several film soundtracks—Szell mouthed to the players, "Like the Philadelphia Orchestra!" The Philadelphia Orchestra was known for its thick, lush string sound, and Rachmaninoff had called it his favorite orchestra in the world and they recorded plenty of his music under Ormandy and Stokowski, so it certainly would have made sense. It's hard for me to believe that Szell would have invoked the Philadelphians so openly in a way that was, coming from him, an implicit put-down. But it's what I remember. It was our first recording together and we were both very high, so perhaps he just got carried away.

What I know is true is that we got the whole thing in the can in one take. I made one single mistake in one of the fast octave runs in what you might call the cadenza, before the last two variations, and I thus had an opportunity to learn, thanks to our producer, Howard Scott, about the magic of splicing. Howard realized that the second time I played the run it was clean. He therefore made a copy of the recording, wound the reel-to-reel tape back through the machine until he found the right segment, cut it out with a razor blade, and laid the good octave in over the bad one, expunging the mistake. All the rest of the performance came out just as you hear it. We were flying. We were also animated by the ministrations of the CEO of Epic Records, a businessman named George Schick. Schick flew out to Cleveland for our recording session, and before the session he came to me in my dressing room and advised me to bear in mind that the session was

costing $10,000 an hour. His words weren't exactly calculated to calm
me down, but at least I know we didn't waste any of his money by
running overtime on that one.

That wasn't actually my first recording. It was my third. My first
recording came about thanks to Peter Diamand, Schnabel's old amanuensis from Lake Como, who was now married to Maria Curcio, my
fellow student who had taken me under her wing so warmly when I
was ten. Peter and Maria had settled in the Netherlands, where Peter,
well on his way to becoming a big-name impresario, had cofounded
and was running the Holland Festival. Soon after I won the Queen
Elisabeth Competition, Peter called me and asked if I would be interested in learning Paul Hindemith's *Four Temperaments* and recording it
with Szymon Goldberg and the Netherlands Chamber Orchestra. I
was a quick learner in those days, so I said sure and made the recording only a couple of months later. That was my first commercial
recording. Then, in 1954, I signed a contract with Columbia Records,
a major step that for me was absolutely thrilling. The first record I
made for Columbia featured the Schubert sonata that, in Paris, had led
me out of despair into the beginnings of confidence: the B-flat sonata,
D. 960. My next recording was with Szell.

I had been conditioned to be distrustful of recording, in that
Schnabel had been ambivalent about it. He felt that playing was a living thing and that to set it in stone, or on shellac, was to kill it off, ren-
dering it airless and barren. When he started recording the Beethoven
sonata cycle—a project that lasted a decade—he was unhappy with the
quality of the sound, felt artistically stifled, harried the engineers, and
referred to the studio as "my torture chamber." It can't have helped
that in those days a record side lasted only about four minutes, so he
kept having to stop in the middle of the piece while the technicians
changed the disks. His Beethoven cycle remains a landmark of classical
music recording, but though he got more reconciled to the recording
process over the years, it always held, for him, some of the features
of a straitjacket.

By the time I came along, though, the situation was quite different. Recordings have shaped the ears and the musical knowledge of the last few generations, and artists are used to the idea of committing their interpretations to posterity. In fact, the ubiquity of recordings has contributed to the increase in technical ability I've seen take place during my own career. Young artists today believe that any mistake or slip can doom an interpretation. The kids who are coming along now have unbelievable technical mastery of the instrument; it seems to get better every year. Interpretation is another matter. That's where I can be of some use.

Anyway, I had no problem with recording. Indeed, as I got more used to it, I may have gotten overconfident. Once when Szell and I were playing with the New York Philharmonic in the late 1950s, I made a recording with the Juilliard Quartet—we were doing the Brahms piano quintet—the same week. The recording sessions took place on Monday and Tuesday, and then on Wednesday I started rehearsing with the Philharmonic for performances at the end of the week. Our recording session on Tuesday went quite late; we finished the piece, but I didn't get to bed until after one o'clock in the morning. I was quite proud of how well the whole thing had gone, and on Wednesday morning, when I came in to rehearsal, I mentioned to Szell—rather foolishly, in retrospect—that I had been recording Brahms until one in the morning and it was really rather good. Szell was not particularly interested in hearing how well it had gone. "Next time," he said severely, "when you play with me, you have no other concerts or recordings or anything that week. You rest, you work, and you only concentrate on what we are doing."

I learned a lesson: not to mention it. It certainly didn't affect my playing. I was young. I could do anything.

Those of us who worked with Szell felt a certain unspoken bond. It was like coming through the wars together, victorious but battered. The experience led to a number of connections over the years. I shared it with Peter Mennin, a composer who appeared to represent a bright future of the field and who had a new symphony premiered on a program that I appeared on. I shared it with the violinist Jaime Laredo and the cellist Lynn Harrell, both Szell protégés. And I immediately hit it off with the violinist Berl Senofsky, one of a particularly illustrious line of assistant concertmasters who served under Szell's concertmaster, Joseph Gingold. Berl was a tremendously talented violinist, built like a tank and gleefully irreverent. In rehearsal, he was always needling Joe Gingold under Szell's nose, trying to get him to laugh. Szell appreciated his talent but didn't think too much of his character. Berl and I complemented each other musically. He was the kind of player who takes a lot of expressive liberties with the music, and I was more straight. The combination worked well.

In 1955, Berl left the orchestra and went off to try his luck at the Queen Elisabeth Competition in Brussels, and he became the first American violinist to win it. I happened to be in Brussels during his competition, and we hung out together at the times he was allowed to mingle with the public. One night I went by his pension to pick him up for dinner, and the family that ran the pension brought me into the kitchen while Berl finished getting ready upstairs. The family matriarch, a grandmother, was sitting by the fireplace wearing a bonnet, and there was something tantalizingly familiar about her, but I couldn't imagine where I might have met her. I mentioned this to Berl after we left, and he laughed and said that he'd been informed that the family was somehow related to Beethoven. That was it. The grandmother was sitting there wearing Beethoven's face.

My career had taken off. After winning the Queen Elisabeth Competition, I was launched into a brave new world.

It started with the telegram from Arthur Judson, instigated, as I said, by Willy Kapell. As soon as I agreed to be his client—I didn't hesitate—Judson sent out a telegram to every major orchestra in the United States. Getting bookings for me was facilitated by the fact that he managed most of the conductors in those orchestras. Indeed, he even managed some of the orchestras himself.

Judson was a towering figure on the American classical music scene, literally and figuratively: physically, he was a huge and imposing man. He had something approaching a monopoly in American music, since in addition to managing a healthy percentage of classical music's biggest stars, he was for a time also the manager of the New York Philharmonic and the Philadelphia Orchestra, putting him in the comfortable position—for him—of having to negotiate artists' fees with himself. In 1930, he united a group of independent agencies into the firm that was later to be known as Columbia Artists Management, CAMI, still one of the powerhouses in classical music. Not surprisingly, he hired a lot of his agency's artists as soloists with the New York Philharmonic—including me and George Szell, performing that Brahms D Minor concerto together in early 1954.

It would have happened sooner had I not decided to postpone my American comeback for a year. It was a calculated decision. First of all, there were a lot of concert obligations in Belgium and Holland as a result of winning the competition. It seemed that Dot and I spent half our time in the car driving from one small town to another. We didn't mind, because we were quite enjoying the Low Countries. We liked seeing the Dutch on their bikes, pedaling, upright, along the canals. We liked it that the food was good and that life was cheaper than it was in America. We liked being close to Maria Curcio and Peter Diamand, who became the center of a lively circle of friends. We liked having some distance from our families. And we liked it that there were eleven symphony orchestras in Holland—including the Concertgebouw, one of the greatest orchestras in the world—making it ripe territory for a concert pianist. So I put off my American concerts until the 1953–54 season, and Dot and I moved from Paris to Holland instead.

Holland was also a better climate for a baby. In 1953, Dot gave birth to a baby girl whom we named Deborah. Actually, we traveled back to the States for the baby to be born. It was a Cesarean section, which for some reason kind of scared me, but everything was fine. Debbie was healthy and, of course, the most beautiful child who had ever been born, with dark hair and big green eyes. I got to see her during a break on what amounted to my comeback tour.

I had something like twenty-two American concerts that year. It was a wonderful tour: audiences were excited, the reviews were glowing, and I felt pretty set up by the whole thing. At the end of the season, I went into the Columbia Artists offices in New York, which were run on a day-to-day basis by two women named Ruth O'Neill and Ada Cooper. They were harpies, straight out of one of the more sinister Greek myths. They peered at me over their desks, ignoring my sheaf of press clippings and my calendar of engagements, and intoned, balefully, "Beware second-year slump."

My heart sank; I quaked in my boots. I thought, I'd better really work hard to avoid any problems. My next tour, however, went off without a hitch—at which point the harpies, in the same dire tones, exhorted me to beware of third-year slump. By the time they were warning me about ten-year slump, I had started to get the idea.

Winning the competition after my long drought had slightly changed my attitude toward the piano. Specifically, I thought I'd better practice. Before, I had been only too happy to accept Schnabel's dictum that the most important thing is understanding the music, which kept me to a relatively modest (for a concert soloist) four hours a day. But the abortive end of my first, teenage piano career had showed me where a lack of practicing could lead.

I didn't have the ferocious technical chops of some of my colleagues. Jacob Lateiner, for instance, was a hand crusher. When he shook your hand, it appeared to be with intent to break it, and he went at the piano keyboard the same way. I didn't like the sound he made, but it was certainly impressive. Willy, too, had that kind of power when he started out, though he stopped focusing on it so much when he found other things that interested him more, musically.

This virtuosic power, the kind of power that makes people refer to "a black belt in piano": that I didn't have. Some pieces were still beyond me. I was not at all confident, for instance, that I could get my fingers around Beethoven's twenty-ninth sonata, Op. 106, called the "Hammerklavier," which is one of the hardest pieces in the literature.

And I had never practiced like a New York pianist. Schnabel wasn't an advocate of overpracticing, those nine- and ten-hour days that Rudi Serkin and his students would put in. Now, though, I finally had a career going that seemed to be taking me in the right direction. I wasn't about to let it slip away again. I had a family to support, and I felt the responsibility keenly. So I began putting in more hours at the keyboard than I ever had before. It didn't dawn on me that all that work might be taking a physical toll.

Szell wasn't the only conductor with whom I was reunited in the phoenixlike rise of my new, flourishing career. I also continued playing with Pierre Monteux. At this point in my life, it was rather like coming to see Grandpa, with Grandma Doris imperious and wonderful backstage. I once counted up and discovered that I performed with Monteux a total of eighty-two times. That's quite a lot of orchestra concerts. During one run of the Brahms D Minor concerto that we did in Boston, I realized it was the thirteenth time we had done that concerto together. I told him that with some amusement. Monteux, however, was rather disturbed. "Oh, we have to find another one this season," he said. "We have to get over the thirteenth." Thirteen was unlucky.

I was playing with Monteux in Amsterdam in February of 1953 when my mother died.

My mother had reconciled herself to my being in Europe. She knew I was doing well. She approved of the fact that I was married and sent us long letters filled with advice. And of course, she strongly approved of my winning the competition, although I think she viewed it as only my due, or even hers.

But I was far away. Ray was the son who stayed home to take care of my parents. This meant putting his own life plans on hold. Ray wanted to be a chemical engineer, but after he came back from the war Dad desperately needed help in the factory and asked if Ray could oblige for a while. Ray did, and a year turned into two years, and five became ten years, and it wasn't so easy to move on. I, meanwhile, after a childhood in which all the family's attentions were focused on me, was gallivanting around Europe. There must have been some resentment, but to Ray's credit he never, ever showed it—except, perhaps, by bugging me incessantly about why I wasn't more famous. Why didn't I get more publicity? Why wasn't he reading more about me in newspapers and magazines? That went on nonstop for most of my life.

Ray was also united with my parents in trying to protect me from bad news. As a result, I didn't have any idea that my mother was in bad shape. I couldn't have done much for her if I had known. In those days, women were often reluctant to go to the doctor about complaints in certain parts of their anatomy. My mother knew she needed to go, but put it off and put it off. When at last she went and the doctor confirmed that she had developed breast cancer, it was too late. Ray finally wrote me a letter and broke the news to me of just how serious things were. I responded by writing my mother a heartfelt letter about all the things she meant to me, and all the things she had done for me, and my gratitude, and my love. She didn't live to read it.

I was playing with the Concertgebouw, a tremendous career opportunity. We had finished the first of three scheduled performances when Ray's telegram came. My mother had died.

The reality was almost more than I could handle. I was far away, and helpless. What should I do? Cancel everything and run home? Stay, and feel callous? My first instinct was to cancel, but Monteux and his wife advised against it. What could I achieve by going home? It was too late for a final good-bye; I wouldn't even make it back for the funeral. Everyone told me, with some justice, that my mother herself would have been violently against my canceling. Ray's telegram was specific on that point. He begged me not to come home and insisted that Mom wouldn't have wanted it.

So I stayed in Amsterdam and played the last two performances with the Concertgebouw. But somehow that remains, for me, an enormous regret. I felt perhaps I owed it to my mother at least to have made the gesture. My mother was in many ways not an easy woman. Her vision for me was often constricting. And she had certainly had trouble letting me go. Even after I moved to Europe, she treated me as her little boy whenever I came home, and it used to drive me crazy.

But she was also utterly devoted to her family and to doing her duty by them. I thought of her cooking three meals a day, week in, week out, trudging back and forth to the grocery store, lighting the Sabbath candles, and sacrificing everything, including at times her family's comfort, for her piano-playing son. At least she lived long enough to know that I had won the Queen Elisabeth Competition and to get a whiff of the big career that was heading my way. You could say it represented the culmination of her life's work. She didn't get the first Jewish president, but she got the concert pianist.

For the next few years, our lives followed a certain pattern, though hardly a predictable one. Dot and I made frequent trips to the United States to perform, see our families, and show off the grandchildren; in 1956, our son, Richard, known to all as Dickie, joined the family. But we stayed based in Europe. We just liked it better. Of course, this meant that Dot was often left alone with the two children while I was off on tour. I can't say I was a wonderful father. In those days, child raising was viewed as women's work, and I was so consumed with my new career that I didn't involve myself as much as I could have. I don't think Dot was crazy about being left alone so much, although that would have happened no matter where we were based. One of the difficulties with a concert career is that much of one's life is lived on the road.

There were, though, considerable compensations. I was being introduced to some of the greatest figures in the music world: the eccentric, outsized personalities who were the leading conductors of the day. Many of them had direct connections back to the Golden Age, to Brahms's Vienna or Tchaikovsky's St. Petersburg. They were not quite of our world. They came outfitted with their own sets of quirks and foibles, to prove it. I learned that dealing with conductors was like dealing with high-strung horses: each had to be managed in a very particular way.

I played the B-flat Beethoven concerto with Fritz Reiner, the great maestro of the Pittsburgh and then the Chicago Symphony Orchestra. Boris Goldovsky, the impresario and radio host, once said of Reiner, "He had a gimlet eye that could pierce you like a dagger, even when he was looking at you from the side, and he had a tongue to match." I remember Reiner's tongue in particular, since throughout our entire performance his mouth was open and his tongue was hanging out. It wasn't an especially inspiring sight; in fact, it was rather awful. The music making, though, was terrific; Reiner was a brilliant technician.

I played with Igor Markevitch a number of times. Markevitch was a dapper Russian émigré who started out as a composer and was known, in his youth, as "the second Igor," the first being Stravinsky. Markevitch later switched his focus entirely to conducting, and when I knew him his own music had fallen into oblivion, though he made some attempts to revive it shortly before his death.

The first time I played with Markevitch, we did the Rachmaninoff Paganini Rhapsody with the radio orchestra in Cologne. Markevitch missed the first rehearsal because he had to attend the funeral of the titanic German conductor Wilhelm Furtwängler in Heidelberg. He showed up the next day, apologizing profusely, and we got to work. But he was possibly a little flustered; it was his first time conducting the piece, and he wasn't that sure of himself. This became abundantly clear in the performance during the fifteenth variation, a particularly rapid one in which the soloist runs all over the keyboard and the orchestra comes in halfway through. Markevitch brought the orchestra in wrong. There was nothing I could do about it: I had my hands full just keeping up with my passagework. And it took Markevitch a moment to realize what had happened. For a couple of bars, therefore, it sounded as if we were playing Schoenberg rather than Rachmaninoff, until Markevitch simply stopped the orchestra and I finished the variation myself.

Because it was a radio orchestra, the actual performance was only for a few hundred people. The real point of the exercise was the broadcast, which was scheduled to take place the next day. Driving home to Holland, I turned on the radio to listen, with some anxiety. To my astonishment, the fifteenth variation sounded perfectly fine. When I got home, I called the station in bewilderment and was informed that they had recorded the rehearsal, just to be on the safe side, and for the broadcast had replaced our disastrous take with a perfect one.

The night before, after the concert, the director of the radio had taken a group of us out for a meal. Markevitch was the last to order and couldn't make up his mind what he wanted to eat. Finally, he settled on "*cinq huitres*," five oysters. It seemed to me the epitome of a bygone species of Russian czarist elegance to be so particular about what one ate that one wouldn't simply go for half a dozen.

But the conductor I most wanted to play with was Otto Klemperer. Klemperer was one of the greatest of them all. He had known Mahler, and in the 1920s and 1930s he had introduced a lot of new work by people like Janáček, Hindemith, and Stravinsky. He got away from the Nazis in good time, emigrating to America in 1933 and settling in California, where he was for a number of years the music director of the Los Angeles Philharmonic. Unfortunately, he was operated on in 1939 for a brain tumor—which it turned out he didn't actually have—and the surgery left him prone to somewhat erratic behavior, though it didn't stop him going on to maintain an important career in postwar Europe.

Klemperer was like Prometheus. He was a huge man, standing six five or six six, so tall that he didn't use a podium when he conducted but stood on the same level as the orchestra, and he still towered over them. His conducting technique was never much to boast of, but he looked at you—often balefully—and, like osmosis, you were somehow able to play what he wanted. He cheated death any number of times. Things kept happening to him that would have killed a normal man: he fell down the gangway coming out of an airplane; he accidentally set a fire while smoking a cigar in bed and got badly burned when he tried to put it out with a glass of Scotch. But he kept coming back. The stories about him were legion. This was a man who, when he was dissatisfied with the service in a hotel he was staying in, went out and pissed on the hallway rug to show his displeasure. How could you not want to play with a figure like that? I longed to perform with him, and I let it be known that I'd be willing to travel whatever distance it took to have the opportunity.

My wish came true. When I was in New York on one of our stateside visits, I got a call asking if I would like to come play the Beethoven G Major concerto—the fourth—with Klemperer and the Cologne Radio Orchestra. There was only one condition, they said: Klemperer insisted on having four rehearsals, a rather large number for a standard concerto. They were rather apologetic, as if having extra rehearsals with Otto Klemperer were something I might balk at rather than seeing it as the opportunity of a lifetime.

I didn't have to be asked twice. I went over to Germany for four rehearsals and a single performance.

Any intimidation I felt about playing with the great Klemperer was only intensified by his noncommittal air when we actually met. He shook my hand and didn't say much. And at our first rehearsal, he didn't look at me once. Nor did he say a single word to me. The same thing was true at the second rehearsal: not one look. After the third rehearsal, I was starting to feel a little down about the whole thing. I had come all the way from the United States to work with one of my idols, and nothing appeared to be happening.

During the fourth rehearsal, though, at one point in the music, Klemperer turned around. He opened his mouth. And from the cavern of his chest emerged a deep, sepulchral, gravelly "Jaaaaa," *yes*. I was flooded with joy. That single word of approval made it all worthwhile.

The next morning, I went back to the radio station to record the Brahms Händel variations, which the director of the station had set up for me to help fill out the fee for the trip. As I was playing, the door of the studio opened and in walked Klemperer, accompanied by his daughter, Lotte. Without saying a word, he took a chair at the side of the room and settled in to listen to me play.

The only sign he gave that he was listening came from his cane. While I played one of the variations, he began beating time with it, rather vigorously. It might have seemed like a sign of participation, or approval, but Klemperer was a conductor. A conductor beats time only when he wants people to follow him. He didn't like my tempo. He wanted it slower.

After a couple of years in Holland, Dot and I were ready to move on. In 1956, my old patron, J. D. Zellerbach, was appointed ambassador to Italy and suggested that we might like to come live in Rome. This sounded like a good idea to us. We were up for anything. The circumstances were pretty ideal, too; after some initial searching, we ended up living in a wonderful big apartment on the Lungotevere delle Armi, right on the river Tiber. We had two maids, one for the house and one for the children. They started squabbling, though, because each thought the other had an easier assignment. Finally Dot had them switch places for a day. After that, they were perfectly happy to go back to their original jobs.

We also bought a car, a Fiat, which was delivered to us in Rome at the end of one of our American sojourns. I picked it up and drove it down to Naples to collect Dot and the children, who were arriving by boat, and to visit Maria Tipo, my friend from the Queen Elisabeth Competition. We all went out for a meal, and when we came back we learned the true meaning of *rubato*, a term used in music to denote slowing down for expressive purposes in places that are not marked in the score: you're stealing a beat or two. This meaning was driven home when we learned that our car was *rubata*, stolen. It was found a few days later, with all its tires gone, but at least we got it back. Later, when we left Rome, we gave the car to a lawyer to sell for us, and he stole all the money. We decided that the car was clearly bad luck and we had been lucky not to be killed in it.

Moving to Rome may actually have been a bit of a mistake. It was in Rome that I first realized that it was somewhat ludicrous for a grown person to spend six or seven hours a day at a big black piano when there was so much else you could be doing with your time. You could, for instance, be out in a café in a piazza somewhere, listening to the soft plashing of the water in the fountains and watching beautiful people walking past you. Such beautiful people. The Italian women were gorgeous. These attractively beguiling possibilities put me in a bad space and definitely cut down on my desire to work. I suppose I had had issues with practicing before, but Rome made them acute again.

Still, I was making music all the time. There were all kinds of musicians in Rome, including Americans who had come over with Fulbrights or Guggenheims or the Rome Prize, a fellowship to work for a year or two at the American Academy in Rome. One composer who overlapped with us there was already a good friend of mine: Leon Kirchner. Leon was something of a maverick: his work was difficult but very expressive and emotional. He never embraced the twelve-tone system of Schoenberg—though Schoenberg was one of his teachers—or serialism, the idea of using systematic arrangements of rhythm or tone or dynamic markings as a basis for a musical work that was such a cornerstone of serious composition at midcentury. Leon wrote rigorous music, but he always went his own way. I had actually met him back in the late forties, when I was a teenager in New York and heard him play a recital at Columbia University's Miller Theater. His piano sonata made such an impression on me that I went backstage to introduce myself after the concert and ask him if I could play it. He was happy to give me the music, we discovered that we both had roots in California, and it was the beginning of a lifelong friendship.

Now we were able to continue it in Rome at our leisure. We used to play four-handed piano pieces at the grand piano in our apartment. Our page turner for one of these sessions was a teenage piano prodigy whom we had met through a friend of his parents; his name was Danny Barenboim. He grew up, of course, to be one of the most acclaimed soloists and conductors in the world; then, he was just a talented kid. We had an enormous living room, with casement windows that opened out over the street, and we would throw open the windows and play for hours, sending our music out into the night. Below us, on the street outside, the ladies of the night would gather to listen, and between pieces they would shout up "Bravo!" in thin little voices.

I was such a fan of the "other" Leon's music that a few years later, when the Ford Foundation awarded ten musicians grants to commission a new concerto, Leon was my obvious choice. As a result, Leon wrote his second piano concerto, a big bruiser of a Romantic rhapsodic declaration. It was a good piece. It was also a difficult one. We were scheduled to play it with three different orchestras—the Seattle Symphony, the Pittsburgh Symphony, and the New York Philharmonic—and the Seattle Symphony's music director, Milton Katims, took one look at the score and asked Leon to come out and conduct it in his stead. That worked very well. But Pittsburgh's music director, William Steinberg, wanted to conduct the piece himself, and he was to lead it in New York as well.

Steinberg was a wonderful conductor. He is rightly remembered as one of the greats. He's sometimes thought of as restrained, but I remember him as ebullient, and a little quirky. Once, when I told him about my plans to play a concerto in another city, he asked me, with a twinkle, "Against what conductor?" I had some of my happiest musical experiences with Steinberg, starting with my early performances with him in Ravinia. But he just couldn't hack Leon's concerto. We had two rehearsals, and it was increasingly clear that he was in over his head. The night before the dress rehearsal, we got on the phone to Leon in Boston and begged him to come down and conduct his piece. Leon, who was no slouch as a conductor (or, for that matter, as a pianist), got on a plane and came down and managed to pull the whole thing together in one rehearsal, so that we were able to do justice to it in performance.

Steinberg was abashed. He swore up and down that he would learn the piece properly for the next season, with the New York Philharmonic. But when the concert date rolled around, the same thing happened all over again. Leon had to come in and save the day. I did the piece once in Cleveland with Louis Lane, who was George Szell's associate conductor, and to the best of my knowledge he's the only other conductor who actually managed to sit down and learn it.

By 1958, we had been in Europe for eight years. And we had two children. Rome was certainly not agreeing with my piano practicing, and Dot would get homesick for her family when she was alone in Italy and I was off on tour. So we decided to move back to America. I think both of us regretted it almost as soon as we got back. For our marriage, it proved fatal.

First of all, we lived with Dot's parents in her family apartment. That wasn't ideal. Dot's parents traveled back and forth a good deal to St. Louis, but we were still all cooped up in the apartment together with the children and my practicing, and things could get a little crazy. And New York seemed chaotic and constricting and dirty after all those years in Europe. Rome wasn't clean, but it was a lot prettier than New York. The situation began to take a toll on our relationship, though neither of us was the type to discuss that kind of thing. When I was home I didn't have the inclination, and Dot, raising young children, didn't have the time.

After some months of this, we decided to buy a house in the country. Prices were cheaper outside of New York, and it would be better for the children to live somewhere where they could run around. They had pretty well exhausted the confines of a New York apartment, especially Dickie. I enjoyed horsing around with my son; having a boy meant you could wrestle and roughhouse in ways that you didn't, in the 1950s, with a daughter, though Debbie had grown into a cheery, exuberant little girl. Furthermore, we were expecting another child: Leah, our second daughter, was born in 1959. We all needed space. We found a house in Yorktown Heights, in Westchester County, about an hour north of New York. To us city kids, it represented an idyllic country dream: a house on the hillside, with seven acres and a brook, and a big barn out back. When you stood on the porch at night, you could see the distant glow of the city lights on the horizon.

When you buy a house, you need a mortgage. And to get a mortgage, you have to have a job. I didn't. No matter that I was one of the most successful young pianists in America, giving prestigious concerts all over the world and earning very good money. The money actually got quite a bit better in those years, in part thanks to Van Cliburn. Van was the American pianist who won the Tchaikovsky Piano Competition in Moscow in 1958 and became an overnight superstar. When he got back to the States, he was welcomed in New York with a ticker-tape parade, which is not something that often happens to classical musicians. He was on the cover of *Time*. In short, he was a celebrity, and he started getting paid like one. Before he won the competition, Van was getting $500, which was the going rate for a concerto performance by a young artist at the time. After he won, he was scheduled to play with the New York Philharmonic, but now Judson informed management that his star was no longer going to play for a mere $500, contract or no contract, and he managed to get Van's fee doubled, or even tripled. As a result, everyone's fees started to go up, because no other star pianist was willing to play for less than Van Cliburn got. Artur Rubinstein said that Van was the person responsible for allowing us all to make a decent living.

Certainly breaking four figures for our fee for an evening's work seemed to all of us an event that called for a celebration. Eugene, Gary, and I took turns taking our whole group out to New York's best restaurant, the Café Chambord, for dinner when each of us passed this particular benchmark.

Regardless of how well I was earning, though, I was technically unemployed. I couldn't get a mortgage. I couldn't even get a credit card at Macy's.

My need of a job made me reconsider an offer that had recently come my way. Peter Mennin, the composer I had met in Cleveland, had just been appointed the director of the Peabody Institute of Music in Baltimore, and he was trying to lure me down to teach. Now, faced with my unexpected status as a member of the unemployed, I rethought my initial reluctance to take him up on his offer. In September 1959, I became a faculty member at Peabody. I had one single student. His name was Reynaldo Reyes, and he went on to become quite a respected teacher himself. As for me, coming to Peabody turned out to be a significant step. I am teaching there to this day, more than fifty years later.

Now that I had a job, I could get a mortgage, and a credit card, and all kinds of grown-up things. I wouldn't give Macy's the satisfaction, though. I got my first credit card from Gimbel's, instead. Little did I know that Gimbel's, then one of New York's largest department stores, would ultimately vanish.

I needed one more thing: a place to stay in Baltimore during my weekly sojourns at Peabody. At this point, very helpfully, I ran into another old acquaintance in Baltimore, Elliott Galkin, Dot's fellow patient from the Trudeau Sanatorium, who was now the music critic of the *Baltimore Sun* and a music professor at Goucher College (and who would later run Peabody himself for a few years). He was also a useful contact who knew the town better than I did. I mentioned to Elliott that I was looking for a room one night a week, and he said he had a friend who was doing his medical residency, which meant he was often out all night on call at the hospital. The friend, Max Weisman, turned out to be perfectly happy to have me stay with him every Tuesday.

Max's apartment was in a walk-up building right across the street from Peabody. And on the top floor of that building lived a beautiful, vibrant twenty-four-year-old girl.

Her name was Risselle Rosenthal. Everyone called her Rikki. She was slender, and opinionated, and athletic, and highly intelligent. She painted, she wrote poetry, she was studying English, she read Proust, and she knew Baltimore, where she had been born and raised, like the back of her hand. I first encountered her when I heard the strains of Bartók's First Piano Concerto wafting down the stairwell of our building, coming from the record player in her apartment. A few days later I came into Max's and there she was: intense, dynamic, amazing. After we had met a couple of times, I asked her to show me around Baltimore. She took me to the Washington Monument, which is actually older than the one in Washington, and to an antique store where there was a wonderful mechanical clock in the window, and then she took me bowling, Baltimore style, with duckpins and small croquet-sized balls, which I had never seen before. Rikki didn't actually manage to knock down all that many pins. But she sure looked great trying.

I had never met anybody like Rikki before. I was absolutely fascinated. I had no business being fascinated, of course. I was married. My youngest daughter was a few weeks old. Rikki had a boyfriend. And yet I felt that something was happening that I had no power to resist. I was always eminently crushable in any case, and now, after feeling

bogged down in all the responsibilities of family life and home owner-
ship, I suddenly felt a new lease on life. And if there was one thing I
knew how to do—that I had been trained to do my whole life—it was
to go after what I wanted.

Rikki listened to early music and contemporary composers like
Bartók, and nothing much in between. I told her she should give
Brahms a try. That fall I played the D Minor concerto with the Baltimore Symphony Orchestra. She went to hear me, but she didn't come
backstage. I called from Washington to ask her why. I was touring
again that fall. I called her from different cities around the country. I
wrote. I sent little presents, souvenirs of the places I was performing.
I knew I shouldn't be writing her or calling her. That made it all the
more attractive, somehow. I couldn't stop. I came back from my tour,
and went down to Baltimore, and went straight to Rikki's, armed with
a recording of Strauss's *Der Rosenkavalier* and a magnum of champagne.
It was Rikki's birthday. It was a big night. The dam broke. All of those
feelings that had been building up poured out in a flood and swept
everything away before them.

This was no ordinary conquest. It felt as if we were made for each
other: looks, brains, talent—an unbeatable combination. And then we
were so intoxicated, and so in love, that nothing else mattered.

For a few months, I led an awful double life. All I wanted was to
be with Rikki. I confided in my old friend Konrad Wolff, who, though
he had become close to Dot, was enough of a ladies' man himself that
he enjoyed helping me achieve my goals and getting to know my new
soulmate. He didn't let Dot know. The following February I left on a
tour of Europe. I had a royalty check from my latest batch of recordings, and I told Dot that I wanted to spend it on myself, and I used
that money to bring Rikki along with me. We revisited all the stations
of my past life. We went to Amsterdam and stayed with a friend of
Rikki's in a big house on the Prinsengracht and saw Maria Curcio and
Peter Diamand and Pierre and Doris Monteux. We went to Paris and
saw Doda Conrad, and the Katchens. We were so much in love that

people weren't too judgmental. It seemed to everyone that I had found what I wanted. And everybody was very impressed with Rikki. Doris Monteux gave her a beautiful bracelet that she wears to this day.

By the time we got back from that trip, it was clear to both of us that our lives were intertwined. We needed to be together. So I was going to have to tell Dot.

I've never been any good at ending things. Discussing personal relationships is not my strong suit. I can talk to you for hours about taking a *ritardando* in a Schubert sonata, but I have trouble wrapping words around matters of the heart. All I knew was I was going to have to end my marriage, because I wanted to be with someone else. So that's what I told Dot. I kind of plunged into it. You have to follow your happiness, I said. It was time for a new start.

For Dot, this was a bolt from the blue—or a punch in the stomach. I don't think, looking back, that I could have done it any more awkwardly. I was in a rush to get it over with, because I knew it was going to be unpleasant. And it certainly was.

I didn't mean for it to be followed up quite so plainly, but a few days later, when Dot was doing our accounts—as she always did—and going through my bills from Europe, she found receipts that reflected the fact I hadn't been alone. "She couldn't do her own laundry?" she said, handing me a hotel's itemized laundry bill that included a listing for a woman's brassiere.

Of course it was especially tough on the kids. I moved full time to Baltimore, and Rikki and I took a basement apartment in the same building we had been living in, while we waited for my divorce to come through. We were wildly, romantically happy in that apartment. But my children were suddenly left almost fatherless. They came and stayed with us for a couple of weeks in the summer, but basically our contact remained quite limited for years. It's hard for me to think of that part of the story without bitter, bitter regret.

My brother, Ray, was horrified. He came to visit us in Baltimore, and he could barely bring himself to look at Rikki. It wasn't that he didn't like her personally; it was just that she stood for something he had trouble swallowing. Ray didn't believe in divorce. He believed that marriage needed to be taken more seriously than that. As the first Fleisher to end a marriage, I was bringing shame on the family. "Our mother would be rolling over in her grave," he told us. Well, our mother was gone.

George Szell disapproved as well. He didn't express it in so many words to me. He didn't need to. You could tell when Szell didn't approve of something. I don't know what bothered him about my second marriage, exactly. He might have seen it as a distraction, something that was taking my attention away from my playing. Or he might simply have thought I had behaved badly.

Szell wasn't exactly a prude. He was married twice, and if I remember correctly, his second wife, Helene, was originally married to one of his friends before Szell and she got together. That second marriage was a good one, though; it lasted the rest of Szell's life. Helene was from Prague, and she was a slender, patrician woman with a cosmopolitan air of Central Europe: a classy dame. At postconcert dinner receptions, she made quite a contrast to Szell, who would hold the dinner plate in the flat of his hand and basically scoop the food into his mouth. At one such function in Cleveland, the evening's host, Horace Rigg, a professor of comparative religion at Western Reserve University who was a prodigious drinker and was, at that point in the evening, fairly well oiled, exclaimed in a loud voice, "Helene, what's it like being married to a god?" Everyone fell silent except for George, who continued to scoop food into his mouth, unperturbed. Helene turned to Rigg graciously, with a gentle smile. "Well, you know, Horace," she said, "it's really rather difficult. Because before a concert, he won't; after a concert, he can't; and he gives six concerts a week."

Whatever Szell's own proclivities, he cast a dim eye on mine. The issue came up only obliquely. I once sat in on a conducting competition sponsored by the Ford Foundation that was held at Peabody. It was a high-powered jury: Szell and Eugene Ormandy, another notable

Hungarian conductor, who ruled at the Philadelphia Orchestra; Max Rudolf, a German conductor who became the doyen of conducting teachers in America; and a few others. For one round, I played the solo parts of several different piano concertos while the contestants conducted, and then I sat in with the jury in the green room during their deliberations. One of the contestants was a kid named Bobby LaMarchina. Bobby was a cello prodigy. He was in Toscanini's cello section, in the NBC Symphony Orchestra, when he was only twenty-one years old, and people still rave about what an amazing sound he could get out of the cello. He was also drop-dead handsome and quite a ladies' man. But Bobby was also one of those tragic cases of a kid who was emotionally crippled by a punishing stage parent, in his case a father who drove him so hard that he was never really able to have a normal life. Anyway, at this point Bobby had decided he wanted to be a conductor, and he was very good at it. During the deliberations, as we were discussing each contestant, Szell brought up the fact that Bobby had come to his attention as a womanizer—I think that was the word he used—which raised questions in George's mind about his character.

I couldn't keep from piping up. I said, "You're not going to penalize him for being a heterosexual?"

George didn't say anything. But he shot me one of his signature looks, a blast of white-hot rage, through his thick glasses, and I withered a little bit inside. After that, I kept my mouth shut. But I still thought it was unfair.

George met Rikki only once, and the circumstances weren't ideal. It was the one time George got really angry at me. It was also the one time I was almost late for a concert. We were in New York, playing the Beethoven C Major concerto (or First) with the Philharmonic, and Rikki wanted to stay downtown. Her favorite hotel in New York was the Marlton, a residential hotel and hangout for artists and writers in Greenwich Village that attracted people like Jack Kerouac. But it wasn't exactly convenient to Lincoln Center, the new performing arts complex that had just opened that season. And on the night of the concert, it was raining. We left the hotel and found ourselves in a classic New York spot: we couldn't get a cab. The minutes ticked by as car after car passed us: no taxis. Eventually, I started panicking, and we got into the subway and went uptown to Columbus Circle or someplace like that where we could finally find transportation that brought us to the stage door at the stroke of eight. I have always made it a point to arrive half an hour before a performance, without fail, but that night, I arrived at curtain time. We rushed into the backstage elevator and rode up to the dressing rooms, and the elevator door opened to reveal the figure of Szell, in full concert attire, bristling with fury, ready to go down and start the concert. On one level, he was relieved to see me—relieved that I hadn't had an accident or something. On another level, he was as angry as I ever saw him. "You're LATE!" he cried.

"I'm sorry," Rikki said, "it's all my fault, Maestro, hello, I'm Rikki," but it didn't make a dent. He swept past us into the elevator without a word. He wouldn't talk to me. He wouldn't say a word—not before the performance, not backstage, not after the performance, nothing. He wouldn't talk to me even though that first concert was marked by another rather dramatic incident. During the first piece, before I came out on stage, one of the sound baffles on the ceiling of the new hall somehow detached itself and crashed onto the stage, delivering a glancing blow to one of the bass players on its way down. I didn't know a thing about it, since I was backstage. When George and I came out for our concerto, George got up on the podium and, mugging for the audience, looked up at the ceiling as if wondering if anything else was likely to fall on him. This got a big laugh. Since I was taking my seat in front of him, though, I didn't see what he did and I had no idea what people were laughing about. My first reaction was to check my fly to make sure I was zipped up. Anyway, the performance passed without further incident, though I was certainly rattled. It's said that Leonard Bernstein, who was touring in Europe at the time, sent a joking telegram to the stagehands saying something to the effect of "No, no, that was the wrong sound baffle; I meant the one in the MIDDLE."

But even this risk to life and limb didn't get George to start talking to me. I got the silent treatment for all four performances. I was racking my brains by then, to think of a way to break the ice. Finally, something occurred to me. In the 1940s, Schnabel had given a series of lectures at the University of Chicago about his career, and these had just been published as a book called *My Life in Music*, complete with transcripts of the question-and-answer sessions that followed each lecture. The first question after lecture number 4 concerned a promising student of Schnabel's whom the questioner had heard that summer; it was obvious that the person they were talking about was me. (The book was recently rereleased in a better-edited version under the title *Music, Wit and Wisdom*, and in that edition my name was left in.) Anyway, I bought Szell a copy of the book, as a gesture toward our shared veneration of Schnabel, and marked the passage about me before I gave it to him, as a reminder that Schnabel, at least, had thought me worth his while. Szell seemed to accept the peace offering. He started talking to me again. He didn't refer to the incident, of course; that wasn't his way. He didn't need to, since it was obvious that I would never be late again, even if I had to set out for the concert hall in the middle of the afternoon.

Another musical highlight of those years was my time in Marlboro, Rudi Serkin's summer institute in Vermont. The basic idea of Marlboro has always been to bring top-notch professional musicians at the height of their careers together with talented younger ones. Originally, it was conceived as a more conventional school, but it quickly evolved into collaborative music making, with the younger players and the older ones exchanging ideas as equals, spending their days playing, and talking about the greatest music in the world. There are no deadlines at Marlboro; the weekly concerts consist of whatever anybody feels his or her group is ready to perform. It's a wonderful, idealistic experience. It's also the most nerve-racking place I've ever played, because everyone else is so good. You're performing in front of the best musicians in the world, people who are going to catch every nuance of what you're doing: they will understand your interpretation, and maybe disagree with it, not to mention hear it immediately if you slip up.

The competition is ferocious. I remember hearing seventeen-year-old Richard Goode and thirteen-year-old Peter Serkin, Rudi's son, playing Stravinsky's concerto for two pianos, an intensely difficult piece, certainly for a couple of kids. It was pretty scary. We didn't know for sure then that both those kids would grow up to be among the most respected concert pianists in the world or that Richard would become one of Marlboro's directors himself, but none of it would have been hard to predict. At one point, a group of us were listening to Richard playing, phenomenally, on an upright piano in one of the dormitories. "How long have you been working on that piece, Richard?" I asked, when he had finished.

"Oh," Richard said, "I was sight-reading."

"I'd better go practice," I said.

The combination of idealism and competition spurred you on to do your best. I remember playing the Weber E Minor sonata, a piece Schnabel had given me as a kid. It's the last of Weber's four sonatas, terribly beautiful, and the final movement is a fiendish tarantella. I'm not sure how I played that. I remember being terribly nervous about it and playing it, actually, rather well. One year, Rudi Serkin and I played Brahms's Liebeslieder Waltzes with a vocal quartet that included the soprano Benita Valente and the baritone Martial Singher; we ended up recording that for Columbia. And I particularly remember a Brahms G Minor quartet with Jaime Laredo, the violist Ray Montoni, and David Soyer, a cornerstone of the famous Guarneri Quartet, on cello. We played the hell out of that piece. I think that's one of those performances that old hands at Marlboro still talk about.

A byproduct of the intensity, and the sense of community, is that there's a lot of kidding around, and horseplay, and practical jokes. You can't always be practicing. Not all of us took to the outdoor life as much as Rudi Serkin, who became such a passionate farmer that the Philadelphia Orchestra once, in a gesture of gratitude, presented him with a tractor, driving it out on stage after a concert to his not inconsiderable delight. But there were plenty of other pastimes. We had a fierce Ping-Pong competition going on over the course of the summer, where I brooked no opposition: I was usually Marlboro's reigning Ping-Pong champion. Another constant were the dining hall food fights. Anything left over on the table in the dining hall, after lunch or dinner, could become a deadly projectile. One summer when Casals was at Marlboro, Queen Elisabeth of Belgium, my old friend from the competition, came to visit him. She was, of course, happy to see me as well, and we ate a meal together in the dining hall. Fortunately, I had had the forethought to anticipate the inevitable food fight, and I came armed with an umbrella, which I opened and used as a shield for Her Majesty while guiding her to safety.

My last two summers at Marlboro were spent as a family, with Rikki and the children. After our whirlwind, passionate start, Rikki and I got married on April Fool's Day, 1962, at a synagogue in Baltimore, only a few days after my divorce from Dot went through. We then went off on another tour of Europe, this time as a legitimately married couple, though our trip was marred by Rikki's bouts of nausea and dizzy spells, for which, we discovered thanks to a doctor in Paris, there was a simple explanation: she was pregnant. Therefore, our first summer together in Marlboro was spent with my three children, and our second summer with four children: Paula, our daughter, was born in February. They were wonderful summers for me but had certain difficulties for everyone. For my older children, it must have been bewildering to be taken off to stay with someone they barely knew. Dickie once went up to Leon Kirchner and asked him, in honest confusion, "Are you my father?"

I did try to be a father to Dickie. I showed him how to play Ping-Pong. But I was such an awful father that I never once let him win a game. Dickie had his revenge: he grew up to be a nationally ranked player, much, much better than I ever was. But I still wish I had let him win when he was a little boy.

Overall, though, life was sweet. I had gotten what I wanted. I was married to the woman I loved, and we were enjoying our beautiful baby. Rikki and I bought a town house on a tree-lined street in Baltimore, with a back garden where we ate our meals in summer, and furnished it with antiques, including some pieces we bought at Marlboro. Rikki was active in political causes, like racial integration, that I fully supported. At one point, as the movement started to really gain momentum, I let my management know that I, like several of my colleagues, was no longer willing to perform in concert halls where African Americans weren't welcome in the audience.

And I kept adding to my list of notable performances—and eccentric characters. One event that particularly stood out was the time I was invited to play a chamber concert in San Francisco with Jascha Heifetz and Gregor Piatigorsky, whom many would have called the greatest violinist and cellist in the world. Heifetz had such a huge reputation that even George Szell was intimidated. Before Heifetz's first appearance with Szell in Cleveland, the conductor was determined to show him who was boss, yet he became downright deferential when the violinist actually took the stage for rehearsal. After the first run-through of the Tchaikovsky concerto, Szell suggested that they work on some particular spots. "I'd rather not," Heifetz said, and left the stage. Nobody had ever acted that way to Szell and lived. But Heifetz was on another level.

Heifetz, when I met him, was in a bad state. He was getting a divorce from his second wife, and everyone was on pins and needles trying to accommodate him. We were performing the Schubert E-flat trio, and the rehearsal was held in Heifetz's living room. We played right through the lunch hour, and then Heifetz excused himself and went off to eat lunch. We were left in the living room to fend for ourselves; he certainly didn't offer us anything to eat. Strange man.

When we got to the last movement of the trio, Heifetz began thumbing through the pages of the music, as if looking for something, back and forth, while we sat there and watched him. Finally, as if recollecting that we were there, he explained that he was looking for a place to cut the last movement. I was affronted at the thought, and I must have showed it, for he explained to me, paternalistically, "An artist's worst sin is to bore his public."

"An artist only bores his public when he is bored himself," I shot back. He didn't like that, and Grisha Piatigorsky rose to his defense. It probably didn't help my future cause with those two artists.

I was no more comfortable when, in the green room before the concert at San Francisco's War Memorial Opera House, I realized, as Heifetz and Grisha began warming up, that there was no piano for me to warm up on. I made some comment about this omission. Grisha, who was a big, genial man, wanted to make me feel better. He turned to me and said in stentorian tones, in his heavy Russian accent, "You shouldn't worry. Warming up before a concert is like doing breathing exercises before dying."

I think a lot of performers feel like that. As much as we love what we're doing, those moments before going out on stage can sometimes feel like the end of the world. You can get yourself into a real tangle of nerves.

Not unrelated was the performance I gave in Cologne with André Cluytens, the marvelous Belgian-born French conductor. We were preparing for a live broadcast with audience, and the orchestra was not treating Cluytens very well, and he got himself into a state, and it got me into a state. It was one of my first times playing Beethoven's first concerto, and I fell into my old familiar terror that I would get lost and forget where I was. As security, I snuck a little pocket edition of the score into the piano, where no one but me could see it. The second movement of that concerto begins with a lovely melody for the piano. As I was playing, I peeked into the piano and my eye fell on a different place in the score, with the result that I played a D-natural instead of the D-flat that was supposed to be there. I knew as I was playing it that it was wrong, and so did everyone else: I could feel everyone's blood run cold. It was particularly unfortunate that that line of music is so familiar that even casual listeners could tell I had made a big mistake. My old friend Piero Weiss, the pianist turned musicologist, happened to be in the audience, and for the next forty years he teased me about the "Cologne D."

But of all my anecdotes and memories, none surpasses the terror and wonder and pure, unadulterated joy of my performances and recordings with George Szell.

The highlight of my collaboration with Szell was a performance of Mozart's twenty-fifth piano concerto, K. 503, that we gave in New York with the Cleveland Orchestra the night before Rikki and I left for Europe on our first, illicit European tour. Dot was there, and Debbie, who was six years old, and Konrad—and Rikki was there, too, so I had an extra emotional spur in the pull of love and excitement and anticipation. Everything came together that night, and it all came out in the music.

The passage that I always wait for in that piece comes in the final movement, where the piano and the oboe have a duet, tossing a tune back and forth. That's always a heartbreaker for me. The principal oboe of the Cleveland Orchestra in those years was Marc Lifschey, an exquisite musician and an Olympian player, just phenomenal. When we started sending that tune back and forth, it was like firebolts across the heavens, except that instead of fire the substance was something immeasurably sweeter, enveloping, like cotton candy. It was one of those moments you wait for as a musician, when you've reached something and you know you've gotten it.

Everyone else got it, too. Rikki got it. And a critic even got it. Jay Harrison, the critic for the *New York Herald Tribune*, was reviewing the concert that night. Jay, by a weird coincidence, had gone to Kamp Kohut with me in Maine back when I was a kid. I think he played the Blue Fairy in one of the musicals we did. Now he was covering me in the Mozart 503. Jay was a fine musician, and he knew what he had just heard. He wrote that it was a performance "such as I never expect to hear bettered in my lifetime."

Me either. If you put me up against the wall and made me choose, I'd have to say that was the best performance of my life.

LUDWIG VAN BEETHOVEN: PIANO CONCERTO NO. 4
IN G MAJOR, OP. 58 (1805–06)

My recordings of the complete Beethoven piano concertos together represent one of the enduring documents of my work with George Szell. It's therefore somewhat amusing to think that we didn't really mean to record the cycle at all. We recorded the G Major first, paired with Mozart's K. 503: that was the second recording George and I made together. Then we decided to record another Beethoven concerto, and suddenly Howard Scott, our producer, said, Why don't we record them all? That was fine with me. I had never done the Third—which happens to be the only one of the five that's written in a minor key—and I had to learn that specially for the project. All in all, those recordings came out rather well. But we certainly didn't go in with the notion of doing a cycle.

The five Beethoven concertos, monumental as they are, are not as clear a map of the composer's work as the thirty-two piano sonatas or the sixteen string quartets. I actually think the string quartets are his profoundest works. The sonatas aren't chopped liver, but the quartets, they're the real acme of his achievement. One year in Jerusalem, at one of the annual chamber workshops Isaac Stern used to organize, we went through a bunch of the string quartets, and I suddenly had this vision that Beethoven would write a quartet that was just divine, and then, to unwind, he'd toss off a piano sonata or two. Then he'd write another string quartet that was monumental—and then another couple of sonatas. That idea loses traction when you get to the last five piano sonatas, which are pretty monumental themselves. In fact, when I was in my thirties, I always felt they were somehow beyond me. I didn't feel I had the solutions for those yet.

The concertos reveal less about Beethoven than the sonatas do, in that they were not written over the whole span of his career. They're younger music: vital, exuberant, even heroic. But I do love them all dearly. The First and Second are quite early works; the second, the B-flat, is the one I started out playing as a child. The Fifth, the "Emperor," is the most majestic: the one that's truly heroic. Its opening is a wonderful example of the way Beethoven puts his music together. You have a huge E-flat Major chord from the whole orchestra. Except that one note is missing. Everyone is playing E-flat and G, up and down the staff, but there's no B-flat in that chord. Then the piano comes in with this big, sweeping arpeggiated entrance up the keyboard, and when it gets to the top it goes straight for the B-flat, over and over, just in case you missed it in the opening chord. It plays that B-flat nine times. As if it were saying, Here it is! Here I am! Get it? Wow! That's what this piece is made of.

But after that opening, the Fifth is a relatively straightforward piece. Its emotions, its character are right on its sleeve. The Fourth is far more elusive. It's been called the "ladies' concerto," because it's more introverted and less showy, which is, of course, absolute nonsense. To my mind, the Fourth is the most difficult of all the concertos. It's the one I have the hardest time expressing verbally, the hardest to put into words.

It signals its differences right from the start. It opens with the piano playing alone, and very quietly—a far cry from the heroic opening of the traditional concerto (or of the "Emperor," for that matter). The opening of the Fourth Concerto sounds almost improvised, and its oddness is emphasized when the orchestra picks it up in a slightly different key. It's an off-kilter beginning, and not only because of the key change. Schnabel helped us students learn to think about how many bars make up a musical phrase. In most classical pieces, phrases happen in multiples of two or four. A theme might emerge over eight bars, made up of smaller individual phrases that take two or four bars to express. The opening phrase of the Fourth Concerto, however, extends over five bars. This, like the key change that follows it, gives the piece the character of a three-legged stool. There's something slightly asymmetrical about it.

The whole movement revolves around a repeating rhythmic motif, three groups of four insistent, pulsing notes, now softer, now mounting to loudness, but never going away. The piano sounds them at the opening; they represent the main material, and they make an elegiac return at the end of the cadenza, in a very peaceful way. Then they segue into long strings of scales, there's a big crescendo, and the movement ends emphatically. It was Klemperer who taught me, at that passage, one of the most important things about the piece. When the scales start, virtually every musician you hear speeds up the tempo, reverting to the tempo of the rest of the movement. But Klemperer said no. He insisted that you maintain whatever tempo you have right at the end of the cadenza when the orchestra comes in. At that point, the music has a spacious, heavenly sense, even sublime, and Klemperer wanted to keep that tempo right through to the end of the piece. The result is extraordinary. If you don't give in to the impulse to get faster but hold out with the more spacious tempo, the whole thing becomes almost like a slow-motion sunrise, except that the sun is right next door. It can blow your mind.

There are different glosses on the second movement, which is a dialogue between orchestra and soloist and conveys the idea of something imperious (from the orchestra) being smoothed out by something gentle (from the piano). I've always thought of it as Jesus and the masses. But there's a long tradition according to which it represents Orpheus taming the wild beasts with his music. The climax of the cadenza, with a big crescendo building up to a trill and these little anguished cries of descending notes, could be the moment Orpheus looks back as he is leading his beloved Eurydice out of Hades and loses her forever. I think it was Emanuel Ax who told me that. Whatever works for you. It's all very good stuff.

Beethoven's last movements are such rollicks. If you're depressed going in, you can't be anything but enlivened going out. The first two concertos have a young, exuberant energy, and that's certainly equally present in the finale of the Fourth. In the same way that the opening of the concerto flips the normal order on its head—with the piano entering first—the start of this movement reverses Beethoven's normal approach: this time, it's the orchestra that enters first, with the piano joining in afterward. The movement—which adds trumpets and drums to the orchestral mix—is the usual last-movement rondo, branching off into slightly foggy, thoughtful byways but always coming back to the springy, bright-eyed central theme: a continual rejuvenation.

Beethoven's music is a doorway to certain things that are hard for us to get to unaided today. I think that a lot of the rapid passages, like the sixteenth, thirty-second, and even sixty-fourth notes in the slow movements of the late sonatas, represent varying states of shimmering ecstasy. In Beethoven's day, there were no distractions—no newspapers, no radios, no automobiles. People had the time and space to tap into other levels of consciousness, of awareness. To a certain extent, we're prevented from doing that today. The dull roar of everything that goes on around us—TV, traffic, Internet chatter—tends to block attempts at thinking, at meditating, at any kind of self-examination. I think part of the attraction of drugs is that they enable one to access another level of awareness. Back in Beethoven's time, people could do that automatically. You can hear it in the music.

CHAPTER 6

CATASTROPHE

Before the crash. (Author's collection)

It began as a sense of laziness in my right index finger, a slight sluggishness in its response when I wanted to play a trill. It continued as a growing sense of clumsiness and a feeling that my fingers weren't doing what I wanted them to do. And it crystallized on a warm, sunny day in the basement of our house in Baltimore when I was trying to carry a patio table into the back garden, banged it against the door, and sliced a chunk out of my right thumb.

A hand can take only so much brutalization before it starts to fight back.

I had probably been overworking my hand for years, ever since I started stepping up my practicing in the wake of the Queen Elisabeth Competition. Not that I ever got into Willy Kapell's league, the thirteen- and fourteen-hour days. I would do six or seven hours, just enough to keep me feeling slightly guilty that I wasn't doing more. It still didn't seem like enough. I was driving myself toward an ideal of perfection. Technique hadn't been the main emphasis of my training: I had the chops to play the Liszt B Minor Sonata or the Tchaikovsky First Concerto, but some pieces still seemed daunting. I wasn't really going for a Jacob Lateiner–style black belt in piano, but I did want to develop the sense of reliability that some of my colleagues seemed to have grown up with. As well as demonstrating my own insight into the music, I wanted to show that I could play the piano. Some of it, I thought, was a question of pure muscle building. I practiced.

I remember one of the few times Szell ever questioned the quality

of my playing. It concerned a passage in the cadenza of the Tchaikovsky First Concerto, one of the biggest virtuoso showpieces in the
literature, which we played up at Smith College in 1958. He felt it
was getting a little muddy and suggested I work more to improve the
octaves. Of course, that sent me right back into the practice room,
even though I thought I played the more famous octave passages in
that piece, in the first and third movements, pretty darn well.

My career was going better than ever. I was building up a body of
work, backed up by my recordings, that was starting to make me feel
I was about to move up to the next level, from "outstanding young
pianist" to (as one critic put it, when I was thirty-six) an "elder statesman." "Leon Fleisher is the finest all-round pianist before the public
today," wrote one critic after a 1963 Montreal concert. It was wonderful
to hear. But I was driven, if anything, even harder by all of my success. There was always more to attain, and more to achieve, and more
musical depths to plumb, and, lurking behind it all, the terrifying risk
of failure.

But with all the practicing I was doing, my right hand was starting
to feel numb.

In the winter of 1963, I played in New York on the prestigious
recital series at Hunter College, a series that had a particularly strong
focus on piano. All the greatest pianists in the world appeared there
when they were in town. My program was devoted exclusively to
Franz Schubert, a composer I still felt was underappreciated. Schubert's
music is profound in part through its simplicity. There aren't many
really virtuosic pieces in his oeuvre. The big exception is the "Wanderer" Fantasy, a work that makes such extreme technical demands
that Schubert, who wasn't a great pianist, couldn't manage it himself
at all.

To my horror, as I practiced, I found I wasn't doing such a great
job with it either. I knew what I wanted to do with the piece, but my
fingers weren't cooperating. The "Wanderer" is a question of stamina.
You get through the first movement, and the second movement has its

stresses, and then there's a really agile, dancing, leaping third movement, which ends with a lot of physical stress; and then you're confronted with a fourth movement that has to be bigger than all of the
big movements that have come before. I couldn't maintain the energy.
After a few minutes of playing, a creeping numbness would set in.
My fingers, particularly the fourth and fifth fingers of my right hand,
were cramping up, as if I had writer's cramp. It wasn't painful. But it
was intensely annoying.

I actually postponed the concert for two weeks—something I had
never done before—to give me more time to work on it. For a solid
month—two weeks before the scheduled concert, plus the two weeks'
grace period—I sat at the piano all day, every day, working on the
"Wanderer." In the short term, it worked. I made it through the recital,
and it was something of an artistic triumph. But my musician friends
who were there heard that I played some wrong notes. They shrugged
it off. Schnabel, after all, was known for a clinker or two now and
then, and it didn't affect the profundity of his playing. It's all right to
be less than perfect if something else, something vital and real, is happening in the music. Yet I felt, inside, that I wasn't entirely in control.

And as far as my hand was concerned, those intense practice sessions represented a final indignity. All that repeated work certainly
had an effect. I just didn't realize yet what that effect would prove
to be.

The 1964–65 season was supposed to be one of the greatest years
of my life, the culmination of my career to date. It was the twentieth
anniversary of my debut with the New York Philharmonic. Twenty
years ago I had burst onto the scene, a gangly teenager; now I was one
of the leading concert pianists of my generation. The whole season
was planned as one long celebration. In New York, Steinway & Sons
organized a small exhibition about my career, and I was to play a raft
of concerts, more than twenty times in New York alone. The crown-
ing point, though, would come in the spring, when I was leaving
on a historic tour to the Soviet Union with Szell and the Cleveland

Orchestra, an American cultural ambassador to Russia at a time when such embassies were rare and epic. It could be a breakthrough season, sealing my place at the top of my field. To prepare, I practiced harder than ever.

Then the accident happened.

It was a warm day in the summer of 1964, and Rikki wanted to eat outside and I didn't. We were fairly strong in our desires, Rikki and I. That was, after all, how our whole relationship had gotten started. The fierce passion that made our time together so intense could also lead to spectacular flare-ups. On this particular day, we locked horns over the question of where we were going to eat. We had a walled garden at the back of our house in Baltimore, with a little porch built out from the kitchen and a built-in grill, and Rikki wanted to cook outside. I didn't. As usual, there were some strong words exchanged in the debate and, as usual, Rikki won. I found myself down in the base-ment, wrestling with our patio table, in a foul mood. The table was wider than the basement door, so you had to tilt it at a certain angle to get it out, and, angry as I was, I was having trouble maneuvering it. The table got stuck; I lost my temper; I banged it into the doorframe; and the strip of black trim that ran around the edge of the table sliced a flap of flesh out of my right thumb.

As a pianist, you spend your whole life protecting your hands. No baseball, no contact sports, nothing rough that might injure the fingers on which so much of your career is riding. Now, at the age of thirty-five, I stood frozen, looking down at the hanging chunk of thumb, with blood everywhere, while Rikki, who had heard my shout and come down to see what was wrong, stood in the doorway, mute with horror. *Well,* I thought, *it's happened.*

Rikki and I moved with the efficiency of people at the eye of a storm. We didn't even say much. We found towels for the blood, and Rikki found her address book and called a friend of hers, a plastic surgeon named Bernard Kapiloff, who lived a few blocks away. Come right over, Bernie said. Somehow, we got into the car and drove over to Bernie's apartment, and right there in his kitchen he stitched my thumb back together. It was only five or six stitches, but it meant I couldn't play the piano for at least ten days. Still, we were almost weak with relief. It could have been a lot worse. The thumb healed. I began practicing again. Story over.

But the practicing wasn't quite the same as it had been. I had an extraordinary feeling in my right forearm. Usually, when you work a muscle you can feel it growing tighter, like a rope twisting into a strong band. But I felt as if everything were unraveling. The more I played, the more strung out and flabby my arm felt. It was like writing on sand and immediately seeing the traces of what you'd done smoothed over by the waves. I had more and more trouble reaching a point where I felt as if the work were actually achieving something.

And the last two fingers of my right hand were becoming harder to control. They were curling ever more strongly toward my palm. The feeling of writer's cramp was intensifying: not painful but powerful, so that it took a tremendous force of will to get them to do what I wanted. When I played, I had to spend a lot of my energy focusing on simply hitting the notes.

At first, I didn't have the objectivity to really understand the scope of the problem. We pianists are always fighting with our hands, trying to lengthen our reach, strengthen our fingers, improve our trills. And if it isn't the hands, there's always some aspect or other of reality that interferes with our quest for musical perfection. I had spent my whole life struggling with such obstacles. A conductor who didn't agree with my interpretation. A piano that was poorly tuned. A slip of my own, too fallible memory. Or even an actual problem with my hands. On my first trip to Europe with Rikki back in 1960, I had gotten some kind of infection that swelled my right hand up to a considerable size and threatened my performance for the first couple of concerts. So whatever was going on with my fingers now seemed like just one more hurdle in a career that was filled with them.

That August, I played Beethoven's "Emperor" Concerto, the Fifth, with the conductor Seiji Ozawa at Lewisohn Stadium, an open-air stage in Upper Manhattan that was at that time New York City's main summer concert venue. Seiji was a young and energetic Japanese conductor, not yet thirty, who had already gotten a lot of attention from the luminaries of the music world and was just about to take over the Toronto Symphony Orchestra. He had an extraordinary natural talent for connecting kinetically with music and getting orchestras to play with energy and verve. I always liked playing with Seiji, and everyone around me said the concert went well. But the *New York Times* review gave me pause. "In the solo part, Mr. Fleisher seemed to be having trouble making his fingers behave and hit the right notes," wrote the critic. He went on to say that this was "a negligible aspect" of a performance that he liked very much. But it wasn't negligible to me. I felt as if a dirty secret had been exposed.

Thus began my triumphant anniversary season.

Playing in public is hard enough when you're in perfect condition. Gary Graffman's teacher Isabelle Vengerova used to say you have to be 200 percent prepared, because you will forget 100 percent of what you know as soon as you step out on stage. Now I wasn't feeling I was capable even of 100 percent. And things were getting worse.

One highlight of that busy season—at least, it was supposed to be a highlight—was, in January, a cycle of the Beethoven violin and piano sonatas at the Metropolitan Museum with Tossy Spivakovsky, a former concertmaster of the Cleveland Orchestra who had left before Szell took over and for a while made something of a splash in a solo career. Tossy played with rather a strange style, his bow hand caved in along the bow, but he got a good sound and was very well respected. My own playing was more of a problem. My fingers were curling and cramping in their own strange ways. Unlike many other sonatas, Beethoven's present the piano as an equal partner rather than a mere accompanist, but I was aware I was playing cautiously, holding back, while Tossy, a more Romantic player to start with, emoted all over the place. I knew I hadn't done my best.

It wasn't the kind of problem you could hide. I'd been concerned about my hand for a while, but now my friends were able to see and hear that something was wrong. Audiences were still excited by my playing, some critics praised my artistry, but musicians, when they heard me, honed right in on that right hand. I didn't know how to answer them. What was going on? And how could I fix it, as soon as possible, and get back to concentrating on what was really important—making music? What had begun as an annoyance was starting to become an insistent problem. Unfortunately, nobody seemed to have any answers.

Fortunately, the leading hand doctor in the United States happened to be based in Baltimore. Dr. Raymond Curtis was based at Baltimore's Union Memorial Hospital, where the hand clinic still bears his name. Dr. Curtis thought that he knew what the problem was, and he thought that he could help me. He gave me an injection in my wrist of lidocaine, or some comparable form of anesthetic. It was like magic. For the first time in months, my fingers felt like themselves again. They regained their old length: no curling, no cramping. There was a little upright piano in one of the patient waiting rooms at the hospital, and I sat down and tried it out. A few notes. A scale. The opening of the Brahms D Minor concerto. Everything worked. There was no question about it: my hand was as good as new. Dr. Curtis had fixed me, and the nightmare was over.

That lasted for a few hours, until the injection wore off. Dr. Curtis tried to repeat his success. Once we rode in a cab together over to Peabody, and he injected me in the cab and again when we got to my studio. He tried another twelve or thirteen times to reproduce the effect of that first shot. But it never worked again. My arm, he told me, was like a fuse box, and I seemed to have blown a fuse.

There were other doctors, of course. I went to orthopedists and rehabilitation experts and specialists up and down the East Coast.

Some people said they'd seen similar problems before. Others looked at me blankly and shook their heads.

They had plenty of ideas. I was tested for a pinched nerve, for neurological diseases, for problems with my vertebrae. But all the tests came back negative. Several doctors wanted to try surgery. Operating on the C5 and C6 cervical disks, I was told, would clear up the problem. I drew the line, though, at cutting into my body. It seemed too irrevocable. And none of the diagnoses seemed certain enough to take the gamble of a surgery. In fact, there didn't seem to be anything actually the matter. I was healthy, I wasn't in pain, I was eating normally. I just had these two fingers that wanted to make a fist all the time, as if taking refuge from the keyboard in the safety of my palm.

For some other people, the obvious conclusion was that the problem was all in my head. Maybe I had some kind of psychological block that was keeping me from playing. It was caused by my relationship to my mother. Or Schnabel's philosophy of playing from the head rather than the hands. I really didn't want to hear this. It added to the sense of stigma you develop when something's wrong: you feel tainted, unhealthy, outcast. It doesn't help to feel that it's your own fault.

Still, I was willing to test out the powers of mind over matter. Two doctors at Johns Hopkins suggested I try hypnosis. It didn't seem so far-fetched when you consider that a trance state is akin to the place of extreme inner focus that I sustained for long periods when I played the piano. One psychiatrist gave me a nifty demonstration of how under hypnosis you could bypass the brain's commands and have your limbs do things that didn't seem to be under your control—involuntarily raising your arm, for example. That sounded like just what I needed. Maybe turning off the anxiety, the focus, all of the layers of extraneous concern that had come to surround playing the piano was the way to free up those two errant fingers. After my first few visits to the hypnotist, I complained that he hadn't put me under yet, whereupon the hypnotist took my arm and told me to open my eyes, revealing that he had stuck a needle all the way through it. I had gone under, all right. In fact, I was evidently a very good subject. I learned some basic principles of self-hypnosis. I wasn't sure I was getting results, but it might, I reasoned, take time. After all, the problem hadn't appeared overnight.

But if hypnosis was helping, it wasn't helping fast enough. There were two events that season I was especially looking forward to. I had been invited back to Hunter College, to give another solo recital. And I had finally gotten another chance to perform with Klemperer; we were going to do the Beethoven Third Concerto in London with the Philharmonia Orchestra. I wanted to play that concerto with every fiber of my being. But my hand wasn't going to cooperate. There was no point in going over to London and offering Klemperer less than my best. Danny Barenboim, the kid who had turned pages for me and Leon in Rome, by now a star in his own right, substituted for me for both those gigs. They went really well for him. He got rave reviews for his Hunter College recital, and Klemperer fell so in love with his playing that they ended up recording all the Beethoven concertos together a couple of years later. I was happy for Danny. But it was awfully hard to sit by and watch that happen.

I felt, in fact, the beginnings of anguished despair. How could I keep my career going if I couldn't play? I tried to fight down panic. I tried to work my hand out every day. My official excuse was that I had a pinched nerve, which was the best explanation any doctor was able to give for what was going on, even though the tests clearly showed that I did not, in fact, have a pinched nerve. Maybe the tests were wrong. I canceled all my performances for a month. And I focused on getting ready to perform in Cleveland with George Szell, to see if I would be able to go on the Russia tour we were so looking forward to.

Trips to the Soviet Union were always big news. Cleveland was the first American orchestra to visit the country in six years, and the press was going into high gear. Rikki had already arranged for her mother to look after Paula while we were gone and had started packing for the trip; the press reported on the clothes she was bringing.

That was the kind of interest that swirled around a trip to the Soviet Union in those days. Nikita Khrushchev had been deposed the year before and Leonid Brezhnev was already showing signs of swinging the country back in a more conservative, not to say Stalinist, direction, so it seemed a particularly opportune time for the kind of cultural diplomacy that a tour by a Western orchestra represented. But the tour wasn't only to the Soviet Union; the orchestra was scheduled to play across Europe. We would be gone for three months. Would be, that is, if I was actually able to play.

I had let Szell know I was having problems. He would have noticed in any case, the minute he heard me. I told him I was taking the month off. I told him I was working on it. I was sure I would be ready by April, when we were running through our tour program in Cleveland. The orchestra was taking two pianists on tour: John Browning was playing Samuel Barber's piano concerto, written for him for the opening of Lincoln Center in 1962, which he had already recorded with Szell and Cleveland, and I was playing my beloved Mozart K. 503. Or trying to play it. I was sure it would all be fine. Only I wasn't sure, because otherwise I wouldn't be telling Szell about my problem. "Well," Szell said, "let's see how 503 goes." Then we could decide whether or not I was in shape to go on tour.

I hadn't played in Cleveland with Szell for more than two years. The knot of dread in my stomach when I landed at the airport was worse than it had ever been. It was March and drizzly, and I was alone. Rikki had wanted to come with me, but I said no, I needed to do this one by myself. I needed all my focus on my hand. Severance Hall, the orchestra's home base, is a little bit out of town, and there weren't any really good hotels in the area. I was staying in a rather shabby Best Western motel. I went to my room and pulled down all the blinds and lay in darkness, trying to hypnotize myself so that my hand would start to work again.

Severance Hall is one of the most beautiful concert halls in America, a real temple of music. The great performances that have

taken place within those walls give it a kind of reverential feeling.
I was playing one of my favorite pieces, which had been one of
my greatest triumphs. Marc Lifschey, the oboist, was about to leave
the orchestra—he was one of many musicians who had a turbulent
relationship with Szell, and Szell had fired him, effective at the end
of that season—but he was still there to pass those glorious colored
swathes of music back and forth with me in the final movement. But
it all felt hollow.

I did get through it. I focused with an almost superhuman effort
on making my fingers work. I got through the rehearsal, though I
noticed the tension on Szell's face as he heard me struggle. And,
after a long day lying alone in my darkened hotel room, visualizing,
hypnotizing, and fighting off despair, I got through the first performance. I was in a fog. The audience applauded, as they always did.
The reviews were warm. "Fleisher's finger work was perfect," said the
Cleveland Plain Dealer. That was nice—but it wasn't true. My finger work
was a long, long way from perfect. And fighting with my fingers to get
them to function was no way to make world-class music on the level
to which I, and George, aspired.

For years, my greatest experiences as an artist had involved being
attuned to every nuance of what Szell did, responding to the slightest
change of mood, trying to achieve perfection. Now, I was just hoping to hit the right notes. I couldn't hide from it anymore. Something
unimaginably awful was happening.

Every bit of my consciousness was focused on getting through
those concerts. That first performance took place on our third wedding anniversary, April 1, 1965. Rikki spent all day at home waiting for
me to call, gradually giving way to panic that something might have
happened. She was right. Something had happened. It was true that
I had forgotten our anniversary. I had forgotten everything except the
need to fight the battle against my hand that I was clearly losing. I
lay in the dark hotel room and worked, and worked, and worked on

making my hand better—rather like someone lying on the train tracks trying to use his brain to stop the approaching train.

Szell and I went into his office after the last performance. He was uncharacteristically subdued, and very serious. He was not unkind. But he wasn't unduly solicitous, either. The bottom line, for him, was always the standard of music making of his orchestra. "I don't think it's possible for you to do the tour in this state," he said. "You can't play." I couldn't say anything. I had to agree. He was right. I couldn't meet our standards anymore.

So the Cleveland Orchestra went off to the Soviet Union and Europe on a three-month tour with Grant Johannesen as the piano soloist in the Mozart 503, and the tour was a wonderful, historic success. And I descended into the valley of the shadow. Because now I had to admit I really couldn't play. And I didn't know how to fix it.

I don't remember how I got back to Baltimore, or how I told Rikki, or how I got through the next days and weeks and months. I kept up appearances. I kept functioning in the world. I ate, and slept, and taught, and talked, and went through my life somehow.

The reality, though, was entirely different. I was living in a nightmare. I would wake up happy and then remember: You can't play. I would get caught up in a lesson and start to demonstrate on the keyboard, and the curling fingers would serve as a reminder: You can't play.

Ever since I could remember, the most important thing in my life had been playing the piano. Everything in my life had been subservient to that one thing: making the best music it was within my power to make. It was more important than anything else in my family when I was growing up. It was important enough to justify my leaving Dot: getting what I thought I needed would help me make music of the angels. No relationship, no activity—not even my wives or my children—held the same central focus in my life, the same hold on my waking hours. At thirty-six years old, I was coming into my own. I was growing more confident in my ability to understand what the music needed. I knew it was a lifelong quest, but it was starting to get to a particularly good part. And now, because of two stubborn fingers, it was all being torn away from me.

I didn't understand what else I could do with my life, or my brain, or my heart. I couldn't stop thinking about the music, working out its problems and challenges and coming up with ideas about how to approach and solve them. And yet when I sat down at the keyboard, I couldn't realize any of my ideas. I had to deal with the mechanics of uncurling my fifth finger instead of channeling the voice of the sublime. What good was it to have reached this point, to have worked so hard, to have so many insights, if there was no way to let anybody know about them?

All of the energy and focus that had driven my performances for so many years was still there, but now there was nowhere for it to drive me. I was battered by aimless determination, a need to do something, anything, that led me to keep searching—on to another doctor, another psychiatrist, another treatment—but left me feeling impotent and spent. Nothing I was doing seemed to change anything in my hand. It wasn't fair. It wasn't fair. I wondered if there was any point to living, if I wasn't able to play. I gave serious thought to ending my life. That, at least, would be an action that would bring a solution, and an end to the suffering.

I couldn't talk about it. There wasn't much to say. There wasn't anything anybody could do. Putting words around what had happened only intensified the pain. I'm not much of a whiner; I don't believe in unloading my problems on the people around me. But that's not to say I was particularly stoical, either. Inside, I was in a black depression. And if I wasn't very good at talking to Rikki about it, I certainly showed my state of mind by being irritable, and inaccessible, and withdrawn.

There were basic practical problems. I had to cancel my scheduled concerts. How was I going to feed my family? How was I going to pay the bills? Rikki and I had to start economizing in ways we'd never had to before. And I had to suspend my alimony payments to Dot. It wasn't bad enough that I had abandoned my oldest children: now, I couldn't even take care of them. Dot was one person who never questioned what had happened to my hand. As far as she was concerned, it was a case of bad karma coming home to roost.

Following the patterns of normal life was at least superficially comforting, even though it all—the bridge parties, the dinners, the evenings out with friends—felt slightly false. I would keep up appearances and then retreat back into my cloud of despair. All of this social stuff, the interactions with other people, had always served as a pendant to music, a way to balance out my life. But everything was thoroughly out of balance.

Still, while I weighed my options and thought seriously about suicide, I went on. I did my best to hide the rage and despair and anguish behind an imperturbable exterior. I kept teaching. I took on a lot more students, in fact, because now that I wasn't making any money from concerts, my job at Peabody was my only way to earn a living. At that fall's auditions, I took on more students than I had ever worked with before. I had to. I had four children to feed—nearly five children, because Rikki soon got pregnant again. At least some things were still working.

Life at Peabody kept me busy and to some extent distracted me from my problems. I did my best to contribute to the community. I played a role in the hiring of both Berl Senofsky and Konrad Wolff, something of which I was inordinately proud: I felt that both of them would enrich the community immeasurably. For me, of course, it was wonderful to have access to two close friends. Berl and I led informal Ping-Pong matches, violinists against pianists, fighting to the death. Berl threw himself into his teaching with equal energy. His performing career had not panned out as he had imagined it would, and he never quite understood why. There was no question that he was a fabulous fiddle player. He harbored a certain amount of bitterness about that, which seeped through from time to time. But he was a formidable musician, and his students got the benefit of it.

I also had some exciting students. One, in particular, was a rising star. In 1963, he had made a phenomenal and much-acclaimed debut with the New York Philharmonic at the age of sixteen, just as I had done. He came to me afterwards to continue his studies when he wasn't off performing around the globe. His name was André Watts. André was the son of an American GI who was out of the picture by the time I met André and a Hungarian mother who was very much present, living with her son and touring with him and working to support him. He needed less and less support, because he was embarked on a major concert career. Shortly before he started working with me, he had won a Grammy award as "Most Promising New Classical Recording Artist." "What did you promise?" I kidded him. When it came time for his final juries at Peabody, he was scheduled to perform a solo recital at the Lyric Opera House, so the professors just went up the street and listened to him in the concert hall. Not surprisingly, he passed.

Even at such a dark time, it was exciting to have such a gifted student. In the studio, the focus was still on music; I could still talk about it, immerse myself in it, or bring it back to life on the rare occasion when André came in with something like a Mozart sonata and played it on automatic pilot, with complete facility but no thought about how he was performing it. At times like that, I was able to wake him up.

And I challenged André to tell me why he practiced. Why do finger exercises? Why practice on concert days, if the piece has gone well the night before? I was on a crusade against mindless practicing. Practicing should serve a purpose: it develops facility, but it should also bring the performer closer to the music. I was against overpracticing, too, though I wasn't able to bring myself to talk to my students about the reasons why. They knew, of course. Everyone knew there was something wrong with my hand. But nobody ever mentioned it. That was the way I wanted it.

That fall, shortly after the Cleveland Orchestra returned from its tour, I was a judge at the twenty-fourth Leventritt Competition, as part of a star-studded judging panel: the fourteen judges included George Szell and Rudi Serkin, Leonard Bernstein and William Steinberg, and my friends Leon Kirchner, Claude Frank, and Gary Graffman. On one level, it was business as usual—listening to the candidates, taking notes, debating in the green room after the performances about their relative merits. But I was keenly aware of the new difference between my colleagues' lives and my own. For them, it really was business as usual: serving on the jury was squeezed into a crowded schedule that included the usual concerts, tours, receptions, reviews. But I, now, was sitting on the sidelines. The others were certainly sympathetic, to the extent that I let them mention it at all. They all hoped I'd get better soon. Still, nobody really thought that whatever was wrong with me was more than a temporary setback. I would surely get better in time. Of course I would. I thought that myself. But how much time?

I kept on going to doctors. One doctor tried shock treatment, trying to jar the hand into working the way it was supposed to. Another doctor put my hand in traction for six weeks, so that I went around with my arm in a sling. At the Rusk Institute of Rehabilitative Medicine at New York University, I was fitted out with a special device that was meant to strengthen my wrist and fingers. One doctor stood me on my head to test my spine. The suggestions got wackier the longer I looked. A colleague swore by Tiger Balm, the Chinese preparation that sells in corner delis for a dollar or so, which I dubbed "Oriental Ben-Gay." At least that was cheap. It didn't do anything, either.

Could it be, after all, in my head? This was another inner terror of mine. The stigma of having something wrong only seemed worse if there was some mental component to it. Did I have some kind of block, or trauma, or repressed fear that was keeping me from playing? Some psychotherapists speculated that I had what is known as conversion disorder, which has also been called hysteria: I was demonstrating symptoms with no known physiological cause. Perhaps the stress of my broken first marriage, the ups and downs of my second marriage, the financial drain of supporting two families, and the demands of my performing career had gotten to me. I couldn't rule it out. I visited a few different shrinks. But after a dozen visits, the main psychiatrist I went to felt that the problem was not psychosomatic. It was at least nice to have somebody to talk to. Outside of a doctor's office, I wasn't doing very well at that.

I know that the stress took a toll on our marriage. Externally, Rikki and I seemed as solid as ever. We had two beautiful children: our son Julian was born in 1966. We lived in a house filled with antiques and kept up an active social life, with Rikki, highly intelligent and dynamic, at the center. Life was going on. And yet I was wrapped in a cloud of swirling despair, wondering what the point of anything was and if life was even worth living. It was like leading a double life. I'm not sure Rikki was aware of how deeply I was suffering.

The dark side of our energy and dynamism was our bitter fights. I don't know if the hand was the whole problem. I now wonder if music had always represented a kind of "other woman" in our relationship. My involvement with music was so intense that I may not have had enough time and energy left over to sustain the kind of relationship Rikki wanted. My inability to communicate wasn't calculated to help. It certainly didn't help when I tried to combat my feelings of impotence by seeking solace from actual, flesh and blood "other women" as well. The less said about that, the better.

The clearest sign of my inner state was my hair. I did have power over my appearance, and I showed it. I stopped shaving. I stopped cutting my hair. Within a relatively short time I had a wild, scraggly black beard and a thick mane that I occasionally corralled into a ponytail. On my more sedate days, I looked not unlike the poet Allen Ginsberg. It was the late 1960s, and young people everywhere were rebelling against the status quo. Well, I had plenty to rebel against. I wasn't happy with the way things were either. I bought a motorbike and began riding around like Marlon Brando ("What are you rebelling against?" "Whaddya got?"), except that my two-wheeler was a Vespa, putting a more Continental twist on my brand of rebellion. I shared the Vespa experience with my friends (Gary Graffman, when he came to town to play with the orchestra, hung on to my waist for dear life as I negotiated the turns) and my family. (My son Dickie, after riding with me, caught the bug, and he has been riding motorcycles ever since.) Unfortunately, social change, or long hair, or even rebellion wasn't going to do much to solve my problem.

I kept playing the piano, every day. Even without the use of two fingers, I didn't know how to stop. Music had always been the thing I used to make sense of my life. Whatever else was going on, there was some higher truth accessible to me through the notes, like a door you could pass through into thinking about some other realm. Even if I couldn't make music any more the way I wanted, there was nothing to stop me from thinking about it. As painful as it was, it was also reassuring. My fingers might be lamed, but the music didn't live in my fingers. It was in my mind, and my heart. It was still there.

It really was still there.

At some point I realized that it had been more than a year since I had played a concert. A year in which I had been deprived of the thing I cared about most. I had gone through the torments of hell. I had thought about ending my life. And yet I was still here, and I still felt the same way about music. I was even still leading the life of a musician. I wasn't playing, but I was teaching all the time. I was surrounded by music. I still had a musical gift. Whatever my life as a musician was, it wasn't over.

The one thing I had been steadily resisting, for many months of that initial black period of mourning, was the idea of playing pieces written for the left hand.

There are quite a few piano pieces for the left hand alone. There are études and studies written as stunts, or exercises, or experiments.

There is also, most famously, the series of concertos commissioned from leading twentieth-century composers by Paul Wittgenstein, a pianist who lost his right arm in World War I. Wittgenstein (the brother of the philosopher Ludwig Wittgenstein) was a difficult personality, at once fiercely possessive and fiercely dismissive of most of the works he commissioned: he didn't like them, but he wasn't going to let anyone else have them, either. Still, he left the world quite a legacy, above all the Ravel Concerto for the Left Hand, which is such a great work that it's often played by pianists whose right hands work perfectly well. I knew about the Ravel. But I didn't want to work on it. It seemed to me that learning the left-handed repertory was an admission that whatever was wrong with my right hand was more than a temporary condition. I wasn't going to give in.

Finally, though, the need for activity won out. I missed playing. I missed performing. More prosaically, I missed making money. It was time to stop moping around and do something with myself. I pulled myself together and learned the Ravel concerto and Benjamin Britten's *Diversions* for left hand and orchestra, another piece written for Paul Wittgenstein that Wittgenstein didn't like and that I knew because Julius Katchen, my old friend in Paris, who had been quite close to Britten, had recorded it for Decca. It's an extraordinary piece, totally original, filled with great imagination. Armed with these works, I let my management know that I would be willing to get some gigs as a left-handed pianist.

In the spring of 1967, I reemerged onto the concert stage with Seiji Ozawa and the Toronto Symphony, which Ozawa was now leading as music director. I hadn't toured for almost two years. I looked completely different. Sometimes I could hear a bit of a rustle in the auditorium as I strode out on stage with my scraggly beard and my ponytail. But I did my best not to sound different. I played that Ravel concerto as if it were Brahms, pouring all the pent-up force of my enforced silence into those rich chords.

I didn't start quietly. If I was going to play again, I wanted to play at the level I'd been at before, in terms of my own music making and in terms of the caliber of my collaborators. I appeared with the Toronto Symphony in Washington and New York. That summer, I joined William Steinberg for a few performances of the Israel Philharmonic's three-week U.S. tour, playing both the Ravel and the Britten. And in the fall, I went back to Europe to try out my new repertory there, in Italy, in France, in Germany, in Belgium. I played the Ravel in Paris, with the radio orchestra, and touched base again with old friends like Julius and Doda. The critics were encouraging. I wasn't too forthcoming about the problems with my hand, but it was impossible to hide that they were there. There were a number of different explanations. I had a displaced finger muscle, according to one source. Another averred that I had gout.

I had proved that I could still do it. I wasn't sure, though, exactly what that was going to get me. I had conquered the same stages and seen my old haunts, but it wasn't clear whether I was saying hello to a new life or bidding good-bye to the old one. I had gotten away with something, but it didn't seem like a basis for the future. I couldn't make a fully satisfying career playing the same handful of pieces—always using the same hand. It was only provisional, anyway. I was going to do it only until my right hand got better.

In the meantime, though, I kept appearing with the Ravel concerto. In 1968, I even went back to the Cleveland Orchestra. Not with Szell, though, and not in Cleveland itself. I played it under their associate conductor, Louis Lane, on a series of run-out concerts to smaller towns in the area. We played at the auditorium of Michigan State University. We played at the Akron Armory. We played in a gym at Kent State University, where the audience was seated on folding chairs. It was three years to the day since my last two-handed concert with Cleveland. And Severance Hall seemed very far away.

At the last performance of that run of concerts, in London, Ontario, as I took my place at the piano I glanced out into the auditorium of the University of Western Ontario and saw George Szell sitting in the audience.

I saw him sitting in that modern, unfamiliar theater. I saw him take in my ponytail and my scraggly beard. I saw that these were things he was not entirely pleased with. And I tried desperately to fight down the rise of panic.

I had been to Szell a kind of musical son, and to me Szell had been a kind of musical father. I thought of our Brahms concerti. I thought of our Beethoven, of our recordings, of the way I could get him to smile by making a little musical joke at the keyboard or adding a little extra *Schwung* to a phrase for effect. I thought of everything I had learned about music making from him, and I thought of his laser-beam ears, trained on my playing. And Western Ontario or no Western Ontario, right hand or no right hand, I determined to rise to his standards. I came to that concerto with everything I had.

Szell was not naturally warm. He was a little aloof, particularly when he wasn't sure of himself. Those moments of warmth I teased out of him when we played together remained, to me, his best self. I didn't quite get that self that night in Ontario. But he came back to speak to me after the performance. And I sensed that, in spite of my long hair, my divorce, my lost right hand and canceled tour, approbation was there.

Szell died not long afterwards, in 1970. That meeting in Ontario was one of the last times I ever saw him.

My parents, Isidor and Bertha Fleisher, and my brother, Ray, a year or so before my birth. *(Author's collection)*

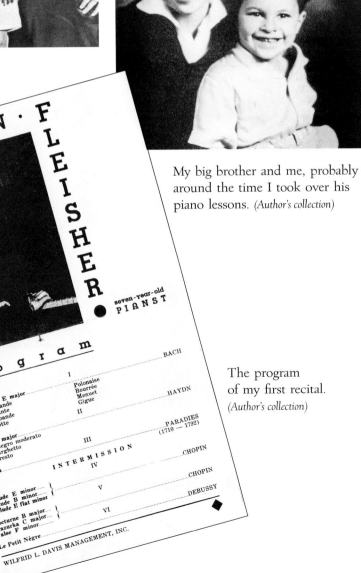

My big brother and me, probably around the time I took over his piano lessons. *(Author's collection)*

The program of my first recital. *(Author's collection)*

L E O N · F L E I S H E R

seven-year-old
PIANIST

THURSDAY EVENING · APRIL 9th · 8:20 P. M. — CON

p r o g r a m

I

.......BACH

French Suite E major..........
  Allemande
  Courante
  Sarabande
  Gavotte

Polonaise
Bourrée
Menuet
Gigue

.......HAYDN

II

Sonata F major..........
  Allegro moderato
  Larghetto
  Presto

.......PARADIES
(1710 — 1792)

III

Toccata..........

.......CHOPIN

INTERMISSION

IV

.......CHOPIN

Prelude E minor.....
Prelude B minor.....
Prelude E flat minor.....

V

.......DEBUSSY

Nocturne B major.....
Mazurka C major.....
Valse F minor.....

VI

Le Petit Nègre..........

WILFRID L. DAVIS MANAGEMENT, INC.

(Below) Lake Como, 1938. I am seated, center, with my arm locked through Maria Curcio's. Schnabel, Therese, and Karl Ulrich are standing behind me, to the right. Peter Diamand is standing, third from righ[t]. Noel Mewton-Wood is kneeling, at right. And Stefar[n] Schnabel, his arm around Sylvia Kunin, is behind m[e] with his foot on my shoulder. (Author's collection)

(Top) My mother and me on the deck of the Conte di Savoia, on our way to Italy. (Ella Barnett / author's collection)

(Above) With Artur Schnabel at Lake Como, 1938. (Schnabel Foundation / author's collection)

(Right) Ruli (Karl Ulrich Schnabel) congratulates me after my debut with the New York Philharmonic, 1944. (© Musical America)

(Facing pa[ge])
The program of my Carnegie Hall deb[ut]
(Author's collect[ion])

Leonard Bernstein and I go over a score around
the time of our performance at Ravinia, 1945.
(Author's collection)

The finalists at the Queen Elisabeth competition,
1952. I am at left; Philippe Entremont is fourth from
right; Maria Tipo—the blond angel—is next to him.
(Author's collection)

(Above) My brother and me,
all grown up. *(Author's collection)*

(Below) Queen Elisabeth of
Belgium congratulates her laurea
(Author's collection)

...t and I celebrating ...e Fourth of July in ...olland, 1952, with ...usician Simon ...doff and Janet Reed ...the New York City ...llet. *(Partican Pictures, ...sterdam / author's ...ection)*

One of the last pictures of my mother, taken in June 1952. *(Author's collection)*

...erre Monteux and ...e, in colloquy. ...uthor's collection)*

Eugene Istomin, Gary Graffman, and me at work . . .

. . . and at play, with Naomi Graffman and Dot.
(Photos courtesy of Graffman Collection, International Piano Archives, University of Maryland)

on Kirchner and me, engrossed in four-handed repertory in Rome,
ᴴile Danny Barenboim turns pages for us. *(Author's collection)*

ᴴe did not want to be chucked under the chin, even by the great and
ually fearsome George Szell. *(Author's collection)*

(*Above*) Dot with Dickie Leah, and Deborah, shortly after my decampment. (*Inger Elliot / collection of Deborah Fleisher*)

(*Left*) With Dickie and Deborah. (*Courtesy of Sony Music Entertainment*)

kki and me, radiant in
vitzerland on one of our
ropean trips. *(Anthony
affer / author's collection)*

Me, newly hirsute, as the Associate
Conductor of the Baltimore Symphony
Orchestra. *(Baltimore Symphony Orchestra)*

or better or worse:
hrough the growth of
y beard, the end of our
arriage, and the stylistic
:cesses of the 1970s,
kki and I maintained a
iendship. *(Collection of Rikki
isher)*

Rikki and me, postseparation, crossing the Atlantic with our kids, Paula and Julian, and Rikki's mother. *(Collection of Rikki Fleisher)*

With André Watts, my former student. *(© Steve Sherman)*

thy was beautiful, and smart, and talented, and . . . beautiful.
uthor's collection)

athy and I wait backstage at the Meyerhoff before my abortive
vo-hand "comeback," 1982. *(© Susan T. McElhinney)*

My five kids strike a pose at my wedding to Kathy. Left to right: Leah, Deborah, Paula, Julian, and Dickie. *(Author's collection)*

Leon Kirchner and I take to the streets of New York after our disastrous rehearsal of "L.H." *(Author's collection)*

Dan Gustin, Seiji, Phyllis Curtin, and I sing "Allelulia" at the opening exercises of Tanglewood, 1996. The harmony was only in the music. *(Walter H. Scott / © Scott Photos)*

_na Koston and I go over yet another
_ore for the Theater Chamber
_ayers. She is smiling; I am not.
uthor's collection)

At the Leon Fleisher Carriage House at Tanglewood. I wasn't sure the sign was permanent. *(Author's collection)*

Kathy coaches Zakeebah (Keekee) on a dance move, shortly before Keekee's audition for the Baltimore School of the Arts. She got in but then her great-aunt moved her away. *(Author's collection)*

Kathy and me, settling for a "godparent" role with Quashawn. *(Author's collection)*

Gary Graffman and I are still posing after all these years. *(Author's collection)*

My brother and me: really, really grown up.
(Photo: David Weiss)

My kids and I gather at Julian's country house: Deborah, Julian, me,
Paula, Dickie, and Leah. *(Author's collection)*

The Kennedy Center Honorees of 2007: Steve Martin, me, Diana Ross,
Brian Wilson, Martin Scorsese. Not bad company. *(Author's collection)*

MAURICE RAVEL: PIANO CONCERTO
FOR THE LEFT HAND IN D MAJOR (1929–30)

I was very lucky. It just so happens that Ravel wrote a concerto for the left hand that is one of the masterpieces of the whole piano literature, whether for one hand or for fifteen hands. I calculated once that I've played it around a thousand times. It's still fresh. It's still challenging. It's one of the great works.

Ravel wasn't a composer I focused on in my studies with Schnabel. I discovered him, really, after I left Schnabel and became exposed to a lot of different music through my travels, through my friends, and through Eugene Istomin in particular. Eugene had an LP set of the opera *L'enfant et les sortilèges* (a tale about a naughty child who is surrounded by inanimate objects—the teapot he has broken, the lessons he hasn't learned—come to life), which he played for me one afternoon on Shirley and Ned's turntable in the apartment on rue de la Harpe in Paris. Eugene's method of instruction was to prepare me for the ecstatic highlights and then sit and watch my reaction with satisfaction, like a musical voyeur.

It wasn't difficult to react. It was such great stuff. Ravel brought colorings to music, and a sensuality, that I found intoxicating. He was a contradictory figure. On the one hand, he was petite (like Chopin), crisp and fastidious, a dandy who dressed to the nines and slicked back his hair. On the other hand, he wrote music that was languid, succulent, oozing the most sensual of harmonies.

One of my friends in Baltimore, a German psychiatrist, once defined Ravel to me as a hysteric. I asked him to give me an example of what a hysteric was. He thought for a moment, and then, in heavily accented English, he said, "Vell, you see, you have a very beautiful girl, in a bathing suit. And on the sides of the suit there are openings, all up and down the suit. And in each opening is written, No! No! No! No! No!" That defined Ravel for me for life.

Ravel is a great musical colorist. "Color," in music, refers to the different kinds of sounds that different instruments can make. Germanic music often focuses on structure; Ravel's, like that of Debussy and some other French composers, also luxuriates in the range of possibilities in the way that sounds touch your ear. It's about the sensation of sound, the tactile experience of it. The surface of the music is constantly shifting, and a single gesture may be made by several different instruments, each picking up part of the phrase and passing it to the next one while lending it their own particular sounds.

There's a long trill in the middle of the Concerto for the Left Hand that epitomizes what I mean. It starts in the piano. Then the violins pick it up. Then all four horns come in with it, then the flute, then the clarinet. Each instrument is playing the same note, but each one, obviously, sounds quite different. Still, the whole point is that it's one single trill: it just keeps changing the way it sounds. It's a virtuosic demonstration of an extraordinary aural imagination.

It's hard to bring off in performance, though. The whole thing needs to be as seamless as possible as the sound gradually diminishes, particularly when it passes from four horns to a single horn to the flute in one continuous line. The problem is that the first horn usually gets too quiet—because his part is marked *diminuendo,* meaning he should get softer—and then the flute comes in making as big a sound as he can, because his part is marked *fortissimo* and he wants to make a big sound to match the horn. The result is a big accent on the flute entrance that is not at all what Ravel intended. You have to work with the flute and the horn there, to help them understand how to make that handoff with as little break as possible. When it's done right, it should sound like one long line. The whole passage is over in a few seconds. Then it leads into a delicate section that sounds like Chinese dolls taking tiny porcelain steps.

Since Ravel's concept of sound is so different from that of Mozart or Beethoven, as a pianist you often have to use a different kind of attack, a different way of starting phrases and putting your fingers on the keys. Mozart and Beethoven generally want definite beginnings. With Ravel, by contrast, you often have to slow down and soften the way you start the notes, so that you just waft in, joining the flow of the music rather than determining it.

Of course, there are other places in Ravel that are brilliant and virtuosic and require you to enter with a big flourish. The start of the left-hand concerto is one example: it opens with a huge jump that's an extraordinary gesture of unsheathing one's sword. This comes off only if you take your life in your hands and fling your left hand up the keyboard—and risk missing the jump entirely. It's quite an embarrassment if it doesn't come off. When that happens—and it does, occasionally—you spend the rest of the piece trying to live that down.

Ravel's attention to detail and the mechanics of a piece—he was a meticulous craftsman—led Stravinsky to call him a "Swiss watchmaker." This was not intended as a compliment. There was a side of Ravel that was fond of mechanical, repetitive patterns (think of his famous orchestral piece "Bolero," which is basically one idea drawn out to amazing proportions and which he once said he would like to have played in a factory). Ravel collected gadgets and automatons; he even had a mechanical bird named Zizi, which he kept as a very low-maintenance pet.

But Ravel also loved color and warmth, the sunniness of Spain, the rhythms of jazz. The Concerto for the Left Hand is full of syncopations, juxtapositions of one rhythm or one key against another. It has moments of delicate detail—like the chinoiserie I've mentioned—but there's nothing restrained about it, particularly in the piano part. Ravel said that his goal was that, if one listened to it with closed eyes, one would detect nothing amiss. I love that phrase. It was, after all, my goal as well.

The piece is born out of the murk. Ravel likes to lurk down around the bottom of the orchestra and let pieces grow out of that darkness. It starts with a rumble from the double basses and cellos, the lowest string instruments in the orchestra. There's something very primal about the sound of open strings on the double bass. Ravel divides the basses into three sections: two of them play on open strings, and the third fills the space in between with a running flow of rapid notes, very softly, so that the chord resonates and shimmers. Then, out of this primordial slime, there rises the gravelly, guttural, impossibly deep sound of the lowest wind instrument, a contrabassoon. (The conductor Sir Thomas Beecham once, while conducting a less than first-rate orchestra, said at the end of a solo contrabassoon passage, "You may now pull the chain," without missing a beat.)

This opening leads into another of Ravel's seamless transitions, because the contrabassoon hands off to the horns. It's the second horn, the lower one, that needs to be emphasized here; the first horn is just a kind of overtone, but the first horn player is not usually too pleased to cede pride of place to his subordinate. If you can get it right, though, it's fantastic. I remember playing the piece with André Previn and the London Symphony Orchestra at the Edinburgh Festival, and the horns made their entrance with this sense of distance, as if from a long way away, and the whole thing became one long line of shifting sound. It was absolutely magical. I'll never forget it. I work toward that sound every time I have a chance to conduct the piece myself.

Playing the solo part, though, is the real challenge. It's a ferociously difficult piece. Anxiety about getting it right has always made for a lot of preconcert stress for me, in the hotel or backstage, in the hours leading up to the concert. The first cadenza is difficult because there's a lot of jumping around and it's easy to play clinkers, and the second cadenza seems to have about fifteen thousand notes. I was always concerned about memory slips, and the Ravel concerto presents you with an awful lot to remember.

Ravel wasn't immediately sure about taking on the commission for a left-hand concerto, but the challenge intrigued him, as did the $6,000 Paul Wittgenstein offered him to write it. That was a considerable amount of money in 1929. In any case, he really understood how the left hand works. He grasped, so profoundly, that the fingers take care of the harmony and the activity while the thumb takes care of the tune. The thumb remains independent. This is why all the one-handed piano music is for the left hand, why there isn't a right-hand literature. If the melody is higher than the harmony, it only makes sense to have it played by the strongest finger, the thumb.

Ravel got the left hand to work overtime, too. When you play the piece, you're constantly leaping from treble to bass, creating the illusion that both lines are happening at once, and you often have to play chords of seven or eight notes, which means that a single finger has to play two notes at once. You also have to plunge in without any preparation: the solo part opens with a long cadenza that leaves the pianist completely exposed. ("If I had wanted to play without the orchestra, I would not have commissioned a concerto!" the hard-to-please Wittgenstein said after he first heard it.)

In that cadenza, after the opening arpeggios and just before the first statement of the theme, there's a little transition section of a measure or two where everything slows down, ending with three emphatic chords. For years, I really took advantage of the resonance down in the bass to make as big a sound as possible on those chords before releasing the pedal and clearing out all the resonance, so that when I came in with the theme it felt like I was starting again fresh. But after a while, I'd had enough of that approach. I decided it was better to let the whole thing settle down a bit before starting the theme, so I started playing those three chords more softly. I butted heads about this with Daniel Barenboim when he conducted the piece with me in Paris in 1987. Danny thought the *diminuendo* was a mistake. He was all for the grand gesture. We went back and forth about it quite a bit. In performance, though, he couldn't keep me from doing what I wanted.

The concerto is highly dramatic. It never lets up. Its three sections are compressed into a single movement, less than twenty minutes long, but it's one long emotional statement. It's as if Ravel were compensating for the limitations of the single hand by being more assertive, more forceful, more beautiful than ever. It leaves you drained, especially if you're the one playing it.

It also incorporates a lot of jazz elements—something that particularly put Wittgenstein off. (Wittgenstein initially did quite a bit of gratuitous rewriting and revising of the piece to make it wholly his own; it took him a while to appreciate what a masterpiece he'd gotten.) Ravel was fascinated by jazz. A trip to the United States he made in 1928 gave him some direct exposure to American jazz, and its influence shows up in several of his pieces, including the violin sonata.

Unfortunately, these rhythms can be particularly difficult for classical musicians to grasp. I've played the concerto with ensembles who obediently play what's written on the page but wholly fail to grasp the underlying swing. Students seem to have a particularly hard time, which is ironic, because we stereotype young people as being naturally hipper. But for people who have been trained only in the more orderly rhythms of the standard classical tradition, this kind of thing doesn't come naturally and they can sound awfully square, dutifully counting out the beats.

Me, I love the jazz elements. My greatest wish, if I could really do anything I wanted, would be to have the gift to sit down at the piano and improvise: to play real jazz. I can't improvise at all. I was trained, like most classical artists, to read notes off the page, and once you've got that ingrained in your mind and fingers it's hard to liberate yourself and improvise without actually sitting down and working hard to learn the rules. But to hear great jazz players fills me with awe and delight. And not only the greats. In fact, any cocktail pianist who can improvise sets me off.

CHAPTER 7

The
Conductor

A new métier: leading an orchestra.
Steven Tavares (Author's collection)

The first problem I had with conducting was coming out on stage and turning my back on the audience. It was an utterly foreign sensation. I always felt as if my rear end were hanging out. That particular portion of my anatomy suddenly seemed enormous, living a life of its own, engaged in its own relationship with the public behind my back. For the first couple of years I conducted, I sat on a chair in front of the orchestra, to help quell that particular discomfort.

It wasn't my idea to start conducting. It really started with a suggestion from one of my students, Dina Koston. I had a few private students over the years—including Joanne Rogers, the wife of Fred Rogers, the host of the kids' show *Mister Rogers' Neighborhood*—and Dina was one of them; she came up from Washington to take lessons. She was married to a superb and highly respected psychiatrist, Roger Lee Shapiro, a very sweet man. He was a long, long drink of water, and Dina was tiny, and dark, and intense. She also had an extraordinary musical ear. She could make connections between Webern and Bach that I found revelatory and that I wouldn't have heard myself.

With me, Dina worked on the standard keyboard repertory, but she was primarily a composer. She had studied with Nadia Boulanger in Paris and spent a summer at the Darmstadt International Summer Courses for New Music, an annual composers' retreat whose name, particularly in the 1950s and 1960s, was a synonym for a particular strain of modernist musical orthodoxy. As a result, she knew a tremendous amount about the cutting edge of the European avant-garde, the music of people like Luigi Nono and Luigi Dallapiccola and György Ligeti (who inadvertently won new fame when his music was used in the soundtrack to Stanley Kubrick's film 2001). She was, however, far less dogmatic than the mainstream of the Darmstadt school. She also had a healthy musical curiosity; she was constantly on the lookout for new scores, new instruments, new composers. This was largely unknown territory to me. I had always performed some contemporary pieces, and I had close friendships with a couple of composers, like Leon Kirchner. But in general I didn't have the same kind of emotional connection to contemporary works that I had to the older stuff.

Dina had another idea. As my student, she had been taken with my ideas about rhythm and tempo, which are a particular cornerstone of my approach. Dina thought they might serve me very well in another form of music making: as a conductor. She thought that my understanding of rhythm might be a boon in some of the intricate contemporary scores that appealed to her.

She also had a very clear idea about where I could conduct. She wanted to found a new chamber ensemble in Washington, D.C., devoted to juxtaposing contemporary music with the old.

Chamber music was fairly regimented in those days. There were established string quartets, like the Juilliard Quartet, and piano trios, and chamber orchestras. There weren't, that Dina and I knew of, any groups with a flexible core of artists who could perform the wealth of literature that's been written for other groupings of instruments, for anywhere from two to eighteen players. And there weren't any groups that we knew of—certainly not in Washington—with contemporary music as a main focus. The Library of Congress had been devoting a lot of energy to new music since the days of Elizabeth Sprague Coolidge—who played a pioneering role in commissioning chamber works from contemporary composers and whose legacy continued even after her death in 1953—but it didn't have an ensemble of its own. Dina had been to Marlboro, and she was inspired by that model. She thought we could find a market for an ensemble of gifted players who came together to perform living composers side by side with the composers who had influenced them—a programming idea that seemed not only informative but organic.

Two or three players can rehearse a piece and read one another's cues and listen and generally manage fine on their own. But music for larger ensembles or music that's particularly tricky rhythmically—written in two different tempos, for instance—often needs someone to conduct it, in order to keep it together. And I, Dina suggested one afternoon over lunch at the Mount Vernon Restaurant in Baltimore, could be that conductor.

Dina was older and more mature than most of my other students, and Rikki and I sometimes saw her and Roger socially. She was, consequently, more aware of what I was going through with my hand: my despair, my lack of motivation, my sense of purposelessness. And I think that her idea of founding a chamber ensemble was also motivated—not entirely, but in part—by a desire to help get me out of my funk.

I wasn't at all sure about conducting. I had, after all, been warned off it by Monteux himself, during the summers with him in Maine. Szell hadn't been very encouraging either. He himself had been a brilliantly talented piano prodigy, but once he opted for conducting, he turned his back on a solo piano career. In the old-school view, you had to make a choice. Conducting wasn't supposed to be good for pianists. The real issue wasn't control; it was grasping the baton, which could lead to a kind of tension in the hand that wasn't very helpful when you sat down at the keyboard to play.

But at that point, my hand didn't seem to be good for much anyway. And Dina's idea held a glimmer of hope. Maybe this was another way I could have a productive life in music. I could conduct it. I could invite other leading musicians to play with us. We could develop our ensemble into something really fantastic, something that no one else was doing, something that represented vital music making. The more I thought about the idea, the more intrigued I got. For the first time in many months, I had an idea of a possible future, something I might be able to look forward to when I got up in the morning. Dina and I walked around Baltimore all that afternoon talking about what we could do.

Thus the Theater Chamber Players was born.

It was a tremendous amount of work. Dina and I spent hours on the phone planning, plotting, discussing, strategizing, before rehearsals had even started. Dina oversaw much of the practical side of things: the fund-raising, the administration. She would come to me with armloads of scores, and I would look through them, and we would discuss what we might want to play and how the pieces might fit together. And she was always making connections in the most unexpected places. One day, for instance, she was marching in an antiwar protest as part of a group called Artists of Conscience—Dina was a committed left-wing activist—when she met a woman named Hazel Wentworth, who had founded a group called the Washington Theater Club. The upshot was that we used the group's small theater on O Street, which was conveniently dark on Monday nights, for our own performances. Hazel even helped us get a foundation grant to help launch our new season. Thus Dina's social conscience found us a performance space, and a name, and a way to start.

We opened in June of 1968 with a program that we thought was a canny blend of the familiar and the new: Haydn and Debussy, Bartók and Stravinsky, Dallapiccola and Dina herself. All but one of the works was written in the twentieth century. A soprano named Jeannette Walters sang the vocal works (Dallapiccola's *Due Liriche di Anacreonte*, Stravinsky's *Three Songs from William Shakespeare*, and Dina's *Rhetoric and Lyric*). I took the stage in my unfamiliar role, lifted my hand—I wasn't crazy about using a baton, which seemed to take on a life of its own when it was in my grip—and conducted. And the next day's review praised us for "an unusual, engrossing, and wisely planned concert." We were on our way.

The Theater Chamber Players became an outlet for a kind of

music making I'd never done before. I found myself conducting scores of terrific complexity. Like one of the Improvisations on Mallarmé by Pierre Boulez, who was a dogmatic serialist composer but later mellowed and even went on to add the role of mainstream conductor (and New York Philharmonic music director) to his portfolio. Or two short chamber operas by Ligeti, *Aventures* and *Nouvelles Aventures*, tongue-in-cheek explorations-cum-send-ups of avant-garde sounds, including the sandpapering of the cover of a book, the mixing of marbles in a bowl, the tearing of newspaper, and, finally, the raising of a tray of glassware that comes cathartically smashing to the floor. Beethoven, it wasn't. But it was exciting as hell.

The mechanics of what I was doing were also unfamiliar. I could delve into a score and do my best to try to understand what the composer was going for, in his or her terms. This wasn't all that different from what I did when I played the piano, although it was slow going sometimes to make sense of these unfamiliar musical languages. I could also advise the performers on how to approach the music; that was like what I did as a teacher. But then, somehow, I had to help them actually realize the music, in performance. One big challenge of this new métier was figuring out how to make that happen: how the different instruments worked, how you went about cueing them, what players needed from you.

It was challenging, but it was powerfully refreshing. Turning so much thought and energy in new musical directions had the effect of cleaning out my ears; when I turned back to music I knew well or a student brought me a familiar piece, it seemed newer and fresher as well. That was, in fact, the whole point of the way we were putting our programs together, juxtaposing the contemporary and familiar in ways that were meant to be illuminating. It may not have always worked, but audiences were not disinclined to follow us. It didn't hurt that I was able to bring in some big-name friends and colleagues. In 1970, André Watts and Jaime Laredo came in to play the Prokofiev F Minor sonata on a program that also included Mozart, Hindemith, and Harrison Birtwistle as sung by the soprano Phyllis Bryn-Julson, another TCP regular. With names like those, we found ourselves turning people away at the door. Fortunately, the Theater Club soon moved to a larger home.

We had a whole roster of pretty formidable players. Pina Carmirelli was a brilliant violinist who was a close associate of Rudi Serkin's and had met Dina at Marlboro, and she used to come over regularly from Rome to play with us. Berl Senofsky played with us. And I enlisted some of the students I worked with at Peabody, like the guitar player David Starobin, the violist Kim Kashkashian, and the cellist Sharon Robinson, who are all now established soloists in their own right. At that concert where André and Jaime played the Prokofiev, Sharon played with Jaime in a piece by Hindemith, "Des Todes Tod," that's written for voice and what I call the perfect string quartet: two violas and two cellos. That's a string quartet that really makes some sound. Jaime was so struck by Sharon's playing—so he said—that he recommended she go to Marlboro. A couple of years later, she did; by then, Jaime was divorced, and the two of them got together and eventually formed the Kalichstein-Laredo-Robinson trio, one of the best-known trios around today, and, yes, got married. They've always seen me as responsible for bringing them together. I don't think Ruth Laredo, Jaime's ex-wife, ever really forgave me.

As the Theater Chamber Players was getting launched, another conducting opportunity came my way. One of my students at Peabody, Michael Campbell, was a cellist as well as a pianist, and he played with the Annapolis Symphony Orchestra, a community orchestra not far from Baltimore. (Nothing is far from anything in Maryland.) He had spoken to the orchestra's conductor about playing a solo concerto, but the conductor, sadly, was diagnosed with a brain tumor and died shortly afterwards. The orchestra, a largely volunteer ensemble, was hastily searching for a replacement. Michael, knowing of my nascent conducting abilities and eager to play his concerto, wondered if I might be able to step in and conduct the concert instead.

It was one thing to get up in front of a few chamber players and help guide them through a score. It was quite a different thing to get up in front of a full-sized orchestra and lead pieces from the standard repertory that called for a kind of style and nuance that I had no experience in getting from a group of players. Still, the orchestra badly needed leadership, and if there was one thing I had experience in, it was the standard orchestral repertory. I agreed to conduct the concert.

To demonstrate that I was compromising none of my musical standards by performing with a small semiprofessional organization, I programmed—ambitiously—Paul Hindemith's *Symphonic Metamorphoses on Themes of Weber* on my first concert. I'm very fond of Hindemith, whose *Four Temperaments* was, after all, my first-ever recording. He sometimes gets a little pedestrian, but he can be quite inspired and he wrote some wonderful stuff. The *Symphonic Metamorphoses* is brilliant, but it's also thickly orchestrated, and it's easy for it to sound plodding when it should be bouncy and springy and delightful. Some people even think it's supposed to sound plodding. People tend to play it in a very heavy, Gestapo-like manner. I remember a cellist coming up to me once in Frankfurt after a performance of Hindemith's piano concerto for the left hand and saying, outraged, "That's not Hindemith!" He then pounded out a chain of heavy beats, explaining, with emphasis, "This–is–Hindemith!" All I could think was, No wonder more people don't appreciate Hindemith's music.

That cellist might well have been happy with my maiden Annapolis essay in conducting the *Symphonic Metamorphoses*. I still didn't quite know what I was doing. I had in my mind's eye the model of all the great conductors I had worked with over the years, especially Szell, and I had plenty of ideas about how one needed to go about conducting. I just wasn't quite sure how to put them into practice yet. I conducted with such exaggerated motions that my stick seemed to reach from floor to ceiling, from one wall to the other of the gymnasium where we rehearsed. It was kind of a crazy concert all around. Michael was playing not one solo piece but two, both the

Liszt A Major concerto and the Franck *Symphonic Variations*, and when he started playing the Liszt, the piano started to move. Evidently someone hadn't locked the wheels. Fortunately, it settled down before creating too many difficulties.

I must have settled down, too, because after the concert the orchestra offered me the position of music director.

Annapolis is essentially a bedroom community for Washington and Baltimore. The orchestra represented a cross-section of the spectrum of musical talent, from people who had played in their youth and were participating solely for the love of it to brass players in the Naval Academy Band who moonlighted with the orchestra to bring variety into their musical diet. We weren't talking about an ensemble of crack professionals. Yet it was tremendously exciting and satisfying music making. In a way, it's far more exciting to get people to play better than they know they can, to unite everyone in the energy and beauty and thrill of the music, than it is to play with skilled but jaded professionals. In the twelve years I was there, we did some bang-up concerts. I brought in lots of my students from Peabody, both in the orchestra and on the podium. One of them, Hugh Wolff, became my assistant in Annapolis. I guess Monteux's advice against conducting would have applied to him, too, because he developed such a taste for conducting that he left the piano and went on to make a notable career. All this new blood helped elevate the level of the orchestra's playing, though there was some muttering from people who felt they were being edged out. There are always growing pains in a situation like that, but the payoff was undeniable: the group got better.

They also got to play with some superb soloists, because I invited my friends to come in and play concertos. André Watts played in Annapolis, and Eugene Istomin. Gary Graffman tried out some concertos with me that he hadn't played before, like the Mendelssohn G Minor and a Mozart concerto that was new to him—which might have accounted for the surprising number of wrong notes I heard him play; it wasn't like him. Jaime Laredo played the Beethoven violin concerto.

I even got the violinist Isaac Stern to come in and play the Bruch concerto. To document the big event, there was a photographer in the hall during the concert, working his way down the aisle. He distracted Isaac, who actually stopped in the middle of the piece and reamed the guy out. "We spend a lot of time doing concentrated work," he said, "working very hard to get this music and communicate it to the public, and you're preventing that connection from taking place." There were no more photographers in concerts after that.

All of this activity was very encouraging to me. Buoyed by my experiences with the Theater Chamber Players and Annapolis, I jumped into a conducting career with both feet. By 1970, I was signed up to conduct all over the place. The Seattle Symphony. The Boston Symphony Orchestra, at Tanglewood. The Mostly Mozart festival in New York. That was the first of them. Anyone in the music business can tell you it's pretty foolhardy to make your formal debut as a professional orchestra conductor in New York. You're supposed to work your way up to that.

But I was so eager at the thought that I was finding a new outlet, a new way to be an active musician, that I threw caution to the winds. In the eyes of someone like George Szell, who worked his way up through the ranks, I would have been no more than a dilettante. I didn't care. I was working again, and these engagements meant I didn't have to remain totally sidelined while I waited for my hand to get better. I even started talking to the press about my hand, which was a subject that for the previous few years I had studiously avoided. I knew my hand was going to get better, of course. But in the meantime, I had this other exciting new career.

My New York debut went pretty well. I was playing with top professionals, so my job was easier than it might have been. And despite my inexperience, I had very clear ideas of what the music was about. That gave me a directness of intention that fooled people into thinking I knew what I was doing. If it walks like a conductor and swings a stick like a conductor and gives orders like a conductor, it must be a conductor. Well—other conductors have learned in the same way. A lot of players seemed to appreciate what I had to offer.

It was good to have some distraction. For all my optimism, my hand certainly wasn't getting better yet, though I kept trying cure after cure: acupuncture, meditation, physiotherapy, cortisone injections. Some doctors at the National Institutes of Health in Washington thought I might have a form of something called torsion dystonia, which contorts muscles of its victims, typically young, intelligent Jews. They put me on L-dopa for a while. It didn't help. Nothing helped.

Meanwhile, my marriage was falling apart.

Rikki was smart and attractive and hugely energetic and involved in social causes in a way that I applauded and sought to follow. She was the kind of person who could make things happen. She was an activist. She knew all the local politicians. She got herself to the 1968 Democratic Convention as an alternate delegate, over the protests of the governor of Maryland, who so much didn't want her there that she had to stay in a different hotel from the rest of the delegation (from her bedroom window she was able to see where the riots started). Her energy and brilliance were terrific. But on some level we were also inscrutable to each other. And she and I had become locked in a vicious cycle of fighting. She was aggrieved. I was withdrawn and uncommunicative. My attempts to console myself elsewhere naturally infuriated her, and the fights wore me down.

I didn't want to let go, though. I wanted my family. I hadn't abandoned one family and started another only so that I could lose that one, too. I may have been inaccessible, I may have strayed, but that didn't mean I wanted it to end. At first, I felt I would do anything to keep the marriage alive. I would panic when Rikki started to get angry. Once, when she threatened to leave and stormed out to the car, I ran after her and threw myself across the hood to try to get her to stay. She kept driving, unmoved, and I finally slid off the hood and fell into the road. Luckily, I wasn't hurt.

Things didn't get any better, or less operatic, after that. One night

I was heading out to a rehearsal at the Annapolis Symphony and Rikki began with the laundry list of terrible things that I had supposedly done. I got more and more agitated about being late to rehearsal, which as a musician you simply can't do but which she clearly didn't care about at all. Finally, in rage and frustration, I put my hand through a window. As gestures go, it was memorable, but it didn't exactly help matters. We both got pretty good at this sort of dramatic but self-sabotaging statement. Once, when Rikki wanted to accompany me on a trip to Vancouver and I didn't want her to come, she started burning her passport in some kind of furious marital protest. As she tended the flame, sobbing, on our little hibachi grill, I walked past her and observed, drily, "You know, that's a felony." It was not a good scene.

We separated for a period in 1969 and then tried again, resuming relations with a brittle care that was hard to sustain over the long haul. We went up to Cape Cod with the kids in the summer of 1971, when I was teaching a summer course at Harvard; I commuted back and forth to Cambridge while Rikki and Paula and Julian stayed near the beach. Rikki and I treated each other with exaggerated courtesy that felt totally artificial. I would phone to let her know if I was going to be twenty minutes late for dinner. When I was home, though, I was often closeted for hours on the phone with Dina, planning out the Theater Chamber Players' next season. Yet even in adversity, we had lost none of our athleticism or our ability to put up a good united front. That summer, we were the mixed doubles champions of the West Falmouth Tennis Club.

But we couldn't keep it going. I wasn't really available to her. And my diversions were too much for her. That fall, she threw me out.

I started out my bachelorhood with the same sense of temporary accommodation that marked my thinking about my hand. Clearly this couldn't last forever. I moved into an SRO kind of place a block away from Peabody called the Stafford, which at the time was practically a way station for homeless people (though it's been renovated and gentrified considerably since). When it became clear that this state of affairs was going to last for a while after all, I bit the bullet and rented a place in a big red-brick building of soulless little apartments up by the main Johns Hopkins campus, called the Carlyle. Not that the Carlyle didn't have pretensions to higher things. My apartment had mirrored sliding doors on the closets in the bedroom. I think those cost me an extra few hundred dollars a month in rent.

It was still quite a change from our comfortable town house. I had no idea how to go about decorating a home. I got a sofa from somewhere, and a stereo, which sat on the floor, and a bed, where we sat to watch TV when my children came to visit. And, of course, there was the piano, in the middle of everything. That seemed about to cover my needs. I did try to keep the junk limited to one room. And I tried to keep focused on my musical activities.

But it was a struggle at times to keep a sense of pointlessness at bay. I'd been through two families and hadn't been able to make either one work. I was now free to have girlfriends openly, but it didn't feel very satisfying—the thrill of possibility, the excitement of conquest, followed by the realization that this wasn't what I really wanted either. I hung out with my students over late-night hamburgers, discussing the meaning of life. I was living like a student myself. I devoted a certain amount of time to practicing on my piano, which, like the picture of Dorian Gray, was starting to reflect some of the ravages of what had been going on inside me: ivories off the keys, the intonation sagging. I kept meaning to do something about it.

My children came to stay with me on weekends. I loved them, but I had no idea what to do with them. I had never had to deal with them like this before. How do you entertain two children (Paula and Julian came nearly every weekend), or four (Dickie and Leah also visited on occasion, though Debbie, by now, was already off at college), in a small apartment? I could think great thoughts about Beethoven, but when it came to family life I was as helpless as many other divorced dads of my generation. There was a lot of sitting around involved. I took the kids out to eat every weekend in a local mall, at a cafeteria called Horn and Horn, and then we would go back to the apartment and sit on the bed and watch bad TV shows.

Rehearsals provided some respite. I often rehearsed on the weekends, both with the Chamber Players and in Annapolis, and since I didn't have anything else to do with the kids, they came along. Julian was an active, curly-haired little boy full of energy who got to know the backstage areas of every theater I performed in. Paula would immerse herself in her books. There was a trampoline backstage in the gym we used for rehearsals in Annapolis, and when the two of them had exhausted their other resources, they would take turns jumping on that. There was usually a lot of bickering by the end of the day. Once, when I had taken them down to Atlanta with me for a performance and was testing out the piano—fortunately there was nobody else in the hall—the fighting led to an unusually loud wail from Julian, and my patience suddenly ran out. I snapped. I jumped up to discipline Paula for whatever she had done to Julian. Paula, startled, took off running, and I took off running after her, in a kind of Keystone Kops vignette, though both of us, briefly, were in deadly earnest. After a few rounds of the hall, I finally managed to corner her behind a row of seats. Now that I had her, though, I wasn't quite sure what I meant to do about it. "Don't do that any more!" I barked at her, and walked away. The episode has gone down in family lore as the time Daddy lost it.

The separation from Rikki did give me a chance to reconnect with my older children—the set I had dubbed Opus 1, with Paula and Julian being Opus 2. They had visited us from time to time in Baltimore, though "time to time" had grown even more infrequent when Dot moved down to Florida with them in 1967 to be near her own parents. By now, they were growing up and heading for musical careers themselves. After Dot's father died, the family moved in with Nettie, the kids' spitfire grandmother, and she became a huge influence on all three children and taught them all to play the harp. In 1972,

Debbie—now Deborah—had gotten into the Curtis Institute of Music, following in her uncle Eddie's footsteps. I was tremendously proud of her, and the fact that she was nearer meant that I got to see her more—mainly because she was working on getting to know me a little better. I even brought my kids to Annapolis sometimes to perform. Once, for Ravel's *Daphnis and Chloé*, which calls for two harps, I had both Debbie and Dickie playing with me in the orchestra. That was a lot of fun.

We had another, and perhaps better, taste of family life when I began teaching in Israel in the summers and brought the kids along, in different combinations. I started giving master classes at what was then called the Rubin Academy and is now the Jerusalem Academy of Music and Dance. It was a good gig, and it gave all of us a chance to explore Israel a bit; we had no actual family ties there, but I felt an undeniable pull to see it. And it gave me some quality time with the children. The first year, I brought Debbie and Julian, the second year Dickie, and the third year Leah and Paula and Julian, which gave Leah, the baby of my Opus 1 set of children, a chance to test out the unfamiliar role of big sister. We went on a camping trip in the Sinai on an amphibious vehicle, reclaimed from the military forces and made over, that could drive across the sand and right into the Red Sea, where we went swimming off the side. We slept in the desert and awoke one morning to the gracious sight of a herd of camels gliding soundlessly across the sand in the near distance. There were more prosaic memories as well. One afternoon I had fallen asleep after lunch on the sofa and awoke to the sound of intense giggling. Leah had told the other children that if you dip a sleeping person's hand in warm water, he will pee. They found it highly diverting to have been able to test the theory out on their father. Kids.

It was sometimes a relief to be able to take refuge from the challenges of fatherhood and immerse myself in music. I was still reluctant to do too much with the left-hand repertoire. For one thing, it seemed a little gimmicky, particularly for someone who was, like me, stubbornly focused on regaining the use of his right hand. For another thing, I was starting to get sick of it. Still, I played the Ravel concerto, in particular, with more and more orchestras. In 1972, I had opened the New York Philharmonic season with it, under Pierre Boulez. And in 1973, I played it with the Baltimore Symphony Orchestra, my hometown ensemble, as part of their first-ever commercial recording.

The Baltimore Symphony was going through a growth spurt of its own. For many years, it had been a perfectly respectable regional ensemble. I played under nearly every one of its music directors, including Massimo Freccia, a dapper, largely self-taught Italian, and Peter Herman Adler, who took over the orchestra in 1959. Adler was spry, bald, energetic, and very well connected. As the music director of NBC's opera company—back when radio and television had classical music—he commissioned Gian Carlo Menotti to write *Amahl and the Night Visitors*, which became one of the most beloved operas, and holiday traditions, of all time.

Adler's New York connections were certainly a plus in Baltimore. They were one reason he was able to get his own TV show on our local NBC affiliate. Once he invited the brilliant and eccentric pianist Glenn Gould to play with the orchestra as soloist and had him on his program, and because he knew Glenn and I were friends, he invited me along. I had always liked Glenn. For a while, I was in the select circle of people he would call at odd hours of the night, treating us to disjointed but lively monologues. Before the problem with my hand, I had given a recital in Toronto, and though Glenn couldn't or wouldn't come to the actual performance, he asked if he could come hear me try the piano in the hall the day before and stood by the side of the piano while I warmed up. He was terribly sweet. He would drive me around Toronto—he was an awful driver—talking a mile a minute, leaping from one subject to another, and I was quite content just to look, listen, and watch. And he was very solicitous when my hand problem did emerge. Unfortunately, someone later taped over the tape of that television program, so our conversation on that particular occasion was lost.

Adler was a fine television host, but he had limitations as a conductor. I remember doing the B-flat Brahms concerto, the second one, with him in Baltimore when I was still playing with both hands. At the very end of the concerto, the piece builds with a veritable pileup of arpeggios, followed by two definite concluding chords. There are a lot of notes to get in there, and as we rocketed toward the end, Adler just couldn't seem to get the orchestra to come in right with the piano at the end of the sequence. He didn't get it in rehearsals, and he didn't get it in our Baltimore performances. Our last performance was a run-out in Hagerstown, Maryland, and I could see the determination on Adler's face as the critical point approached. Lo and behold, he got it. He was just thrilled. He was so delighted that he forgot altogether about the last two chords. So there was a rather long and very pregnant pause until he collected himself with a start and hastily brought me and the orchestra in to finish the piece.

In the late 1960s, the orchestra began to move up toward another level. First, it got a new president, a real estate developer and construction tycoon named Joseph Meyerhoff. Meyerhoff had big dreams for turning the BSO—the "other" BSO, to distinguish it from the Boston Symphony Orchestra—into an American orchestra to be reckoned with. To help in this endeavor, in 1969 the orchestra got a new music director, Sergiu Comissiona.

Comissiona was a born performer. The theater lost a great talent when he became a conductor. He had the body of a dancer, moving around the podium with the balletic movements of a particularly animated cat. (His wife, Robinne, actually was a dancer, though I doubt this had more than a subliminal role in his conducting approach.) He was also a great mime, true competition for Marcel Marceau. He spoke English with a heavy Romanian accent, but he would act out his stories with every inch of his body: hands, lips, darting eyes, and veritably prehensile eyebrows. And what stories. He was a hysterically funny raconteur.

He was also an extraordinary conductor. I don't mean to be pejorative when I say that he was the best conductor of second-class music that I've ever known. He had his problems with Beethoven and Brahms, somehow; those performances never quite reached the heights of others I've experienced. But in things other than the mainstream German repertoire, he could be revelatory. He was a fine technician who knew what he was about. And he invested all of that energy and verve and talent in the Baltimore Symphony. They made their first recording. They went on their first European tour. And Sergiu kept insisting he wouldn't be happy until the orchestra, which performed at the Lyric Opera House, had a proper concert hall of its own.

Sergiu and I performed together frequently—as frequently, that is, as my limited repertory would allow. Still, we gave some notable concerts together. For his first performance with the orchestra at Carnegie Hall, I played Britten's *Diversions*. But when the Baltimore Symphony Orchestra had an opening for an associate conductor, it was Rikki who called him up. Rikki and I may have been separated, but (in part through the children) we still had considerable and not unfriendly contact, and we wanted the best for each other. Rikki suggested to Comissiona that the post might be a good fit for me. And Comissiona suggested it to me. Of course, when I had heard about the vacancy, the thought had crossed my mind that I might want it. But I had been shy about asking.

A job like that isn't something you get handed on a platter, no matter what your background. There were ten candidates and I had to audition, just like everybody else. I was as nervous as I'd ever been before a performance. As a pianist, I hadn't had to audition very often. But I got through the selections—which included Britten's "A Young Person's Guide to the Orchestra," a staple of youth concerts and thus of associate conductors everywhere—and the orchestra gave me a unanimous vote. In July 1973, I was named associate conductor of the Baltimore Symphony Orchestra.

It was a thrilling vote of confidence. Not only did I feel I could still be an active musician, but I had a place. I had an orchestra. I had a repertory. My foray into conducting was being validated. An associate conductor's job isn't always the most glamorous engagement: in those days, it involved a fair amount of pops concerts, as well as run-outs to smaller towns all over Maryland. I loved it. I was surrounded by musicians, working together with them, in my element. I already knew a lot of people in the orchestra. One close friend was the principal cellist, Misi Virizlay, a colorful Hungarian émigré of large appetites, particularly for food and women. Misi was a colleague of mine at Peabody and often had me over for his spectacular home-cooked dinners of goulash and stuffed cabbage and other Hungarian specialties, hosted by him and Paula Skolnik, a cellist in the orchestra and one in what was ultimately a considerable sequence of Misi's musician wives. The associate conductor job made me feel even more like part of a family. I rode in the bus with the musicians to the run-out concerts. Everyone was tremendously supportive, down to the stagehands. It was a big boost for me in every respect.

It was also a wonderful way to continue my education as a conductor. Often enough, I had already worked out the solutions to the music's challenge from a pianist's perspective—when I conducted a Mozart concerto, or something else I had played before. The new challenge was to find a way to communicate my ideas to seventy-five or a hundred people. I'm struck by how many of us went on to be conductors after years as soloists: Danny Barenboim, Vladimir Ashkenazy, Christoph Eschenbach, Itzhak Perlman, Pinchas Zukerman, Mikhail Pletnev. There are even a couple of others who, like me, turned to conducting after injury, including the violinists Maxim Vengerov and Peter Oundjian, who had to leave the Tokyo Quartet after fourteen years, ultimately becoming music director in Toronto. You're the same musician you always were; you're just expressing yourself through a different medium. It does help that you've already been there and you know what it feels like to find a solution. You just have to be very clear about what you want, because a lot of times you're facing people who have their own ideas about the music and tend to be skeptical about yours.

A few times, I went up to the Curtis Institute to see my old acquaintance Max Rudolf, who was there cementing his reign as America's premier conducting teacher, continually revising his landmark textbook, *The Grammar of Conducting*. Max was very sweet. He didn't actually have me swing a baton for him, but he generously loaned me some of his scores, which were an education in themselves. Studying them, with all the markings he had put in over the years, was tremendously rewarding.

I was self-conscious about my stick technique, the way I communicated with my baton. It's true that after the exaggerated flailing of my first concerts in Annapolis, my beat got smaller and more manageable. At times, it may be too small. The advantage of keeping your movements more focused is that it keeps the orchestra on its toes; the players have to really watch you in order to know what you want, rather than keeping tabs through their peripheral vision. Naturally, the players don't like that as much, because it requires more effort from them. Fritz Reiner was a great proponent of the small beat. There's a story that he came to rehearsal one morning in Pittsburgh and was conducting as he always did, barely moving, and one of the bass players got out a pair of binoculars—a pointed comment about how hard it was to see those tiny movements from the back of the orchestra. It was an expensive joke, though, because the player was fired. Those old-school conductors didn't stand for insubordination.

Every conductor has his own style. I tend to talk to the orchestra quite a bit and speak in images and feelings. I think that the musicians sometimes welcome information that uplifts them and helps them understand that there's a reason why they're doing something. That's exactly counter to the style of a conductor like Lorin Maazel, who's one of the most brilliant technicians on the planet but who breaks everything down into its technical components. He doesn't want to hear about the poetry of the thing: he cuts it down to louder, softer, faster, slower, and he microbeats everything in his quest for precision.

I could never begin to approach Maazel's technique, of course. I remain in awe of conductors who can go in and make things happen in one of those big, top-tier orchestras. But when I got frustrated about my own technique, I always thought of Klemperer. Klemperer was not a technician at all. His stick technique was almost primitive. And yet he was one of the greatest conductors of the twentieth century and someone I venerated. Klemperer was a perfectly fine role model as far as I was concerned.

Our Theater Chamber Players experiment was proving a success. We had outgrown the Washington Theater Club and moved to the auditorium at the Smithsonian Museum of Natural History on the Washington Mall, which was convenient but rather dingy. In 1978, we took another leap forward by becoming the first resident ensemble of the Kennedy Center's new Studio Theater, a performance space that was built on the center's rooftop level with funds given as a present for the Bicentennial by the Japanese government. (The theater is now called the Terrace Theater.) It made a huge difference to have a regular space of our own, even if the acoustics took a little getting used to.

The Kennedy Center staff had to get used to us, too, particularly Dina. Dina was full of idiosyncrasies, and she could be hard to get along with. She had a fear of sweaty hands while she was playing the piano. She certainly wasn't the only pianist I knew with this issue, particularly after ivory was outlawed and the piano makers began using plastic on the keys instead. Plastic was awful. It was slippery and slidy, and we all did everything we could to try to get a purchase on those slick white keys. We tried pool-cue chalk; we tried spraying our hands with antiperspirant. Eugene went so far as to scrub the keys with steel wool, causing the technicians to pull their hair out. Dina's solution, or attempt at a solution, was to stash bags of talcum powder in the piano. It made a terrible mess; someone would have to go in and vacuum out the piano after every time she played. Being a pianist myself, I was more understanding of this foible than some of her other colleagues. The first time she played at the Kennedy Center, a couple of the stagehands went back to Phyllis Bryn-Julson in her dressing room in great concern. "We think the pianist is on drugs!" they said to her. "Did you see what she has in the piano?" Phyllis had to reassure them that the substance in question was considerably more benign than they thought.

We had also started to tour. We made several trips around the country—Texas, California, Philadelphia—with different groups of players. (Pina Carmirelli discovered nacho cheese–flavored Doritos in Arizona, to her delight, with the result that all our rental cars reeked of the chips for days.) Our biggest step, though, was our debut in New York City, which took place right around the time we moved to the Kennedy Center. It was quite a big deal. Rudi Serkin came down from Vermont to hear the performance, and we got a profile in the *New York Times*. We were even engaged to tape a segment for television: CBS had some kind of arts show on Sunday morning. We chose the Ligeti *Aventures/Nouvelles Aventures*, complete with breaking glassware. Perhaps because of the dishes involved, it was decided that a kitchen would be the appropriate background for the piece, which is how we came to record Ligeti on the set of the soap opera parody *Mary Hartman, Mary Hartman*. Both are irreverent and tongue-in-cheek, so perhaps it fit.

Still, we had our share of problems. We weren't making much money. Our fees were terribly low; the musicians were essentially playing with us for the love of it. We had a regular cadre of players, and when they came in from out of town to perform with us they usually had to stay with Dina, although in fairness that wasn't much of a hardship, because Dina put them up in fine style. Nonetheless, it could be hard to keep up morale, although some artists, like Phyllis Bryn-Julson, performed with us for decades.

One big problem turned out to be Dina herself. In social settings, she was great: funny and warm and gracious. Unfortunately, in a work setting she was bossy and undiplomatic, even tactless, when it came to getting what she wanted. It wasn't malicious on her part. The Theater Chamber Players was her baby, and she wanted everything to be perfect. She knew the things that were most likely to go wrong, and she would try to prepare for them. She micromanaged. She would write out detailed diagrams of where the chairs and music stands should be set for every piece. You have to do that kind of thing if you want your show to work, but everybody thought she was just being overly finicky. I understood and let it roll off my back when, for instance, she complained about the position of my hands when I was conducting a piece she wasn't even playing in. But some of the other players weren't so sanguine about her behavior and stopped performing with us. It was almost impossible to keep a manager. In the thirty-five or so years that the Theater Chamber Players operated, I'd swear that we had at least thirty managers. Working with the Kennedy Center was difficult as well. We had to go in every year and figure out our dates and renew our status, and the whole process got to be like pulling teeth because Dina was cordially abhorred.

I was a busy full-time musician. I was maintaining an active career. Yet I still felt lamed, sidelined, not entirely complete. I kept working at the keyboard on two-handed repertory as well as I could without the real use of two fingers. I never lost the hope that my condition would one day start to go away as mysteriously as it had come. I imagined the gradual uncurling of the fingers, the way it would feel to stretch them out, the first run of notes up and down the keys. Every day, I tested to see if perhaps this was the day that the change would finally start to happen.

I couldn't ever entirely shake a sense of stigma about my condition. Nobody had yet been able to give it a name, I was clearly healthy, and therefore at the back of my mind was the nagging idea that whatever was wrong was probably my fault—or at least, that people thought it was my fault.

One idea was that my failure to learn technique in any systematic way in my years with Schnabel had allowed me to develop bad habits. I made some attempts to go back and redo my technique, seeking out piano teachers who might help. I went for a few lessons to Irma Wolpe, the ex-wife of the composer Stefan Wolpe, up in Morningside Heights. It felt rather strange to be sitting at the piano bench and talking about technique at that point in my career. She didn't have any insights, though, that made my hand work any better.

Another idea was that I had some kind of mental block that I could get around if only I could find the key. My explorations in this arena took me pretty far afield. I discovered the writings of Edgar Cayce, a psychic and clairvoyant of the early twentieth century who laid much of the groundwork for the emergence of New Age spirituality and philosophy. He was said to be able to diagnose people long-distance, without ever actually laying eyes on them. I was particularly interested in Cayce because in his young adulthood he had lost his voice after an attack of laryngitis but, after discovering it could return when he was under hypnosis, managed to cure himself while in a hypnotic trance. Cayce was long dead by the time I began looking into him, but there was a Cayce Institute down in Virginia, and I explored that and read everything about him and by him that I could get my hands on. I found it fascinating stuff. There are many mysteries in this life that we don't bother with simply because we don't happen to encounter them, many levels and dimensions of awareness and ability that we possess but never use. I was willing to believe that Cayce had powers unknown to most of the rest of us.

Reading Cayce led me to an interest in John C. Lilly, the California-based scientist whose experiments in consciousness led him to develop the isolation tank, attempt communication with dolphins, and test the effects of LSD and other psychedelic drugs on his work in both these areas. I was open to some of those explorations, too. And reading about Lilly opened me up to other treatments he had tried.

One of these was a form of bodywork called Rolfing, which feels something like a very intense massage. It's based on the idea that everyone stores memories in their connective tissues and that those memories can be released with proper deep manipulation. A basic Rolfing series involves ten sessions with a practitioner, each focusing on a different area of the body, after which you've been Rolfed: your balance and physical alignment restored, your muscles freed, your sense of well-being improved. Rolfing was very in vogue at the time, and had a reputation for being very painful, probably because there was a general idea that pain was a necessary accompaniment to catharsis. I had ten sessions with an eminent Rolfer named Sharon Wheeler, and felt duly improved.

One reason for Rolfing's emphasis on pain and catharsis at that time was its association with EST, the personal-development seminars established by Werner Erhard in the 1970s. Lots of people who did EST also got Rolfed. I was intrigued by EST as well, and not only theoretically. Rikki did EST before I did, and it seemed to me to have tremendously positive effects. It made her act like a reasonable person. Anything that could do that, I had to try. The EST seminars were held over two consecutive weekends, promising a transformative consciousness-raising experience. I did the seminars, and I thought they were terrific. They reminded me of working with Schnabel, and how after a session you came out with an expanded vision of the piece of music you were working on, except that with EST you came out with an expanded vision of yourself. It tied into my interest in how we function, especially those parts of us of which we are not aware. I was so enthusiastic I even turned a couple of my students on to it. It was an interesting way to learn about yourself. The one thing it couldn't do was fix my hand.

I would try almost anything once. I traveled to Germany to work with someone there who was recommended to me; I went to see a psychic healer in Scotland. I did draw the line at one treatment. There was a healer in the Philippines, essentially a witch doctor, who purported to cure internal ailments in what amounted to a kind of exorcism. He would somehow go inside you without benefit of a knife or any visible tools and withdraw a clump of organs and stuff, a mass of bloody gunk, which he claimed he had pulled out of you. His patients would then claim to be cured. I thought about it, but I wasn't sure I really needed to try that one myself. My appreciation for the unknown mysteries of the natural world has its limits.

And then, unexpectedly, I wasn't alone. Gary Graffman started developing problems with his right hand, too.

Those wrong notes I'd heard Gary play in Annapolis turned out to be more than just an off night. I had thought they were unusual for him, and they were. Gary's problem began when he injured his finger during a performance of the Tchaikovsky First Concerto with the Berlin Philharmonic, trying to coax sound out of a particularly recalcitrant piano. When he started playing again after the injury, he compensated by adjusting his fingerings, and that seemed to trigger a problem that gradually got worse. By 1979, he was essentially unable to use the fourth and fifth fingers of his right hand. He seemed to have exactly what I had—whatever that was.

I felt awful for Gary, of course. But it was a huge relief not to be alone. Gary is the sanest, most down-to-earth, sensible, practical person I know. He certainly wasn't nuts. It wasn't all in his head. And if this bizarre, crazy thing could happen to him, it proved that it wasn't just in my head either. I wouldn't wish this on anybody, but to have it happen to a friend removed some burden that I had been carrying around for years. I went over to see Gary and his wife, Naomi, in their New York apartment shortly after I learned about Gary's problem. We took one look at each other and burst out laughing. Years of anxiety melted away as we chortled in the foyer. "Oh, boy," I said, "are you in for it. Are you going to have fun."

Gary and I approached our problem in different ways. Gary's had set in at a different stage of his life; he had had almost fifteen more years of performing than I had. He was perhaps more philosophical than I had been. He also wasn't all that open to some of the alternative treatments and schools of thought I had been trying out. Gary put his faith in Western medicine, all the way, even though he, like me, had gotten fifteen different diagnoses from the first fifteen doctors he'd gone to. One doctor told him he had Parkinson's, which put things in perspective: at least we didn't have anything degenerative, or life-threatening, or even painful.

Except that now it was. Initially, my cramping had been almost without sensation. By this point, though, the hand was rigid from disuse—I could barely write my name or use a fork properly at dinner. And now, for the first time, it was starting to hurt.

Gary and I started comparing notes on our various treatments, like baseball cards. What have you tried? What did your doctor say? The spirit of competition that was always lurking in a benign way behind our conversations about music was not entirely absent from our discussions of our searches for a cure. I frankly didn't think Gary would find anything I hadn't already come up with. Yet he located two doctors at Massachusetts General Hospital in Boston who were particularly interested in the job-related injuries incurred by musicians. I had to admit that this sounded promising, and I went to them for a physical.

I had already had more tests for nerve damage and pinched nerves than I could keep track of. All the tests had come back negative, year after year. This time, though, something was different: there were signs that the tissue in my wrist was swollen and pressing on a nerve. In a word: carpal tunnel syndrome. It wasn't that the other doctors had missed it before; I had brought this one on myself. As a conductor, I had been gripping the baton too tightly—perhaps in my desire not to let this career, too, get away from me.

The doctors at Mass General didn't make any rash promises. The carpal tunnel was a result of my hand problem, not the cause of it. It didn't have anything to do with the contractions in my fingers. Still, carpal tunnel syndrome is curable. There would have to be an operation, but unlike some of the other surgeries that had been proposed to me, this one seemed to make sense. They knew what was wrong, and they could fix it. It would make my hand hurt less. And it might make it better. The doctors cautioned against being too optimistic. They couldn't promise any results, beyond the fact that my hand would hurt less. I thought it was worth taking the gamble. Who knew? Nobody seemed to be able to figure out what else was wrong with my hand. Maybe the carpal tunnel syndrome was linked, in some mysterious way, to my fingers.

In 1981 I was wheeled into an operating room at Mass General and Robert Leffert, an orthopedic surgeon who was the hospital's chief of rehabilitative medicine, started the Mahler First Symphony on his tape player as I was going under. "By the time this symphony is over," he said, "you'll be out of here."

And when I woke up, the pain was almost gone. My fingers were cramping less. The urge to curl was absent. I felt the sun rise in my heart.

I reached for the phone and called one of my girlfriends in Baltimore. "I think it's better!" I said.

Then the anesthetic wore off and the cramping came back. You'd think I'd have learned by then.

Still, the curling of my fingers wasn't as bad as it had been. In fact, I thought I could detect marked improvement. My hand certainly felt better. Maybe the problem was finally, gradually, starting to go away.

I also had someone to share my excitement with. I usually had a couple of girlfriends around at any given time. But my relationship with one of them was blossoming into something more.

Katherine Jacobson was a pianist who had come to Baltimore to work with me one summer in the mid-1970s for a few fun, flirtatious lessons. It was summer. It was hot. School was out. There was a sense of informality to the whole thing, though when we started talking about Mozart and Schubert, it was serious business. It was even more serious after she transferred to Peabody to work with me full time. I grew a little more distant. I tried—I really did try—to keep appropriate boundaries between myself and my students.

But a few years later, when Kathy was no longer working directly under me, I went to see a lecture-demonstration by the soprano Beverly Sills at Goucher College that Kathy had been enlisted to accompany at the last minute. The place was packed with people eager to see the diva, but I found myself focusing more on my former student. Kathy was, and is, very tall, and blond, and very beautiful, with high cheekbones and a sculpted mouth. Of course, being her teacher, I was also observing how sensitively she played, and I went backstage afterwards to give her my impressions. You wouldn't be a good teacher unless you found something to criticize in your student's performance. "Are you going to the reception?" I asked her.

Oh, no, she answered, she was going out with friends. She hadn't been invited.

"Well," I told her, "you've been invited now."

We went to the reception. And we went out for coffee. But it wasn't until May, when school was out, that we went out on a real, official date. Things took off from there. Eventually, I even broke up with my other girlfriends, which was a huge commitment on my part.

Kathy always stood out from the other students. Most of them were a little sloppy or casual in their presentation, but she was always immaculately put together, perfectly tailored and perfectly groomed. She exuded a sense of organization and focus and drive. She used to go running in the park with her German shepherd, a big dog named Kane, and her blond hair wafting in the breeze. She looked like Diana at the hunt. There was something quite mythical about her. I would wobble along next to her on a bicycle, but she would usually outpace me.

And she was a musician. She was a pianist herself. She understood.

Kathy brought a new sense of freedom, and purpose, and hope to my life. I felt like a new person. I moved out of the rental apartment and bought a condo. I hadn't been so happy in a long time.

It seemed to me that my hand was beginning to work. It didn't work perfectly. Some days it didn't work all that well. But I thought I saw definite signs of progress.

The first postoperative treatment my doctors recommended was training with a biofeedback machine. You hooked up your arm to a bunch of electrodes, and the machine registered the electrical activity in the problem muscles, while you worked with a therapist to try to regulate the activity level. Like most of the other cures I'd tried, this one didn't seem to do all that much. All it showed me was that even in repose my muscles were less relaxed than I thought they were.

Kathy came up with another suggestion. She had worked with someone in Virginia who had helped her tendinitis using a technique called myotherapy—"myo" meaning "of the muscle." Myotherapy was developed in the mid-1970s by a woman named Bonnie Prudden. The idea is that a damaged muscle stores its problems in certain trigger points; by manipulating these, and briefly cutting off the flow of oxygen to the muscle, you can start to work on the damage. Myotherapy was intense and definitely geared to those who subscribed to the philosophy of "no pain, no gain." It hurt, a lot. But it actually got results. My hand, freed up by the surgery, started to move again.

I would test it at the keyboard, a little more each day. At first, it was limping. In addition to my other problems, my muscles weren't used to the kind of sustained activity required to play the piano. But the notes were there. The musical memory was there. I didn't start out with cautious exercises, of course. I wasn't trying to regain the use of my right hand to play finger exercises. I played real pieces. A bit of Beethoven here, a touch of Brahms, or, like healing medicine, the clear runs of Bach. As my fingers moved over those lines of music, I felt something lightening inside me.

At the end of the summer, I went back up to Boston for a checkup. The doctors, at least, called it a checkup; I had something else in mind. I brought them into the hospital chapel, where there was a piano, and sat them down for a performance. Gary happened to be there for an appointment of his own, and so he got to hear as I performed in public—albeit a very small, select public—with two hands for the first time in sixteen years. It was like water after years in the desert. Bach's "Jesu, Joy of Man's Desiring" never sounded so good. I wasn't back all the way. My hand tired quickly, and I played for only seven or eight minutes. But I could perform, for others, at my old level. I was still there. I still sounded like myself. It only added to the sweetness that Gary, with his highly trained ears and intimate knowledge of my playing, could attest to the fact that my hand, at last, was working.

I sometimes say music is as good as drugs. It never rang truer than it did in the euphoria of that afternoon. I finally had an answer. I had a cure. I had something I could do to help my hand, and I was on the road to recovery. The light at the end of the tunnel was in sight and getting brighter.

From here, it was but a short step to the next stage of my recovery: to perform before a real public, in concert.

And what better way to return to two-handed playing than by inaugurating the stunning new orchestra hall, named for Joseph Meyerhoff, that the Baltimore Symphony Orchestra had finally built?

After five years as associate conductor of the BSO, I had reluctantly relinquished my post. I had too many engagements—teaching gigs, left-handed recitals, guest conducting—to be able to keep up my commitments to the orchestra. It was a perfectly amicable parting, insofar as it was a parting at all. I kept performing with the BSO, and I was still very close to Comissiona.

My involvement with the orchestra became closer than ever in 1981. Long troubled by difficult labor relations, the orchestra went through a painful strike. After a number of weeks of no concerts, the musicians contacted me to ask if I could conduct them in a benefit concert. Of course I said yes; I even got André Watts as a soloist. We raised $16,000, and morale.

It was going to take more than $16,000, though, to fix the deeper problem. The difference between what the musicians wanted and what management said it was able to pay was about $600,000. It seemed to me and a few other people that if we raised that money we could make the problem go away. We founded a group called Friends of the Symphony and did everything we could to get the word out, including working with the local news media: I was photographed for the Sunday paper with one of the co-anchors from the local CBS affiliate, showing her the basic papal four-beat—the baton moves as if you're crossing yourself—that's the first step in learning how to conduct. She was a young woman named Oprah Winfrey. Imagine what kind of clout she could have given us twenty years later. I can't say she showed any great promise as a conductor, but we didn't have enough time together to allow her to develop. Three minutes really isn't adequate.

We raised the money. We found a labor arbitration lawyer named Ron Shapiro, who proved his toughness by also working as an agent for baseball players; Cal Ripken and Brooks Robinson were among his clients. And I personally sat with Shapiro and the orchestra management and the players' committee in a marathon negotiating session that began at 9:45 a.m. and lasted till nearly 5:00 the following morning, while members of the press waited outside to hear whether we would manage to come to terms. We did. The orchestra went back to performing, and everything started moving smoothly again toward the opening of the new hall, a night that was to be the fulfillment of so many hopes and dreams.

My only condition, when the symphony engaged me, was that I would play with two hands. It gave me a definite date to work toward as I practiced every day, preparing for my comeback. I had played the Ravel as much as I ever wanted to—eleven times in Baltimore, by then—and I vowed, somewhat prematurely, that I would never play it again anywhere as long as I lived. For my return, I would play the Beethoven Fourth Concerto. It was the perfect reintroduction.

Everything was going beautifully. Kathy and I were in a haze of euphoria. We felt we couldn't be apart, and it seemed to me that she was an integral part of my life's finally turning around and coming back together. To get married felt like the most natural and wonderful thing in the world. We planned our wedding to take place shortly after the Meyerhoff performance, though we decided to keep the news a secret until the big night was over. There was no need to make advance announcements. This time, at last, everything was going to turn out all right.

If only my hand would hold up.

It clearly wasn't what it once had been. You don't come back to normal after seventeen years without playing. It was often a struggle to get my fingers to do what I wanted. And my hand got tired. I kept on working, assiduously but carefully. I had to get into shape, but the last thing I wanted to do was to jeopardize my future once again by overpracticing.

But it was getting better. It had to be getting better. I was so eager to play again. I had pinned so many hopes, against the doctors' advice, on the operation's finally fixing whatever was wrong.

Only it wasn't, really, getting any better. It actually seemed about the same.

Baltimore was gearing up for a huge opening night. The news of my comeback was as big a story as the opening of the new hall—if not bigger. I learned that the concert was going to be broadcast on live television. Offers were pouring into my management for me to play two-handed concerts with orchestra, and my management was accepting them. I had a whole string of performances lined up, a real comeback tour.

But instead of euphoria, I was starting to feel flashes of terror. The Beethoven Fourth loomed before me like an impassable mountain range, and I didn't think I was going to get across. I could make it through those first five exposed opening measures. It was the next several hundred measures I was worried about. The challenge no longer seemed exhilarating. My hand wasn't improving enough to meet it.

Finally, a few weeks before the performance, I had to admit the truth. I called up Sergiu and asked if we could switch the piece. Instead of the Beethoven Fourth Concerto, I suggested Franck's *Symphonic Variations*, the piece I had struggled to learn with Ruli as a child. It had seemed difficult then, but now it appeared a lot easier than the Beethoven Fourth. The orchestra in Franck's piece was more powerful, so you could conceal minor imperfections. More to the point, it was shorter.

I tried to keep up my optimism. After all, I would still be playing with two hands. But in my heart I was starting to recognize the truth. The hand wasn't where it needed to be. It wasn't "better" or "cured." I wasn't really going to have a triumphant comeback at all.

All the wheels were in motion. Preparations for the gala were well under way. The new hall was being cleaned and polished and prepared. The cameras were coming in. My whole family was gathering to see me play. I couldn't very well cancel. I felt as if so much was riding on me, and I couldn't stand to let so many people down. Whatever it took, I had to go through with it. I might be the only person, apart from Kathy, who realized that, far from a triumph, the whole thing would be only a sham.

So the morning dawned of my first rehearsal with Sergiu and the orchestra, in a brand-new hall, as a two-handed pianist. My family had congregated for the event: three of my five children (Leah, who had just graduated from college, was in Europe, and Paula was starting college herself), and Rikki, and Kathy. They had all come in for my big moment. They all hugged me and took their seats, and the orchestra started the first piece on the program as I went backstage to prepare myself. Prepare myself, hell. I went backstage to find a place where I could be alone, without my children seeing me, and cry.

I barred myself in the bathroom off the conductor's dressing room and hunched on the toilet and cried. I cried for my lost career. For seventeen years of trying to make the best of it. For getting so close to my return and having it again taken away from me. For all the loss, and pain, and suffering of being pulled away from the career that was all I had ever wanted. I wanted it so much. I had tried so hard to do everything right. And I was left, again, with a hollow shell, something that tasted of failure, crying my heart out.

When I heard footsteps, I reached out for toilet paper to wipe my eyes. No fixture is safe in a new building. The toilet paper holder came off the wall. Sergiu found me on my hands and knees, picking up hardware, retrieving the toilet paper roll, crying and laughing at the same time. Sergiu was a great friend. He got right down on his knees to help me pick up the pieces.

And I pulled myself together, and put my game face back on, and went out to face the orchestra, and my family, for a rehearsal.

There I was again, sitting at the piano waiting for the conductor's downbeat. It felt so familiar. It was familiar. I had, after all, been doing it all the time since my injury—in one-handed repertory. Sergiu raised his arm, and I braced myself. Then, with one hand, I leapt up the keyboard in the arresting opening of the Ravel concerto. The whole orchestra burst out laughing. With the ice broken, the moment passed, and my tears behind me, I was able to get through the rehearsal. I wouldn't say it was my finest hour. But I didn't disgrace myself. Julian, now a teenager, gave a penetrating whistle of approval, baseball-stadium style, when the piece was over.

The Meyerhoff opening was like a warped segment of *This Is Your Life* where you are surrounded by everyone who has ever mattered to you and yet feel you're living a horrible lie. Everyone was so excited. There were articles about me in what seemed like half the papers in the country. I got telegrams and flowers from all over the world. And the whole event moved with lightning speed, in Technicolor. I took the stage and felt the dark blur and hum of the people in the seats, beyond the lights. I was almost overwhelmed by the rush of emotion, the ache from the pit of my soul, the taste of doing again what I had wanted so long to do. And then for the next seventeen minutes, the whole duration of the Franck, I focused solely on getting my hand to work and making my fingers uncurl as much as possible.

Playing in public isn't quite like any other experience. It's an opportunity to be connected to the music and to include everyone in a definition of what this particular piece of music is about. You feel a connection to it and a sort of proprietary air: you really know something about this piece, and here it is. Your relationship to the piece crystallizes in an absolutely unique manner that doesn't occur under any other circumstances. The moment is there, and that moment is irretrievable and unlike any other. It's an amazing feeling. And my life, before the problem with my hand, had been filled with just such moments. Now I could barely even enjoy it, because I was just focused on getting through it without messing up. I did get through it and stood there, under wave after wave of applause, feeling as if I were watching from a great distance as something happened that looked very much like what I wanted but that I couldn't really have. I almost resented the ovations. It felt like it was part of a huge deception, a deception that I was helping to perpetrate but that wasn't of my choosing.

I had to play an encore. I picked something that, like the Franck, had been a staple of my childhood: the Chopin Nocturne in D-flat, Op. 27, a piece so securely in my fingers that I at least didn't need to worry that my memory would betray me. It was my mother's favorite piece. It's one of Chopin's beautiful, limpid melodies, spinning out over a gentle bass line, rising twinned in a kind of operatic duet, repeating with increased ornamentation and urgency, never losing its flow. It took me a moment to collect myself enough to begin playing.

It's an achingly beautiful piece. It may never have been surrounded by such feeling as I had that night, as I fought my fingers and spun out the crystalline lines, falling across the keys like tears. But the beauty was tinged with almost unbearable pain. It was like a bad joke, the ultimate cosmic irony: everyone was moved to tears, listening, and everyone was eager to celebrate with me the return of the gift that I knew I wasn't actually going to get.

Afterwards, I could barely speak. There were television cameras everywhere. Sergiu and I wrapped each other in a violent bear hug. Leon, he said, in his inimitable Romanian accent, this Chopin, when I am dying, I want to hear this music. I think that's what he said (and at his funeral, years later, I did indeed play it for him). I couldn't say much of anything. I had to retreat from the crowd, briefly, because I was once again overwhelmed by tears. That was my comeback, and now it was over, and I might never play again. I sat in my dressing room, completely drained. The door opened and my daughter Leah walked in; she had flown in from Europe for the concert, to surprise me. I was so numb and dazed that I looked at her speechlessly, as if she were a stranger, this lovely young woman appearing before me. I couldn't begin to formulate anything to say to her.

My comeback was the biggest news in the music world. The next morning, I was on the front page of *The New York Times*. I was a bigger star than I had ever dreamed of. I just couldn't play properly. I was left with the worst kind of emotional hangover, dealing with the residue of a dream that had exploded like a soap bubble, leaving, it seemed, only dregs behind.

Kathy and I got married a few weeks later.

CHAPTER 8

THE
TEACHER

Working with a young pianist at Tanglewood.
Walter H. Scott (© Scott Photos)

Through all the ups and downs of my professional life, teaching is the one career that I've been able to sustain.

As with everything else in my life, I started young. I gave my first piano lessons when I was fifteen years old. My first student was a little girl named Pat. My mother had a friend who had a daughter who wanted piano lessons, and thus Pat came into my life. Pat's family was Greek, and her mother made wonderful baklava. Sometimes I got paid for lessons in baklava, which was fine with me. I must have done a halfway decent job, because Pat and I are still in touch. Even then, teaching didn't seem like a new or unusual activity. We spent so much time in Schnabel's lessons thinking about music, analyzing it, talking about it, that doing those things with someone else seemed a perfectly natural outgrowth.

I dabbled in teaching after I left Schnabel, when I was trying half-heartedly to support myself in New York before I left for Paris. But it wasn't until I took the job at Peabody in 1959 that teaching started to play a more important role in my life. In a way, it even became a replacement for my lessons with Schnabel: teaching other pianists offered the same kinds of opportunities for me to come out of my own head and give utterance to what I was thinking about music. This was true for me even before the problem with my hand set in. "The greatest teacher for me since Schnabel is teaching itself," I once told a reporter. That was in 1964.

Teaching forced me to be clear. You can't approximate when you're teaching. You have to find words for your concepts—or at least be able to illustrate your point clearly. Sometimes you sing a phrase; sometimes you play it at the keyboard. I use the keyboard a lot during my lessons. Imitation is a useful teaching tool. I don't want my students to sound just like I do, and I don't want to tell them what to do; I want them to learn to figure it out for themselves. But asking them to imitate me is a way to find out how well they're able to listen and able to hear. You'd be amazed at how little some kids are able to hear. They come into the studio full of anxiety and full of ideas about what the music is supposed to be, and they have a terrible time dropping their preconceptions and opening their ears.

One of the most popular misconceptions is that you're supposed to put all your feelings into the music. New students arrive in the studio burdened with the enormous responsibility of expressing themselves. They think they have to demonstrate constantly how much the music means to them. They've been taught that that's what makes them special. I have to work very hard to convince them otherwise. Feelings are important, and, of course, everybody has feelings about music. But whatever gift you have, whatever insight or response, has to be used to support what the music itself is saying, not to inflict your own views on it. What you want to avoid at all costs is playing that sounds as if feeling were being injected into the music, as if through a syringe. You hear that kind of thing a lot, and it's ghastly.

And that really isn't the point of the exercise. I believe that a performer's highest goal is to discover what the music is about. You find that in the score. All the information you need is right there. The printed music is full of clues. Why did the composer use an eighth note here and a sixteenth note there? Why did he omit that note in that particular chord, or write a certain indication over the phrase, or resort to that dynamic marking? What is the point of this musical statement, and why is he making it? Why did he write this line the way he did? Every piece is a unique combination of tones. And any feeling that emerges when you play it is based primarily on that.

Here's how I look at it: the performer needs to have three personae, all the time. Person A hears, before he or she strikes a single note, exactly what he or she wants. Without a clear idea of what you're going for, everything that happens is an accident: you've sabotaged yourself before you've even gotten started. Person B is the player occupied with depressing the keys, attempting to achieve what A wants. And Person C is sitting a little apart, listening, judging, and trying to hear whether B is getting what A intended and helping him or her adjust if not. When the communication between these three personae works, it's a state of ecstasy. And when it doesn't, it's a state of absolute frustration. That's the struggle of the musician.

A lot of new students arrive aware only of B, the player. So much of their concentration and energy goes into simply performing the work that they haven't thought much about how to inform A. They aren't sure how to have a goal in a piece of music. They don't know how to find a reason for what they're doing with it, beyond simply, "I feel it that way." "I feel it that way" is not an acceptable reason. It's not allowed. You almost have to take your feelings and put them in a drawer for a while. Then you can start to see what the music is really about.

It's not that there's no feeling in music, of course. It's just that you draw the feeling out of the music as you're putting it in. When you hit the balance it's a kind of natural cycle, like circular breathing. It's one of the central points of my relationship to music, this balance between what you draw from the music and what you put into it.

But your focus is not exactly on the poetry or tragedy or pathos of the phrase you're playing. You're thinking about the quality of sound you're getting. You're thinking about how to play the rhythms so they come to life. You're thinking about how to depress the pedal—sometimes only halfway or one-third of the way—so that you support the phrase with the resonance of the strings, and then, when the next thought begins, you release the pedal and stop the haze of sound and start again fresh. What you gradually learn is that focusing on the score and learning to understand it and developing an awareness of the music's structure actually broaden your expressive possibilities rather than limiting them. It's only through that process that you start expressing things that are truly worth expressing.

Room 413 at Peabody is up on the top floor of the main building. From the hallway, it looks like any other studio, though when you get inside it's bigger than most of the others. I originally taught down on the second floor, then I moved up to the fourth floor, and eventually they enlarged the studio by breaking down the wall to the next studio, giving me a "double-wide." The room is big enough to fit two pianos, side by side. Surrounding them, against the wall, is an assortment of your standard institutional chairs, a sofa, and an armchair for me not unlike the one Schnabel used to hold court in sixty years ago. Hang-ing on the walls, along with a couple of posters from my concerts, are some images from NASA of galaxies and stars. Those represent the cosmos. We do a lot of thinking about the cosmos in my lessons. That's where Beethoven resides, and Schubert, and the other great composers. But especially Beethoven. That's cosmic music.

The walls are thin, and when there's a break in our playing you can hear music wafting in from the other piano studios: Prokofiev intruding on your Mozart, Rachmaninoff mingling with your Brahms. Lesson times are variable. They depend on my schedule. I may be out of town for a few weeks and then, when I'm back, I may teach three or four days in a row. The kids all come in and sit for four or five hours at a time, with a break for lunch. Most of my lessons are group lessons. I do have private students sometimes, but I still think, as Schnabel did, that group lessons make the best use of your teaching time, and allow students to get the most benefit out of it.

I suppose I've changed my approach over the years. The 1970s had such a different vibe. I would come to lessons in sneakers, jeans, a leather jacket. Over the years, there were periods when I kept a rubber band around my right hand and worked it repeatedly during class, taking advantage of the chance to limber it up, just in case. I would have a pack or two of cigarettes in my pocket—Lark Reds were my brand—and light one slowly, savoring the process, wetting the tobacco with my tongue, while I was thinking about what to say.

When I first started teaching, I was very concerned about how I would teach pieces that I didn't know myself. I worried about not knowing the particular problems and challenges of a piece of music that I hadn't worked on or performed. I didn't realize at first how much my own experience helped me hear music in general. After years of performing, I can hear pretty quickly what's missing in a student's playing—what questions aren't being answered. No matter what the music is, you want vitality, you want meaningfulness, you want eloquence, you want a sense of form, you want balance, you want transparency. Even if you don't know a piece, you can tell if those things aren't there. Still, I can never shake a lingering fear that when someone plays for me I might not find anything to say.

The first lesson establishes a trust, an intimacy, a relationship. That's not to say I come out with a final judgment based on how the student plays in that first lesson. Often, we start by dismantling the preconceptions. Pianists seem to think there are two main modes of expression. Either you play heroically, *fortissimo*, in a revolutionary mode, or you adopt what I call the "I love you" approach, this slurred, pseudoromantic, heightened kind of emoting. I also call that pre-barf: the sense of something rising up irresistibly, about to spew out. Maybe that's just the physical reaction I have when I hear it.

First, I listen to the student play a piece through. Then I come and sit next to him or her, at the second piano or sometimes on the same piano bench. We begin talking about the piece, about the issues it presents and about what the student has—or hasn't—done with it. I question, I give my observations, but I try not to dictate; the point is to get them to start questioning and thinking for themselves. Eventually, I have the student start playing again, but I keep a running commentary. Not only verbally. I play along, with my left hand, at the upper end of the keyboard. Sometimes, over the years, when the discussion got particularly intense, I'd forget and use both hands to play. At certain key moments of certain particularly intense or profound pieces—like Beethoven's late sonata Opus 109—it would be the only way to explain what I meant. I'd play with both hands for a minute and then hit a passage where my little finger wouldn't respond, or I'd just realize, from the quality of silence, that the students were listening with extra attention, and then I'd collect myself and put the right hand back in my lap.

There are so many different things to keep in mind. One place to start is with rhythm. I think the understanding of rhythm, and the approach to it, is a key to my own playing and it's something I seem to be able to explain in my teaching in a way that the kids find helpful. Some people get very locked in to a literal sense of rhythm, a heavy, regular beat. I don't find that very musical. For me, one of the most important things to understand about rhythm is its flexibility. Rather than feel restrained by it, a musician needs to master it, play with it, understand it. You might want to wait to play a note, for instance, until the last possible second that you can play it and still play in time, instead of simply clomping down obediently and rather approximately when the beat comes along. One of the greatest compliments I've ever got was passed on to me from Richard Goode, who said something to the effect that I put every note exactly where it belongs. That meant a lot to me, and I was enormously touched by it.

Tempo, too, needs to be something that liberates rather than a straitjacket. I remember what a revelation it was when Schnabel explained that the same tempo could be either slow or fast, depending on your conception of the piece. You could play with a close-up lens, looking at every detail of the beat, or you could pull back for a wider view, emphasizing, say, only the first beat of each measure. Same tempo, different experience of speed. It was a fantastic sleight of hand.

The score's directives aren't there to hold you back. They give you a certain freedom. In fact, there are meaningful moments in the score that demand that freedom. But you can't get too locked into your moments of freedom, either. Often, I'll decide that at a certain point in the music I need that freedom, and I take a *rubato*—"stealing" a moment or two—and that's very satisfying. But after a week or two, it's no longer satisfying, because I'm used to it. So I do a little bit more, and that, too, loses its freshness after a couple of weeks. After a while, you've done so much twisting and tugging that everything has been pushed completely out of shape. Then, like a fisherman with a fishing boat, you have to take the whole thing out of the water, scrape off the barnacles, and start over again from square one. Otherwise, you wind up with distortions you're not really aware of.

And you don't want to communicate distortion. You want everything to sound like it's falling into place. One of the extraordinary things about Schnabel's playing was the sense that not only was each note where it had to be but it described a state of being that is inherent in the notes. And each piece is a unique combination of tones, so it's different from every other piece. So much of the playing I hear today is kind of generic. That was never the case with Schnabel.

Then there's the quality of sound. How do you create that? How many different colors and sounds can you conjure up just by touching an ivory key with your finger? How do you make a sound on the keyboard that penetrates not only into the concert hall but into your listener's heart? People say that I have a distinct sound when I play, that they can recognize my playing from hearing it. I can't judge that myself. But it's certainly something I strive for.

Then there's pedaling. There are three foot pedals on a piano. One softens the note, allowing the hammer to strike only two of the three strings associated with each key. One allows you to sustain individual notes. And the right-hand one, the one used most frequently, lets all the strings continue to resonate for as long as you keep it down. It's this pedal that pianists, generally speaking, tend to overuse. Students' feet don't seem to belong to them when they're pedaling. They play without fully realizing what their foot is doing. If there aren't any dissonances in a passage, they'll just keep the pedal down, no matter what kind of a whooshing sound comes out of the piano. You have to work on developing that awareness. "Good pedaling develops slim ankles," I tell my students. That has a way of improving their awareness very quickly.

Because trying to keep track of all these things is so overwhelming, and because I've been teaching for so long, I've ended up developing what amounts to a set of adages, things I end up saying over and over. "Practice less, think more," I say. Students get so caught up in the mechanics of playing that they lose the kind of critical ear they need in order actually to make music out of it. "All the notes are equally black," I say. "It's up to us to make the decisions about which notes are of primary importance." They think they're responsible for every note on the page; the real point, though, is to figure out which notes are worth the effort. "Support the composer," I say—often enough that in election years, in particular, it takes on the weight of a campaign slogan.

Remember, I tell them, the stylistic differences between one piece and another. Classical music—Mozart, Beethoven, Schubert—should be played as if you're a part of the universe: man finds his proper place in the cosmos (and I point to the photographs on my wall). By contrast, in the Russian repertory—those big showpieces by Tchaikovsky or Prokofiev—you have to play as if you are the center of the universe. The world revolves around you.

But even in the Russian repertory, a player shouldn't go too far. "Rachmaninoff works better if you don't get too emotionally involved, if you let the music speak," I say. "You want to stay cool, so cool that it's hot, like dry ice. That's the way to generate heat in that music."

After a while, when you really get in a groove with a student, you reach a point where you're almost speaking in music, a hybrid language of sung phrases and words, exchanging ideas without knowing quite how. I call it "angel babble." Sometimes, when the music is taking the discussion into particularly deep waters, I close my eyes to focus better. Often I push my glasses up on my forehead; sometimes I leave them on but have to tilt my head back in order to see the students through my bifocals. This leaves a lot of students looking at my nostrils. My students used to talk about "going up Fleisher's nose" as the sign of a particularly intense lesson.

Over the years, I've taught hundreds of students. I've led master classes in Shanghai and Taipei; I've conducted student orchestras in Paris and Singapore; I've had faculty appointments from the University of Kansas to the Royal Conservatory in Toronto to the Curtis Institute in Philadelphia to the Paris Conservatoire, and the list goes on. Each situation is different. In each case, you try to tailor what you have to offer to the time you have available: an afternoon, a week, a month. You're always looking for phrases that will help the students grasp something essential about each piece—the kinds of phrases Schnabel was able to give me. You want to encourage the talent and keep them excited about the process while you help to guide it. And you want to say something that they can hold in their minds and even, if you can, to inspire them.

Students have enough conflicting information as it is. I remember the annual series of chamber music workshops called Encounters that Isaac Stern used to hold, alternating between Jerusalem and Carnegie Hall. The idea was that there were three or four coaches for each performance, so the kids would benefit from multiple perspectives. Sometimes, though, the multiplicity of perspectives was a little too much of a good thing. A few sessions degenerated into arguments between the faculty members, while the kids sat on stage trying to take it all in, not quite sure whom they should believe. It was great fun for us but possibly a little confusing for them.

I certainly benefited from those sessions, though. I learned a lot about different musicians, different approaches, different instruments. I remember Isaac's talking about how string players, when you ask them for a warm and luscious sound, usually press down hard on the bow, which makes the sound hard and ugly instead. "Tell them to lift the fiddle into the bow," he said. It yields a totally different sound. That kind of thing was fascinating. It was also something I could use directly, in my conducting. Conducting, in a way, is like teaching, and I frequently taught and led student orchestras. Marc-Olivier Dupin, a French composer who led the Conservatoire National Supérieur de Musique in Paris, used to bring me over every year to work with the student orchestra. I'm always sensitive about my technique, but I'm not really there to teach that. I'm there to teach music. My real focus is on the music that lies behind the keyboard, or the baton. My model, after all, was Schnabel: not a pianist but a musician. Over the years, I've worked with plenty of instrumentalists who aren't pianists, and I like to think I've had something to offer them.

After so many years as a teacher, I can hardly keep track of everyone I've taught. I find I've gotten to know several generations of pianists. There have been some notable stars: André Watts, or Louis Lortie, or Yefim Bronfman, who came to me as a great big bear of a Russian-Israeli teenager, already launched on a career and ready to work as hard as necessary, hungry to learn piece after piece, and who followed that hunger to become one of the best and busiest pianists in the world. There have been a lot of hugely talented people who have active careers in music but who aren't as well known outside the piano world. There have been some who left music altogether. The music world isn't big enough to provide careers for everyone.

You fall in love with all of them a little bit, these groups of eager, talented, driven kids, tongue-tied with respect, always addressing me as "Mr. Fleisher." At the same time, you don't want them to get dependent on you. It's most helpful to them if you teach them to learn to think for themselves. Too, my time is very limited. There were times, decades ago, when I spent hours with my students after class, hanging out in coffee shops, talking about God and the world and music over hamburgers. These days, everything moves faster, and I tend to be always on the move, in town for a couple of days before jetting on to the next engagement or teaching gig. So the personal relationships are more limited. We focus on the music.

Sometimes I get concerned that I'm helping to train all these kids for a career that really isn't available to them. Careers are so hard to come by. But then I think, who am I to stand in their way? I think the real point is to live a life in music or with music: to find satisfaction with the art and a way of coexisting with it that brings fulfillment. That can come out in all kinds of ways. I've decided that my responsibility is just to expose my students to what I've been exposed to musically. What they do with it is up to them.

I did, of course, fall particularly in love with one student, or former student, and reader, I married her. It was one of the smartest things I ever did. Kathy has been my Rock of Gibraltar, supporting what I do and helping to keep my life in a state of equilibrium, maintaining the stability when things start to veer out of control. She's beautiful, and smart, and talented, and kind. She understands a musician's life, and she's also wonderful with the public parts of my career, the parties and social activities that surround a concert: she manages all of that fantastically. More important, she understands what goes into music from the inside. We've been married for more than twenty-five years. After my two failed marriages, I finally managed to get it right.

Kathy and I were married in October 1982, in a church—much to the vocal amusement of my children, particularly the Opus 2 set, who had been bat mitzvahed and bar mitzvahed and found this Protestant thing highly unfamiliar, even though we had a rabbi as well as a pastor presiding. The occasion was slightly surreal. I was suffering the crushing letdown of my Meyerhoff performance and trying to shake the familiar feeling of hopelessness. Still, I was marrying this stunningly beautiful woman whom I loved, and moving on from my bachelor life. After Opus 1 and Opus 2, I told Kathy, she was my Eroica. "Eroica" is the epithet of Beethoven's Third Symphony. It means "heroic." It seemed to suit her very well.

Like any married couple, we had our share of bumps at the outset. It wasn't altogether easy to readjust our relationship from its teacher-student beginnings. I had great visions of Kathy's future. With her ability and drive and beauty, and her unlimited access to me as her in-house teacher, she had, I thought, every chance to have a flourishing international career. She wasn't there yet, but there was no reason she couldn't be, with enough hard work. There may have been a certain degree of projection involved in my rosy visions. It turned out that giving lessons to your wife wasn't as easy as giving lessons to your student. It's funny how relationships change once you go through the marriage ceremony and the first flush of romance is dissipated by a dose of day-to-day reality. As Kathy strove to assert her own identity, and I strove to mold her, we sometimes found ourselves butting heads.

My state of mind wasn't calculated to help. I was devastated by the failure of my comeback. I was irritable, and short-tempered, and somewhat unhappy. Kathy was wonderfully supportive, though. And she was very clear-eyed about my career, starting with my planned comeback tour. This was to have been my triumphal return, the victory march around the country, from one great orchestra to another. I understood, after my experience at the Meyerhoff, that I really couldn't play that many concerts with two hands. But I was terribly upset at the thought of having to cancel.

Call the orchestras, Kathy said. Tell them you want to play left-hand pieces rather than two-handed pieces. They don't care whether you play with one hand or two. They want to play with you.

I had trouble believing that.

Call them, Kathy insisted. Try it out.

The first person I talked to about it was Sergiu Comissiona, who at that point held the music directorship of the Houston Symphony as well as the Baltimore Symphony Orchestra.

"Leon," Sergiu said, "we didn't engage one, two, three, or four hands. We engaged Leon Fleisher to play music. We want you to come."

That response almost undid me, because it was so beautiful and warm and supportive. It also gave me great courage. I was supposed to play with eleven orchestras that season. Ten of them were very happy to welcome me playing left-hand concertos. Only the Denver Symphony arranged to get another, two-handed soloist. I was enormously moved by this. It felt like another vote of confidence at a time when I needed it, and helped remove some of the weight of failure.

Kathy showed her support in other, concrete ways as well. She threw herself wholeheartedly into the effort to find a cure for my hand. We had come so close. The Meyerhoff performance had just missed being what it was supposed to be. Kathy had been so involved with the build-up to that, and was so aware of physical fitness and the benefits of various kinds of therapies, that she took on my quest for a cure as a kind of personal mission of her own.

We addressed the motor issues again. We traveled up to Brooklyn to consult with a woman named Dorothy Taubman, who's remarkably intuitive and really understands the biomechanics of piano playing. If you go to her with a specific complaint—a pain, a tightness, a tic—she can immediately tell you what you need to do to alleviate it. It was Dorothy who came up with the idea of molding a foam pad around the ball of my conductor's baton: something that would reduce the tension of my death-grip on the stick. She had some great ideas. The only problem was that, when you work with her, you have to agree that you won't work on any music you've done before. The idea is that your brain has been polluted, and you can only hope to retrain it if you take on music that's completely new, so there are no lurking bad habits. I couldn't quite bring myself to agree to that.

Kathy brought about all kinds of dietary changes as well. She got us both to quit smoking, which was, of course, a great thing, but at the time seemed like an awful nuisance. She had me start eating more healthily; our diet began including all kinds of whole grains and fibers and seeds with various beneficial properties. After a visit to the Golden Temple of the Sikhs in Baltimore to consult with the guru, Kathy tried to eliminate red meat from my diet. She had to give up on that one. There's no question that all of these things did a tremendous amount for my health over the long term. But they were also part of a period of adjustment that didn't necessarily further the cause of marital harmony at the beginning of our road together.

One day, when Kathy and I had been married for a couple of years, we came home and played the messages on our answering machine and found one from a chief administrator at Tanglewood. Tanglewood is one of the leading music festivals in the world. It's the summer home of the Boston Symphony Orchestra; it's also one of the most prestigious summer music schools in the country, the Tanglewood Music Center (TMC), where the cream of America's young musicians go through seven or eight weeks of intensive musical immersion. It's a cradle of America's musical tradition, associated with names like Leonard Bernstein, Aaron Copland, Gregor Piatigorsky, and Serge Koussevitzky, the dynamic BSO conductor who founded it in 1940. And now, the school was without a leader. Gunther Schuller, the composer and conductor who had run the festival for years, had just resigned. Tanglewood's administrators wondered if I might be interested in the job.

Kathy and I burst out laughing.

The idea of me directing the TMC seemed like a joke. For one thing, I had no time: my life was filled with teaching, performing, traveling around the globe. For another, I was certainly not cut out to be an administrator. Running an institution like Tanglewood calls for a skill set that has nothing to do with making music. I wasn't particularly interested in holding staff meetings, or focusing on student diversity, or negotiating with the musicians' union. Nor did I have any particular aptitude for that kind of thing. "What a crazy idea," I said. And we thought no more about it.

At least, we didn't think about it for several months, until they called me again.

I can't say the idea hadn't germinated in the meantime. It's true that I wasn't particularly cut out for the administrative side of the job. But Tanglewood had a new administrator, Richard Ortner, who had been appointed after working for years at Tanglewood in various capacities, and knew its workings well. The job title they were offering me was Artistic Director of the TMC. It would be my task to focus on the art, and the teaching; and in those areas, I thought I had something to offer. I seemed to have developed a kind of reputation over the years for helping to inspire and guide young musicians. Tanglewood offered a chance to work with some of the best young talent in the world. The job was an opportunity to do some musical good. That side of it appealed to me very much. I admit it was also extremely flattering to be asked—even to be pursued, after I had said no.

And pursue they did. One of my most insistent supporters was my longtime friend and colleague Seiji Ozawa. Seiji had risen rapidly through the ranks of North American orchestras until, in 1973, he became music director of the Boston Symphony Orchestra, one of the so-called "Big Five," traditionally the best orchestras in the country. (The others are Cleveland, Chicago, New York, and Philadelphia.) I had played under Seiji with two hands, and I had played under him with one hand, and we had formed quite a strong artistic relationship. Seiji liked me. Seiji likes musical depth, and I was deep: a window into the tradition. Seiji doesn't necessarily access that kind of thing himself, but he certainly appreciated it in other people. I seemed to him more substantial, and also more of an ally, than some of the other candidates. This was one reason that various BSO and Tanglewood top brass—specifically Dan Gustin, the BSO's manager of Tanglewood, and Tom Morris, who was the orchestra's administrative head at the time—came down to Baltimore to talk to me about the position.

I was frank with Dan that there were many things I simply couldn't do. Gunther Schuller used to travel around the country and personally oversee all of the student auditions; for me, that was out of the question. Gunther Schuller used to supervise the contemporary music component of the summer; that wasn't my strength. And I was concerned about my ability to be an administrative leader. I just didn't have the experience. Dan told me not to worry. "We have people who can take care of all of that," he said. What they wanted was someone who could act as a leader among Tanglewood's high-powered, prestigious faculty, and keep the institution's educational mandate on a firm track.

I was also hesitant about my qualifications to carry on the TMC's vision. When Koussevitzky founded the school, he envisioned composers and performers working together side by side, and the school was often run by composers after he died: before Schuller, Copland had been one of its heads. I was no composer. I am essentially a re-creator, not a creator. And though I have played a lot of music by living composers in my time, I don't consider myself a real expert in the contemporary music world. I felt this was a distinct disadvantage.

I had another concern that I talked about less. It was the idea that taking the position would effectively mean giving up on my dreams of a career as a pianist. I was 56 years old. It wasn't clear how many more chances I would have to do what I wanted. Taking over as director of Tanglewood might be seen as a culmination of my career—but also as the end of my search to find a way to use my right hand again. I couldn't bear to see it in that light. I wasn't ready to take that kind of step.

But as I talked to Dan, and Tom, the possibilities began to open up for me. I could work with the best musicians in the field. I could take my place in an exclusive fraternity of artists, in a setting in which it didn't matter that one hand didn't work. The offer was a confirmation that my work as a musician was being recognized, and counted for something. It was heady to be asked to step into a pantheon that included some of the leading figures in my world. It was exciting to be entrusted with the stewardship of a place that was designed to foster teaching and learning and performing at the highest level; to keep music in America vibrant and alive. This was a mandate I could relate to. And the more I thought about Tanglewood, the more it seemed to me that it was a field where whatever wisdom I had accrued over the years, in my many different lives in music, could be sown and, eventually, reaped.

I took the job.

Tanglewood is magical. It sprawls across more than 250 acres in the Berkshires, in western Massachusetts: a symphony of green woods opening up onto sunny glades, with music happening all around. Tanglewood's traditions go back to the nineteenth century, when the author Nathaniel Hawthorne rented a cottage from local resident Lewis Tappan, who christened the cottage Tanglewood after the book of stories Hawthorne wrote there ("Tanglewood Tales"), and later used the name for his nearby estate. The musical tradition started in the 1930s with the New York Philharmonic: a group of music lovers who spent summers in the area persuaded members of the orchestra to come up and play a few outdoor concerts. In 1936, the invitation was transferred to the Boston Symphony Orchestra under Koussevitzky, who immediately began pushing for an actual permanent structure to replace the makeshift tent—and pushing so successfully that at the end of that year, Tappan's heirs offered the orchestra their family estate. Koussevitzky kept on developing the facility, and realized his long-held dream to found an academy of music by establishing the Tanglewood Music Center in 1940.

Koussevitzky's spirit still hangs in the air at Tanglewood. Seranak, his house, is still kept much as he left it, with a kind of museum of the maestro's pictures and papers and even, in the upstairs bedrooms, his personal effects. The grandeur of the house and grounds, with their sweeping view of the surrounding countryside, fit the conductor's image: Koussevitzky, self-taught and self-made, married to a wealthy woman who supported his dreams, sported all of the appurtenances of the grand style, down to the cape he wore to concerts. Leonard

Bernstein, his protégé and no stranger to theatricality, didn't actually inherit Koussevitzky's mantle—when the maestro died in 1951, Charles Munch became the BSO's music director. But he did appropriate Koussevitzky's cape, which he used to wear with relish. He also slept in Koussevitzky's bed at Seranak when he came to Tanglewood himself.

The heart of Tanglewood is the Shed, the main concert hall, its sides open to the air so that birdsong is a not-infrequent accompaniment to afternoon concerts. (It's particularly fortuitous if the bird happens to be in tune with the music, but that doesn't happen often.) The Shed got its name from the architect Eliel Saarinen, whom Tanglewood's trustees approached about building a concert hall as soon as the Tanglewood property was theirs. Saarinen kept submitting plans that were too expensive; finally, he informed the trustees that if they stuck to their budget, what they would get would be "just a shed." They duly got a shed, designed by a local architect, that for more than seventy years has been framing performances by the Boston Symphony Orchestra as well as the TMC orchestra, made up of the best young players in the country. Beyond the walls stretches the verdant lawn where music lovers flock to picnic and hear concerts in the best summer festival tradition. Tanglewood has become a place of pilgrimage for people drawn by the idea of a single site where you can hear so much music, at such a high level, in such a short period of time.

I had a huge amount to learn about the school and its traditions. In 1985, the year I started, I was available only for a few weeks, because my schedule for the summer was already pretty much in place by the time my appointment was made official. Classical music books its artists long in advance. But those few weeks turned out to be a good way to ease into the job and figure out how things worked around Tanglewood. Fortunately, there were plenty of people who could help show me the ropes.

First among those were Dan Gustin and Richard Ortner, both of them old Tanglewood hands. It was they who made sure things ran smoothly and they who helped me integrate into the place. We were in almost constant contact, not only at Tanglewood but throughout the year. I gradually came to realize that you weren't really in the swing of Tanglewood until your whole year was dominated by thoughts of what was happening in the summer, either at the session just past or the one that lay ahead.

There was also a host of old friends. There was Gil Kalish, the pianist, who had been on the Tanglewood faculty almost twenty years by the time I got there and who took over in 1985 as faculty chairman. There was my close friend the composer Leon Kirchner, a Tangle-wood regular. There was Shirley Gabis, once known as Xenia, whose apartment in Paris I had lived in so many years before. Shirley, always something of a femme fatale in our circle, was married for a while to the sculptor George Rhoads, who's done these wonderful perpetual motion machines that involve little balls that run along tracks and up and down conveyor belts in complicated, colorful Rube Goldberg–like contraptions. There's one at the Philadelphia airport and another at New York's Port Authority bus terminal. You can stand and watch them for hours. That marriage didn't work out, though, and Shirley married the composer George Perle, who wrote beautifully crafted serialist works that could sound difficult but were really a pleasure to listen to when you started to appreciate how well they were put together. George became a great friend too. Shirley and George had a summer home in the Berkshires, and we were able to pick up our friendship right where it had left off.

Then there was Lenny Bernstein, the larger-than-life, flamboyant, brilliant, generous, eccentric conductor and composer and mensch, who had taken it upon himself in many ways to uphold Tanglewood's traditions.

When I got to Tanglewood, it had been forty years since Lenny and I gave our first performance together that stormy afternoon at Ravinia. Oddly enough, we had hardly played together after that. I remember one other performance, when Lenny, as part of the festivities inaugurating the new Lincoln Center, led Bach's concerto for four pianos with me, Gary, Eugene, and Malcolm Frager, the only American pianist besides me to win the Queen Elisabeth Competition, who happened to live near Tanglewood. But I'm not sure we did anything else together before that, and within a couple of years of Lincoln Center's opening, the problem with my hand set in and further collaboration was out of the question. We had seen each other over the years, because anyone who traveled in the music world in those days would end up seeing Lenny somewhere or other. To me, he was always Lenny, warm and cordial. Lenny was everybody's best friend. Once I was named to Tanglewood, though, he actively set about embracing me into the fold.

Lenny considered Tanglewood his home—although he also acted that way about a number of musical institutions around the globe. But Tanglewood, where he had been a student of Koussevitzky's in the 1940s, had particular significance for him ("I feel I built the bloody place," he once said). He was eager to show me its ways. My very first summer, he called me up out of the blue and invited me to go swimming over at his house, just the two of us. A few days later, he showed me the best place to hear Tanglewood's orchestral concerts: on stage, right below the trombones. There was a level there where you could sit and not be seen by the audience. Lenny used to have the stagehands put a chair there for him, and when he brought me, he had them place one for me too. Sitting there, you were at eye level with the legs of the trombonists' chairs, and you could see the conductor and the orchestra above and around you. There is nothing in the world quite like being on stage with an orchestra, surrounded by its sound. Lenny and I sat there and basked in it, and Lenny held my hand, in comradeship and understanding rather than with any physical intention—because Lenny was the kind of person who liked to hold someone's hand when he was sharing a musical experience.

Another Tanglewood fixture was Seiji Ozawa. Seiji and I had a fine working relationship. I can't say it was close. Seiji had such a busy schedule it was almost impossible to be close to him. I used to take him a six-pack of beer once in a while. After our years of music making, there was a lot of mutual affection and respect. But Seiji wasn't really around all that much. His role at Tanglewood was actually a source of some friction between him and the BSO's administrators. Seiji did not have an easy time teaching. Some artists—myself included—can draw energy from teaching; working with talented students is a source of inspiration and invigoration. But for Seiji, it represented yet another drain in an already overcrowded schedule. That was no reflection on his teaching: when he did work with students, particularly the conductors, he was very good at it. But it meant he didn't play a very hands-on role in the workings of the Music Center. He was happy to let me keep my own counsel.

He certainly appreciated my approach to music making. He seemed to have a lot of respect for me. In Japan, Seiji was conductor laureate of an orchestra called the New Japan Philharmonic. The musicians were extremely talented but hadn't necessarily had a lot of exposure to Western performance style. How do you go about playing Mozart or Beethoven? Seiji knew that these were questions I loved to explore, particularly with other musicians. He therefore had me go to Japan to work with the orchestra for a week or two every year. It was fun for all of us. Kathy and I would get red-carpet treatment, and I felt I was able to contribute something to the orchestra's development. That had nothing to do with Tanglewood, of course, but I took it as a flattering sign of Seiji's regard.

I didn't want to make sweeping changes at Tanglewood. I had too much respect for the school and the way it had been run and the things it represented to want to do that. But I did have some ideas that I thought might be beneficial. For one thing, I wanted to do opera. The vocal program at Tanglewood was hampered by the lack of an actual opera program. Opera is terrifically expensive. Yet there was an important tradition of opera at Tanglewood. Koussevitzky commissioned Britten's *Peter Grimes*, one of the greatest operas of the twentieth century, and it had its American premiere at Tanglewood (with Lenny conducting). Seiji and I both very much wanted to find a way to revisit that, though it was some years before we were able to do so.

For another thing, I wanted to institute some kind of physical training for the TMC students. I still didn't have a name for whatever was wrong with my hand, but I did see a growing awareness of the wear and tear that a career in music could take on a performer's body. Techniques like yoga, Alexander, Feldenkreis, or even ballet could only help protect students from career-ending injuries, a subject I knew a thing or two about. For a while, I took ballet myself with a brilliant dance teacher named Thomas Hanner, after Kathy and I hit on the idea that this might be a solution to my students' execrable posture when hunched over the keyboard. Hanner, a former principal of the San Francisco Ballet, was really remarkable in the way he could take these kids and instill in them a sense of discipline and idealism and beauty. I won't say every one of us lived up to his standards. I took his class right alongside my students, but my turnouts were never all that great.

But it was difficult to find a program that worked at Tanglewood. I tried a number of different approaches over the summers. I instituted dance classes. I brought in a Feldenkreis teacher, I tried out an eccentric physical therapist named Shmuel Tatz, whom I had seen a number of times in New York; Isaac Stern, in particular, was very high on him. But the students had busy schedules, they wanted to focus on music, and it was hard to find a time that worked for everyone. None of those programs were quite as effective as I'd hoped. I did buy new chairs for the orchestra, since I didn't think it was doing the students any favors, physically, to be sitting for hours on the wobbly folding chairs that were the norm when I arrived.

Part of the excitement of the job was the chance to work with a breathtakingly talented faculty: people like Gil Kalish, or the soprano Phyllis Curtin, who ran the vocal department, or Gustav Meier, the conductor who later became a colleague of mine at Peabody, or the wonderful double-bass player Julius Levine, a longtime collaborator of Casals's. I brought in other musicians who I felt would have something to contribute. I was particularly concerned with getting the right person to oversee the contemporary music that was such an essential part of Tanglewood and that, as I said, I couldn't fully do myself. We solved this by bringing in Oliver Knussen, a student of Schuller's and, like him, a significant composer-conductor. He did a better job than I could ever have done. I also invited some old friends of my own. Doda Conrad came from Paris and gave a lecture. Dina Koston came up one summer, but she was notably unhappy and unsuccessful at Tanglewood—no more a people person there than she was anywhere else.

I was very aware of my responsibility in setting the tone and keeping Tanglewood's traditions alive. One of my duties was to speak at the annual opening ceremony, welcoming the students and outlining for them what they were about to embark on. It was a chance to give a kind of manifesto of my own beliefs about the arts. I used to labor over those speeches. My colleagues called them my "opening exercises." I felt it was important to say something significant. Did the students realize that the United States spent more on its military bands than on the National Endowment for the Arts? Did they realize we had to fight for our rights, to keep our arts alive? I've never been a stranger to taking a stand or speaking my mind when it comes to my beliefs. Nor have I ever shied away from administering precepts. In some ways I'm just a Polonius at heart. After I had had my say, everyone in the room—all the faculty and students and any parents who were up to it—joined in singing Randall Thompson's beautiful choral piece "Alleluia," a tradition that goes back to the year the Music Center opened, when Koussevitzky commissioned the work for the occasion.

After a couple of years, Kathy and I bought a house near Tanglewood, a second, summer home. Tanglewood was not altogether easy for Kathy. For me it was all-consuming, but for her there was no very clear role. She was too talented and active to be content with being simply my wife, but I didn't feel I could hire her, either; I was firmly against nepotism, and I didn't want to expose either of us to criticism on that count. But it left Kathy a little adrift, though she certainly responded to the beauty of the place and to the quality of the music.

Nonetheless, for better or worse, Tanglewood had become an integral part of our lives. It was also a new gathering place for my family. Dickie had married another harpist, Kayo Ishimaru, whom he met in Paris, and Kayo was a fellow at the TMC for a couple of years, so I got to see them quite a bit. Once, at a party at Shirley's, Dickie went up to Lenny Bernstein and asked him why he hadn't written a harp part in *West Side Story*. Lenny's answer was succinct: he couldn't fit a harp into the small Broadway pit.

For my sixtieth birthday, in July of 1988, Kathy threw me a big party at Tanglewood, and everybody came. There were picnic tables set up on the lawn, and there was lobster, and there was corn on the cob, and at least sixty or seventy people gathered for a huge, joyful celebration. Among them was Lenny, who never missed a party—or an opportunity to make a big entrance. He drove up in his convertible when the party was in full swing. "I hope you've got a bottle of wine and a lobster for me!" he shouted as he made his way up our hill.

In social settings, Lenny was in his element. Whether it was a room full of students or a lawn full of partygoers, he was never happier than when he was holding court, emitting a steady stream of conversation, from far-flung ideas to riotously funny anecdotes, and testing just how far he could go in his quest to be outrageous. At my birthday party, he got himself set up at a picnic table with a bottle of wine in one hand and a lobster in the other and proceeded to give the guests around him the full-on Lenny treatment.

At one point in the afternoon, after a certain amount of wine had been consumed, I found myself sitting at the table with Lenny and the conductor Maurice Abravamel and another renowned pianist who had just recorded the Beethoven piano concertos, and was widely seen as the star du jour.

Lenny turned to this pianist with the air of a man who had something to say. "Your Beethoven concerti are really good," he told him. "But they don't measure up to Danny Barenboim's."

An awkward hush fell over the table, which was just the kind of reaction Lenny liked.

"And Leon's," he continued. "Oh. Well. Sublime. No one can touch Leon's. They're in a league of their own." And he grabbed me in a neck lock.

It was an acutely embarrassing moment. Lenny was blatantly, publically dissing one of the most acclaimed living pianists. But of course, Lenny was God, and nobody could argue with God. It was all very flattering for me, of course, but I felt awful for the other pianist. But that was just Lenny. He did that kind of thing all the time.

In addition to that private birthday party, Tanglewood gave me an official sixtieth birthday celebration. The orchestra had put some thought into what I might like to have as a present. Costa Pilavachi, who was the artistic administrator of the BSO at the time before going on to become a big recording-industry mogul, went so far as to ask Kathy for advice. Kathy didn't hesitate. "Give him the orchestra," she said. And they did. I got to play with and conduct the BSO in a program at least partly of my own choosing—Beethoven's "Prometheus" overture, the Ravel left-hand concerto, and Rachmaninoff's Second Symphony—which was a magical, memorable experience, and one of the most wonderful presents I could imagine. It also meant that for my birthday, I had to work like the proverbial dog.

After the concert, when I was still in something of a happy fog, there were speeches and tributes in my honor. It was all extremely moving. I had to respond. I stood up to say a few words and, not finding any very original way to express my thanks, I finished by saying how touched I was. "My cup runneth over," I said.

My brother Ray had come to Tanglewood—his only visit—for the occasion. He evidently felt it was his responsibility to say something. As soon as I had spoken, his gravelly baritone, still with a distinct tinge of a New York accent, rose above the crowd, shouting, "Well, get a bigger cup!"

All of the artistic energy floating around Tanglewood was a powerful motivation for me. I taught. I conducted, working sometimes with the TMC orchestra and sometimes even with the BSO. I used to go to the dining hall regularly and set up at a table so students knew where to find me and could come talk to me about whatever might be on their minds. I felt that the best thing I could do in my role as director was to represent Tanglewood, to oversee everything that was going on, to check in on lessons and master classes, and to make myself available to share what I knew whenever it might be helpful. Of course I gave lessons myself. And when I wasn't doing all this, I was practicing.

Dan Gustin's office was right next to my studio. He knew what I was working on. Dan could hear me trying, with one and a half hands, the Copland piano variations or Beethoven's Opus 101 or the Brahms D Minor concerto. After the Meyerhoff debacle, I wasn't pretending to the world that I was able to perform with two hands. But I was still immersed in the repertory.

"Leon," Dan said to me one day, "you have so many things going on in your life. You're leading Tanglewood. You're teaching all over the world. Your students refer to you as the Obi-Wan Kenobi of the piano. You have a really full career."

His implication was clear. Maybe it was all right that I couldn't play with two hands. Maybe I didn't need to worry about it so much any more.

And it was true. I was living such a full life. So many wonderful things had happened. A lot of them would never have happened if my right hand had kept working. I would have continued as a blinkered pianist, unaware of so much of what the world had to offer.

Still, in my heart, I knew what I really wanted.

"I couldn't live another day," I told Dan, "without believing that somehow I'll play with both hands again."

WOLFGANG AMADEUS MOZART: PIANO CONCERTO
NO. 25 IN C MAJOR, K. 503 (1786)

Schnabel used to say that Mozart was the most inaccessible of the great masters. He sounds simple, but he's elusive. He gives you the least to work with. You have to bring out what's in the notes, and what's behind the notes, and what's in front of the notes. A Rachmaninoff concerto is difficult, but when you play it you're concerned with its acrobatic aspects. With Mozart, there are no shortcuts. There are no fireworks. There's nothing to hide behind. It takes a certain amount of living into it to bring it off.

Schnabel's Mozart was crystalline. He would play Mozart's long chains of notes, those rising, falling, running lines, so that each note had its own little halo around it. The French love to use the word *perler* to talk about those lines of perfectly matched notes, strung like pearls on a necklace. Instead of pearls, though, I prefer to talk about diamonds. Each diamond has its own radiance, and when you string them together, the radiance becomes a single, unified thing. You know that there's a core inside each one, but when they are placed side by side there's a brilliance to the strand as a whole that blurs the distinctions between the individual crystals. To get that effect, I use the pedal, depressing it only the tiniest bit—one-quarter of the way down or even one-eighth of the way down—and changing it frequently. This gives you a glow and shine of resonance that makes those diamonds sparkle.

You also have to find a way to keep the notes moving forward and to convey the sense of centrifugal force. That's a particular challenge of the piano. Most instruments naturally incorporate a sense of the horizontal. The bow of a violin or the breath of a trombonist provides a natural line: it moves forward, horizontally. You stop blowing, and the music stops. With a piano, though, the movement is vertical:

you touch the key, and it makes a sound. Then the sound dies away. How do you create a sense of horizontal movement through a totally vertical activity? To help create a musical line, you have to focus on the way those notes form patterns. Are the sixteenth notes grouped in bunches of fours, or eights? Do those groupings extend across two measures, or four, or many? What you want to achieve is the kind of force you feel when a car goes around a corner: the idea that your body is actually swayed by the propulsion of the music.

Even orchestras can have trouble getting this effect. The natural tendency of an orchestra, with those long chains of sixteenth notes— "railroad tracks," as many people call them, because on the printed page the notes are bound together with a parallel double line like train tracks—is to start slowing down. There are a couple of ways to com- bat this. One is to think very vigilantly about phrasing and fight the urge to start phrasing each new group of sixteenth notes with a new stroke of the bow, sawing back and forth. The overture to *The Marriage of Figaro* is an example of Mozart's rapid playing, little bursts of eighth notes popping out of the orchestra pit, and I think it was Furtwängler who had his string players, instead of playing each episode with an individual bow stroke, do the whole thing in a single stroke of the bow. It changes the whole feeling of the piece. It makes it less choppy. Another thing you can do is have the players, in rehearsal, play only the first note of each four-note set. This gives them a different sense of the way the music is moving forward; after they've done that a few times, then the other notes can fall into place, filling in the gaps.

But you still need to understand the rationale behind each gesture. These aren't just random lines of notes that you invest with your own interpretive ideas. Mozart had reasons for writing the way he did. In the first-movement cadenza to K. 488, for instance, there's a place where a big scale goes zooming up to a diminished seventh chord. This is a shock: diminished seventh chords are dissonant, arresting, and, in Mozart's terms, downright ugly. But I've heard that passage played with a kind of Victorian vapors approach, getting all quiet and pretty as it gets up to that dissonance. It can't have been intended that way. It has to be a snarl, ferocious, violent. What more can Mozart do to indicate what he wants?

A lot of my students, probably as a result of mediocre teaching, come to me using all sorts of Romantic devices in Classical-era music. Musicians play a lot of Romantic music today, and many of them approach Classical music as if it were a slightly paler version of the Romantic idiom. I've heard Pinchas Zukerman give an account of Mozart's Sinfonia Concertante with extraordinary facility, but playing it as if it were Romantic music with about five points less cholesterol. You end up steamrollering the piece if you approach it like that.

I'm not a purist about trying to play in period style. I'm not all that interested, for instance, in playing the kinds of pianos that Mozart played, which were far lighter and softer than the powerful instrument that is a modern Steinway concert grand. We have wonderful instruments today, and I'm happy to use them.

But there are certain stylistic features that you have to keep in mind. Those different musical epochs had their own particular awareness of sound and rhythm. One principle I've uncovered over the decades is that in Romantic music you can hurry over the long notes and stretch out the little notes; this gives you the right sense of *rubato* that the music demands. By contrast, when a Classical composer writes long notes, he wants stasis, and when he writes little notes, he wants activity and movement. It's a different approach. Musicians play so much Romantic music that they tend to slow everything down; they don't realize they're losing the crispness of those little notes. That kind of thing can make an enormous difference. In a way, I feel that the period-instruments approach to Mozart is coming back to what Schnabel was talking about all along. It involves cleaning away all of that Romantic heaviness and hearing with fresh ears.

K. 503 holds a special place in my heart, mainly because of my fond memories of the performances I gave of it with George Szell and Cleveland. It's not one of Mozart's most popular concertos. In fact, when Schnabel played it with Szell in Vienna in 1934, it turned out to be the first time the piece had been performed in public there since Mozart's day. It doesn't have the haunting second-movement melodies of K. 467, the "Elvira Madigan," with which Schnabel made such an impression on me when I was a teenager. It doesn't have the obvious brilliance of some of the other concertos. It therefore took posterity a while to figure out that it's actually one of his greatest.

One of its distinguishing features is its use of trumpets; you don't encounter trumpets in many Mozart concerti. Another, perhaps less obvious, is that it's notably symphonic. The piano and orchestra are locked in a dialogue: the orchestra doesn't merely support the piano while it does its thing. A lot of the difficulty of the solo line involves nuance and subtlety and control rather than flashy fireworks. It's funny how I've always been drawn to pieces like that.

Not that it isn't accessible: it's quite a regal and openhearted piece. It starts with an extended and rather majestic-sounding orchestral section in C Major. I believe it was the composer Olivier Messiaen who said that C Major represented God. That's not bad. But in this piece, the music keeps shifting and changing, like the play of light over water. Time and again, it dips into the minor mode and is then pulled up by chains of ascending sixteenth notes, brought back out into the sunlight.

The second theme of the first movement goes through lots of those major-minor shifts: now a somber meditation, now back to its spritely, vivacious self. It's the same "How dry I am" motif that Brahms so loved, and it evokes other familiar tunes. Once, when I was rehearsing the piece with George Szell, I added a little fillip of notes at the end of the theme that turned it into the start of "Ein Mädchen oder Weibchen," one of Papageno's songs from *The Magic Flute*. The tunes are so close to each other that I could do it without even interrupting the rhythm of the piece. I remember George turning around and raising his eyebrows while a big smile broke over his face, and he continued conducting without missing a beat. He really enjoyed things like that. When the pianist Lili Kraus played the piece, she gave a nod in her cadenza to "La Marseillaise," the French national anthem, which also sounds very similar, though it wasn't written until after Mozart's death. I've since heard other players do the same thing.

The whole second movement of K. 503 is actually quite simple; it doesn't even have a proper development section. Its power lies in its implications: what it arouses, what it awakens. It sparks the imagination. It doesn't spell everything out for you. It works for the same reasons that, for me, radio is more effective than television. When I was a teenager there was a radio program called *Inner Sanctum* that opened with the sound of a creaking door and the host's voice. I found it deliciously terrifying. When they later put the show on television, they presented someone's vision of what might be scary, but for me that wasn't scary any more. You want there to be some mystery, something left unseen. The opening of the second movement of K. 503 has that same evocative quality for me. Those first four descending notes somehow awaken a sense of possibilities.

Mozart's slow movements have a kind of dignity. They address the highest aspects of us. I think you have to respect their simplicity to bring them across. There are these great leaps in that second movement of K. 503, where the piano line jumps an octave or more. Tradition, and the musicologists, will tell us that a pianist in Mozart's time would have filled in those gaps with little improvised scales and arpeggios, those small musical gestures known as ornaments. But the great soaring of the spirit is lost, I think, if you fill them in. I just try to soar up there and come back down, and soar up again. I think a musicologist and pianist like Robert Levin, who is a master of Mozart scholarship, would probably present an almost irresistible case for filling in those spaces. But I won't do it.

The final movement has always been one of my favorite things to play. The section where the piano trades off phrases with the oboe—where I had my greatest moment in Carnegie Hall, when Marc Lifschey played so divinely while the piano danced out chain after chain of rapid notes below him—still gives me goose bumps. But it's a mistake to think of it as too divine. It's in this movement where the horns and trumpets come into their own. I'm convinced that Mozart was always playing around with irreverence. So when the trumpets come blatting in with these decisive, loud chords, right at the end of the concerto, it's like thumbing his nose. He's just having fun with everybody. One of the problems with young musicians today is that they come in with such a sense of high seriousness. The idea of how great this music is tends to fill them with awe. But so much of what we do is about these guys just having fun. That earthiness is a very important part of life. Listen to it. It's there.

CHAPTER 9

THE
LEFT-HANDED
PIANIST

At Tanglewood, Leonard Bernstein attempts to cure my left hand with a direct application of Scotch. Dan Gustin
(Author's collection)

It's no accident that pianists always injure their right hands. You never hear about a pianist with a left-hand injury due to his or her playing. It's the right hand that gives out. Robert Schumann's right hand gradually stopped responding during an intense period of practicing (the injury is commonly ascribed to a contraption designed to strengthen his fingers, but he didn't actually get that until several years after the onset of his problem). Alexander Scriabin injured his right thumb by, allegedly, trying to learn Liszt's "Don Juan Fantasie" in as short a space of time as possible. Both of them became composers. I didn't.

There's a reason the right hand is vulnerable. It has to do the most unnatural work. The left hand gets all the good harmonies, the meat of the piece. The right hand is responsible for the melody, the main tune, which is usually on top. If you have both your hands on the keyboard, the top line is going to be played by the fourth and fifth fingers of your right hand. Those happen to be the weakest fingers, with the least independent motion. And they're trying to make the loudest possible sound on the highest notes of the piano—the part of the instrument where the strings are thinnest and get the least volume. It's no surprise that so many pianists who develop hand problems have them with the fourth and fifth fingers of the right hand.

The left hand, by contrast, is naturally built for the piano. You have four fingers for the harmonies, and you can plunk out the melody with your thumb. My left hand has stood me in good stead. For thirty-odd years, it enabled me to continue a career with only five fingers. I'm grateful to it. It's held up well.

As a left-handed pianist, you have to make a number of adjustments. Your whole center of gravity shifts in relation to the piano. When you're playing with two hands, you sit squarely in front of the keyboard. When you're playing with your left hand alone, you have to shift your body up, since you spend quite a bit of time playing in the piano's upper register, which means your arm is extended across your body. You end up sitting mostly on your right buttock, and you can risk twisting your back when you are doing strenuous things at either end of the keyboard.

Another problem is figuring out what to play. There are not that many pieces out there for one hand, though there are a lot more than you might think. Probably the single greatest work for solo left hand is by Brahms, who was looking for a way to capture the spareness, in a piano transcription, of the unaccompanied violin line of Bach's wondrous D Minor Chaconne. Writing for only one hand allowed Brahms to echo both the limitations of the solo instrument and the way that Bach miraculously transcends them. Brahms wrote the piece for Clara Schumann, who particularly adored the Bach Chaconne and who happened to be sidelined, at the time, with right-hand tendinitis.

Some other significant artists have tackled left-hand music, with slightly less imposing results. Camille Saint-Saëns wrote a set of left-hand études that sound a little bit like a Baroque suite; they were a present for his friend Caroline de Serres, a concert pianist, after she lost the use of her right hand in an accident. Dinu Lipatti, the tragically short-lived Romanian pianist, wrote a beautifully spare left-hand Sonatine. His only reason for writing for the left hand was that he was running out of music paper and thought he would economize by using only one line at a time.

But the cornerstone of the left-handed repertory is the orchestral works commissioned by Paul Wittgenstein. Wittgenstein, as I mentioned before, was the Austrian aristocrat who commissioned the

Ravel concerto and so many other pieces after losing his right arm early in World War I. These circumstances would normally make him a sympathetic figure, but he never made it very easy for people to like him. He was so critical of most of the pieces he commissioned that composers generally ended up with a healthy aversion to him, in spite of the generous fees he paid. He didn't even play some of the pieces, yet lifetime performance rights were a part of his contract and he wasn't about to let anybody else play them, either. When a German pianist named Siegfried Rapp lost his arm in World War II and approached Wittgenstein about playing some of "his" concertos, Wittgenstein turned him down. "You don't build a house just so that someone else can live in it," he told Rapp. To top it all off, Wittgenstein's own playing was questionable. He made only a couple of recordings, one of the Ravel, and they are sadly wanting.

There were some mitigating factors. Wittgenstein came from a bizarrely neurotic family, one of eight children of a domineering father who loved music but didn't want his own children to play it. The Wittgensteins' musical salons hosted the cream of Vienna's musical society: Johannes Brahms, Joseph Joachim, Gustav Mahler. Paul was determined to be a concert pianist, but nobody in his family thought he was anywhere near good enough. He finally got himself accepted by none other than Schnabel's teacher, Leschetizky, who had a few reservations of his own—he dubbed Wittgenstein "the mighty key-smasher"—but ultimately embraced him as a musical protégé. Not that Leschetizky was exactly discriminating about whom he took. As I said, he taught everybody.

Wittgenstein was savvy about his image. After he lost his arm in a Russian POW camp and set out, with the same fierce stubbornness that had marked his relationship to the piano all his life, to be a one-handed pianist, he extended commissions to big-name composers whose works he thought would have a good chance of getting performed: Hindemith and Prokofiev and Ravel and Erich Wolfgang Korngold, who was viewed as one of the leading composers in the

German-speaking world. The problem was that Wittgenstein didn't actually like modern music. His favorite composer was Franz Schmidt, whose music sounds like an Austrian version of Rodgers and Hammerstein, only on a larger scale. Schmidt's piano concerto is a monster. It's as big as the Brahms D Minor. I've played it a couple of times. But it sounds like *South Pacific*, filled with pops-like tunes, highly chromatic, at once imposing and easy on the ear. That was the kind of thing Paul Wittgenstein liked.

So some of the works he commissioned never got played. It was Rapp, not Wittgenstein, who eventually premiered Prokofiev's Fourth Concerto. As for Hindemith's Piano Music with Orchestra, which was written in 1923, it languished until 2002, when it was found in a trunk on the Pennsylvania farm of Wittgenstein's widow, and I played the world premiere of it myself, in 2004, with the Berlin Philharmonic and Sir Simon Rattle. It's a terrific piece. It's got a lot of fun stuff in it: imitations and canons and playful intellectual games like that. Hindemith's slow movement, with a dialogue between the piano and the English horn, even anticipates the Ravel two-hand concerto, several years before Ravel's was even started.

Wittgenstein's commissions made up the bulk of my performances with orchestra. I didn't even learn all of them. I never liked the Korngold concerto, which I think is over-orchestrated, and I never got around to either of the pieces Richard Strauss wrote for Wittgenstein, the *Parergon* and the *Panathenäenzug*. It was hard enough to get orchestras to program the pieces I did know. In fact, it was hard to get them to let me play anything other than the Ravel. I had become so associated with the Ravel that it had become my trademark, or stunt—exactly, of course, what I didn't want. After I'd played it six times with the New York Philharmonic and they asked to engage me again, I begged and pleaded with them to let me play, at least, the Prokofiev Fourth. The Philharmonic's management said that their audience wanted to hear me play Ravel. "Don't worry," I told them. "I'll have a sex-change operation and wear a different gown to each performance. Then nobody will even notice what I'm playing." They let me play the Prokofiev.

With the Theater Chamber Players, of course, I could try out whatever I wanted. There are advantages to having your own ensemble. I did two of the three Franz Schmidt quintets with them. All of Schmidt's mature piano music was actually written for Wittgenstein, including those quintets, so the piano part was all for left hand alone. However, Schmidt was so popular in Austria that one of his students, a composer and pianist named Friedrich Wührer, arranged everything for two hands, and now the original left-hand versions are a little hard to track down.

Less well known than Wittgenstein was another pianist who was injured in World War I, a Czech soloist named Otakar Hollman, who also had several works written for him by his own preferred composers. These include pieces by Bohuslav Martinù and Erwin Schulhoff, but the one that I remember playing is the quirky *Capriccio* by Leos Janáček. Janáček was something of a maverick, and this piece is one of the strangest in the repertory. It's scored for a bizarre combination of instruments: left-hand piano, tenor tuba, three trombones, two trumpets, and a flute in there somewhere, trying valiantly to be heard over all that big brass. The idea is that everyone is doing awkward, unusual things in unexpected registers. It's a lot of fun. I don't play it anymore, though. It's written in several movements, and one of those movements got stuck in my head after I worked on it. It drove me crazy. I was reminded of the Mark Twain story "A Literary Nightmare," about a jingle that gets into his mind so deeply that he loses weight and can't sleep and is at his wits' end until he finally discovers that the way to get rid of such a thing is to pass it on to somebody else. I felt very much like Twain in that story after playing the Janáček *Capriccio*. I thought the safest thing to do was to avoid it altogether in the future.

Although I had kept playing, more or less steadily, for years, it took me a long time fully to shake the idea of its being a gimmick. Paul Wittgenstein used to worry about this too: the idea that there's a circus aspect to what you're doing, that people come to see the stunt

rather than to appreciate the art. You want to be appreciated as a pianist rather than as a left-handed pianist.

But after a couple of decades, you start to accommodate. I hadn't
abandoned the idea that I was, somehow, going to play again with two
hands. But my relationship with the piano was continuing to deepen
and grow. I had already proven that I didn't need my right hand to
keep thinking about, and understanding, and expressing music. And I
started to feel that, even with my left hand, I had more to say at the
keyboard. That series of concerts I did after the Meyerhoff debacle
helped me come to terms with the idea of playing more of the things
I was actually able to play.

Eventually, therefore, I worked up a solo recital. I'd been playing
with the left hand for years, but mainly with orchestra. It was around
1990 that I started increasingly to appear alone. The more I did it, the
more I liked it. It was a thrill to resume that old relationship with the
keyboard and to experience those unique moments when I found a
relationship to the music that I couldn't find in any other way.

One fount of left-hand works was Leopold Godowsky, a Polish-
born pianist and teacher often cited as having had the most impressive piano technique the world has ever seen. Godowsky had decided
views on relaxation and piano playing. For a modern pianist, he wrote,
"the right hand is constantly in a state of tension, while the left hand,
owing to its freedom from cramped muscles, is in a better condition
for the cultivation of the desired relaxation essential to a superior pianistic equipment." This certainly rang true for me. Godowsky's own
compositions, however, seemed calculated to introduce the same state
of tension in the left hand that he describes in the right. He created
some fiendishly difficult left-hand arrangements of Chopin études. I
never tackled any of those. I did spend a lot of time learning the Symphonic Metamorphoses he wrote on waltzes from the Strauss operetta
The Gypsy Baron, which sounds like a light, frothy showpiece and is
unbelievably hard to play. I learned the whole thing, and I played it
many times and even recorded it. Never again.

Another left-hand piece had come to my attention years before, back when I was living in Holland in the 1950s. I was listening to a radio show, and the announcer asked listeners to guess how many hands were used in the piano piece he was about to play. I figured it was a trick question and guessed three. My jaw hit the floor when I learned that a single hand was responsible for everything I'd heard. The piece was an étude for the left hand by Felix Blumenfeld—a once-renowned Russian conductor and pianist now mainly remembered as a teacher of Horowitz—who wrote the piece for his friend Scriabin when his hand was out of commission. The recording I heard was made by another student of Blumenfeld's, Simon Barere, whose considerable career ended when he had a fatal cerebral hemorrhage as he was playing the Grieg piano concerto at Carnegie Hall. What a way to go. But the piece stayed with me.

I worked up a recital program that I felt comfortable with, and I stuck to it for a long time. I played the Brahms/Bach transcription, and the Saint-Saëns études, and the Lipatti Sonatine, and the Blumenfeld étude, and I finished up with the Godowsky *"pour épater les bourgeois,"* to throw a little vulgarity, one might say, into the highbrow mix. I didn't tackle every left-hand piece I came across. I bypassed Max Reger's challenging suite for the left hand, which actually ends with a four-voiced fugue. That's basically one finger per voice, with the remaining finger devoted to making connections between the others. The recital I had worked out hung together pretty well. I did eventually get a little tired of it. "I feel a bit like Nathan Hale," I used to quip. "I only regret that I have but one recital to give for my country."

Gradually, though, composers began to write pieces for me. Very often I was presented with works as gifts, in one form or another. One work I usually included on my recital program was by an English composer named Robert Saxton—a student of Britten's—who wrote "Chacony" for me after he heard me play the Brahms/Bach. It's a very tricky piece: beautiful, and one of those far-out pieces that you have to hear many times before it might begin to make some sense. It became a cornerstone of my solo programs. I also often played "Silk Water," written for me by an American composer named Jean Hasse.

Dina Koston wrote me a beautiful piece called "Messages," which I loved. Dina had taken a long hiatus from composing, in part because she was giving so much to the Theater Chamber Players, but she started to return to it later in her life, to great effect. I found "Messages" fascinating. In it, she got a lot of effects on the piano with what you might call finger pedaling: separate lines of sound that blend and melt and pass back and forth without the pianist's resorting much to the actual pedal. There was a purity to its sound. This was music I could relate to.

I couldn't relate to all of it. Generally speaking, as a pianist, I can't say I was always a big fan of contemporary music. The challenge of late Beethoven, or Mozart, or Schubert seemed to me to be somehow greater or more worthwhile than that of learning difficult, ill-placed notes. To me, the kind of transcendence in the older pieces really was more interesting. That's not to say I didn't love the contemporary pieces I did play. I became very attached to the ones I learned, and I played them with pleasure and absolute commitment. It may be terrible to say this, but playing some of that music is like having a handicapped child. You love it all the more for the problems that it gives you.

One piece that gave me particular problems was a gift from Leon Kirchner: "L.H." The problems weren't with the piece itself, though. Leon presented it to me as a surprise at Tanglewood in the summer of 1995, a few months before I was scheduled to give my first solo recital at Carnegie Hall in more than thirty years. It seemed like perfect timing. The piece wasn't long—it lasts about seven minutes—and the obvious thing to do was to learn it in time to give its world premiere at my "comeback" performance.

Each of my left-handed solo recitals was heralded as a "return" or a "comeback," because I was taking the recital stage again. I didn't care so much what they said about it afterwards. It was the buildup before that I was anxious to avoid. My experience at the Meyerhoff in 1982 had made me allergic to buildups. But of course, a return to Carnegie Hall is not easy to downplay. I'd been at Carnegie a number of times playing left-hand concertos with this or that orchestra, but a one-handed solo recital was something else again. So there was a certain amount of nervousness.

The first problem with "L.H." was Leon's handwriting. It was virtually illegible. Simply deciphering the notes was a difficulty. The next problem was with what was actually written on the page. Leon was one of those composers who don't manage to get on paper exactly what they want the music to sound like. To him, it was perfectly clear what he intended, but those intentions weren't always expressed in the markings he wrote down. He was a notable pianist himself. He had a very peculiar physical way of approaching the piano: fingers out-stretched, with all of his gestures motivated from the arm. You might have thought his playing would sound choppy, but it didn't; he played with great delicacy, and the unusual style gave great energy to his attack. In his music, he was generally looking for a rhapsodic quality and a feeling of spontaneity. But it usually took a couple of sessions of going through the piece with him in person for him to get you to understand what he wanted.

Unfortunately, it was hard for us to find time to meet. Leon was a sought-after professor at Harvard, in addition to his own composing and performing, and I had my schedules at Peabody and Tanglewood, as well as conducting, playing, and teaching around the globe. The upshot was that we didn't manage to get together to go through the piece until literally the eve of the recital.

I was already nervous, and a little on edge. Leon, however, knew no compromises when it came to his work. He was as picky and persnickety as ever. I should have been used to his manner, because I remembered it from working on his piano sonata and, of course, on his second piano concerto, the one I commissioned. But in those cases I had had enough time to process his directives. Now, he just started to depress and upset me as he kept growling No, no, that's not right. At the end of the session, instead of feeling better about the piece, I was thoroughly rattled.

I stayed rattled, too. In fact, I was so upset that I screwed up the whole recital. I simply did not play well. The whole time I was on stage, I was aware that Leon was behind me in the box. It made me feel slightly off for every piece. It should have been a thrilling occasion. The audience was ecstatic, and the critics raved. Most of them felt that Leon's piece and the Brahms/Bach Chaconne were the highlights of the evening. But I felt I hadn't done as well as I could. I learned my lesson. I vowed never to play for a composer again so close to a performance.

Leon was intractable. Gary Graffman got very much the same reaction when he tried to play "L.H." himself. He learned the piece and played it for the composer, and Leon was fiercely disparaging. The difference between me and Gary is that Gary vociferously defended himself. "But this is what's on the page!" he said. He didn't convince Leon, who bad-mouthed him afterwards as ungifted. It was unfortunate, and unfair. But the music itself is wonderful. And I think I play it pretty well now.

The first left-hand piano concerto that was written for me was by a composer named Curtis Curtis-Smith. It was a fun concerto, based on changes in the ringing of the bell towers in the British Isles; I wish I'd done more with it. More concertos came out of my connection to Tanglewood and the Boston Symphony Orchestra. Gunther Schuller wrote an extraordinary concerto for three hands for me and Lorin Hollander; Gunther somehow made it sound like a regular piano that has simply been extended by one-third. And in 1994, the Boston Symphony Orchestra commissioned a piano concerto for me, to my enormous delight. They have a lovely tradition of doing things like that, stretching all the way back to Koussevitzky, who was an energetic champion of new music and commissioned things like Bartók's *Concerto for Orchestra* and Stravinsky's *Symphony of Psalms*. "To the glory

of God and the Boston Symphony Orchestra," ran Stravinsky's dedication.

My own concerto was written by Lukas Foss. I was delighted with
the selection. Lukas was another old Tanglewood hand—he had been
a student alongside Lenny in the 1940s—and when he was composer
in residence there in 1989 we had a chance to rekindle our friendship.
He, like me, had traveled a long way from the days when we drove
with Dot to Belgium in 1951. At that time, I was pretty obscure and he
was one of the hottest young composers around. He even succeeded
Schoenberg at the University of California after the great man's death.
Later, though, Lukas's restless musical intelligence led him to probe
many different musical styles and different career directions, including
the music directorship of a number of orchestras (the Buffalo Philharmonic, the Brooklyn Philharmonic) that he really helped put on the
map. He was always respected in the field, but I think his music fell
somewhat out of sight in his later years, which is a shame, because it's
awfully good. I wonder if his curious absentmindedness had anything
to do with it. He was an absolutely brilliant man, and yet even at the
height of his powers, he was not all there all the time.

That left-hand concerto is creative, and original, and imaginative.
It has tremendous rhythmic vitality, which I always respond to. It has
a whole range of musical references, from the Ravel left-hand concerto
to Minimalism. Foss also makes some great sounds. In the first movement, he re-creates, in the horns, the sound the ambulances in France
used to make—a nod to our Parisian past. In the second movement,
there's a bowed vibraphone. And in the third movement, he has a special quote that was a tribute to our friendship, going back to his summer at Tanglewood in 1989. Lukas's birthday is in August, and there
was a party, and I wasn't sure what to get him. I finally hit on the
idea of a T-shirt emblazoned with the words "To L.F. from L.F." The
impact of my gift was somewhat muted since, on opening it, Lukas
didn't understand what it meant. Only after I spelled it out did he get
it, and then he was absolutely delighted by it. He was so delighted, in

fact, that he quoted it in the concerto, having some of the orchestra musicians call out these words aloud as they play. "It's undoubtedly the first time a T-shirt has ever been set to music," he told a journalist.

Another memorable concerto was a work called "Gaea" that William Bolcom wrote for me and Gary Graffman: a piano concerto for two left hands. Since each of us had one good hand, we could join forces and make a whole pianist. The idea was more intricate than that, though, since what Bill Bolcom actually did was write two independent concertos for left-hand piano and chamber orchestra that could be played separately or together.

The whole thing was the brainchild of David Zinman, who had taken over as the Baltimore Symphony Orchestra's music director in 1985. David is a fantastic conductor, in my opinion one of the great ones of our time; he's had a respectable career, but I still think he's woefully underrated. Isaac Stern once said that when he played with Monteux he had the feeling that if he were to sneeze a year later, Monteux would have the handkerchief ready now. That's how alert he was, not only to what you were doing but to what you were going to do. I feel exactly the same way about David Zinman. Playing with him is a delight.

David is also an avid champion of new and recent music. He knew that the French composer Darius Milhaud had written two of his quartets in such a way that they could be played together as an octet, and he knew that Bill, who won the Pulitzer Prize for music in 1988, had studied with Milhaud. Bill is a composer with flair, a sense of humor, a streak of American irreverence, and a deep knowledge of the piano. Still, he evidently took some convincing before he agreed to an idea that was so challenging it sounded nearly impossible. It was, in truth, a fiendishly difficult idea. Gary thought it was a long shot too. I thought it sounded like fun.

Practicing for the premiere of "Gaea" gave me and Gary a chance to play together in the Steinway basement, as we had done when we were teenagers, ready to take on the world. Gary had settled into acceptance of his one-handed state. Like me, he had turned to teaching as a response to his crisis. Actually, the first thing he turned to was a longstanding interest he had in Chinese art and archaeology, sitting in on classes at Columbia and traveling to China on several digs. He also wrote a memoir called *I Really Should Be Practicing*; his friends immediately, with our customary supportive instincts, projected a sequel that would bear the Yiddish title *Svet Gornisht Helfen* (It Wouldn't Help). At the same time, though, Gary joined the faculty of his alma mater, Curtis, and within a few years, unexpectedly to those of us who knew him, he had become the school's director. It actually made a lot of sense. Gary, sanguine and levelheaded and practical, is a perfect leader. He was Solomonic in his ability to deal with the problems of two or three hundred kids from all over the world. And he was quietly, insistently tenacious when he wanted something—for instance, when he wanted me to join the Curtis faculty. I didn't need or want another teaching position, but Gary kept after me, promising that if it was too hard for me to come to Philadelphia they'd send the students down to Baltimore. Finally I gave in.

Unlike me, Gary wasn't looking for a cure. But he was certainly continuing to play with his left hand. He had commissioned some new works of his own, including a left-handed concerto by Ned Rorem. He had even learned a few of those Godowsky Chopin studies I had so carefully avoided. So our repertoires were somewhat divergent. Even Bill Bolcom's concerto characterizes our two parts quite differently.

There were a few business questions about setting up the contract. The world premiere extended over three days: Gary played his piece on Thursday's program, and I played mine on Friday, and then we played together on Saturday. At some of the other performances, we played all three pieces—his, mine, and ours—on one program. Gary and I agreed that we wouldn't ask for more money, above our regular fee, for the extra work. Gary asked for a gin gimlet, instead. For my part, I specified a vodka martini with as many olives as they could spare. We actually worked that into the contract. I thought this was such a good idea that I kept on doing it. Today, I have my manager, Frank Salomon, specify that I need a little bit of Chivas Regal at the end of a concert. Isaac Stern used to have a rider like that as well, except that his drink was a "Sternini," which was basically a very dirty martini that nobody but him could stand.

It felt wonderful to embrace performing so fully. And everyone was very encouraging. Seiji and I made a recording of the three main Wittgenstein concertos: the Ravel, the Prokofiev, and the Britten. And I made a solo recording of my recital program. I thought I might as well bite the bullet.

My home life with Kathy was tranquil too. She had found a wonderful home, a three-story house on a hill in a green suburb of Baltimore, with gardens and a little fishpond outside, and we eventually built on an addition that could hold two concert grand pianos, back to back. (My own old, battered Steinway was relegated to my studio on the third floor.) Kathy and I are great animal lovers. Over the years our house has become a haven for rescue dogs, home to a cavalcade of loving, shedding, barking quadrupeds. We've hosted benefit galas to raise money for them, and loved them, and mourned them when they've died, and shepherded them out into the back garden when we've used the house for other purposes, like political fund-raisers for causes we believed in. During some elections, if a Democratic candidate is in a particularly tight race, our place can become a veritable command central, filled with volunteers working the phones.

Kathy also continued building her own career, continuing an active life in music. She performs concertos and recitals around the country and the world. One of her connections is an organization called the Piatigorsky Foundation, which sends artists into communities that don't often get to hear live performance: senior centers, schools, even prisons. It's a contrast to the concert halls where we usually appear. In Baltimore, a few years after our marriage, I put together a marathon fund-raiser with the orchestra: I conducted all five Beethoven concertos in one evening, each with a different female soloist, and gave the evening the outrageous title of "Leon, Ludwig, and the Ladies." Ann Schein played the "Emperor." Israela Margalit, who was Lorin Maazel's wife at the time, played the Fourth. Idil Biret did the C Minor, Lilian Kallir did the C Major, and Kathy got my old standby, the B-flat. It was quite an event.

One thing we did not have was children. I had been explicit from the first. I didn't want any more children. I felt it keenly that I hadn't done a very good job with the five I had, though they were all turning out to be really terrific people. Sometimes they are even colleagues. Dickie is a member of the orchestra in Naples, Florida, while his wife, Kayo, plays with the Jacksonville Symphony, as well as the Grant Park Orchestra in Chicago. One summer when I was playing the Ravel concerto in Grant Park, I walked out on stage for rehearsal and there they both were, having arranged to come up and perform as a surprise. The conductor that night was my former student Hugh Wolff, so it was very much a family affair. And that turned out to be just the first in a series of Fleisher family performances.

But I am not sure I had much of a hand in their turning out so well. They had had to deal—particularly my Opus 1 set—with a considerable amount of abandonment and neglect. One of my great regrets in life involves my shortcomings as a father. I tried to do what I could, later, to make up for them. But I didn't want to keep perpetuating the same mistakes. Even during my marriage to Rikki, I had put my foot down: no more kids.

Kathy knew this. But it was also hard on her. She would have liked to have children. And on some level, I think she hoped to change my mind. She certainly did a lot of work with children herself. One spring, she and another talented pianist, Kwang-Wu Kim—who was my assistant for a while—performed a few four-handed piano programs for kids in the Baltimore city schools, and she had the idea of giving some of those kids a chance to take piano lessons with her over the summer, if any of them wanted to learn. A handful of them took her up on it. So that summer, instead of going to Tanglewood, she stayed home and taught piano to a group of children—giving, in effect, a summer institute of her own.

At the end of the summer, one little girl named Zakeebah didn't want the lessons to stop. Kathy had gotten quite attached to all the children, but Zakeebah—Keekee, for short—was particularly adorable, and Kathy said she'd be willing to go on teaching her if her guardian was willing. Keekee lived with a great-aunt and a little brother named Quashawn. The great-aunt at first said that there was no way to get Keekee to and from lessons, and Kathy offered to pick her up and started running over to West Baltimore—a pretty rough neighborhood—to get the little girl. On one of her first visits, she met Quashawn, who was just as smart and beautiful as Keekee was, and eventually Kathy started bringing him to our house as well. One thing led to another, and the children came to our house to spend Thanksgiving weekend that year, and we all had a wonderful time. I took them over to a school near our house and taught them how to ride a bike in the parking lot. It was fun to have kids in the house again, and it was very silent after they had gone. I said to Kathy, "We should do something to help these children." And we tried.

It wasn't immediately clear how we could proceed. We did see, though, that the kids' family didn't have the means to give them certain things, and we established what we called the Fleisher-Jacobson International Children's Education Foundation, which allowed us to help them with schooling and other needs (we later helped a few other kids as well). Kathy had Quashawn tested for the Gilman School, one of the leading prep schools in the country, and he got in. Unfortunately, his great-aunt wouldn't let him go. That was the first sign of trouble. At first, the aunt had been happy to have the kids treat us like family; she even encouraged them to call Kathy "Mommy." The kids, whose mother had at that point essentially abandoned them, were quite excited at the idea of having a mommy, but Kathy thought we should be careful about taking things too fast, and it turned out she was right. We did want to adopt the children, and we acted in many ways like parents. We took them with us to Aspen, we helped with their schooling, we had them in and out of our house. But gradually the great-aunt got jealous. And it's hard to push an adoption through when the children's guardians don't want to let them go.

The process became a veritable tug-of-war. At one point, Zakeebah was all set to start at the Baltimore School of the Arts, where she was already involved in a serious after-school dance program that trained kids for a career in the field. Then the great-aunt decided the kids would be better off living with another great-aunt, in South Carolina. We tried to get a court injunction to block the move, but the court couldn't do much. Quashawn called, begging for help, and Kathy had to tell him there was nothing she could do. South Carolina didn't last long, though, and the kids ended up living with an alcoholic grandmother in New Jersey. All of the moving around and the changes in school didn't do them any favors. Quashawn has had a particularly hard time. After a couple of expulsions, he came and lived with us to finish his last year of high school, but he had already grown more distant. I couldn't really be a father to him, and the lack of a father figure made itself felt; he struggled a lot to find his place in his young life. We both always hope he will eventually find some way to realize his potential. Keekee, though, is flourishing, and working full-time while continuing her education to become an elementary school teacher.

Keekee and Quashawn brought us a lot of joy. They also brought heartache. The pain of having them almost like our own but always out of reach, of being able to help, but not enough, was a somber leitmotif running through some of the years we spent with them.

For the most part, though, everything was going well. My sixties were proving to be a time when I really was able to start reaping what I had sowed. Time and again, I would look at my life and marvel that so many wonderful things had happened that never would have happened if my hand had not been struck down. I couldn't imagine my life without conducting. I couldn't imagine life without teaching so intensely. I couldn't imagine my life without Kathy.

I also couldn't imagine life without Tanglewood. Of course, in an institution with so many people and agendas, there were bound to be some problems. It was sometimes awfully hard to read what Seiji wanted. Seiji was not very communicative (in part because he never learned to speak English very well) and not very present, and occasionally he telegraphed his wishes by springing decisions on us as faits accomplis. One of these involved the jazz trumpeter Wynton Marsalis, himself a Tanglewood alum, who came in 1994 with a project that was billed as a great opportunity for Tanglewood students to get some exposure to the varieties of musical experience in the real world. Marsalis and his band would join the TMC orchestra for a televised series called *Marsalis on Music*, a spiritual successor to Lenny's famous Young People's Concerts with the New York Philharmonic in the 1960s. The whole thing would be taped by Sony Classics; it was, in fact, the brainchild of a newly-minted Sony executive named Peter Gelb, who within a decade would take over as general manager of the Metropolitan Opera.

A number of us didn't think this was a very good idea. The TMC has only a seven- or eight-week session, and this project would tie up the students for at least two of those weeks, a healthy part of the summer. And I didn't think it would bring them any musical benefit, which was supposed to be the reason they had come to Tanglewood in the first place. But Seiji loved the idea. This project was the kind of thing that really turned him on. He overrode everybody's objections, and he made the project happen. The result was pretty feeble stuff, and there was a lot of complaint from the kids who had come to Tanglewood to study with the greats and instead ended up spending the better part of two weeks sitting in a darkened studio playing unilluminating orchestral excerpts. It was an awful waste of their time. The fact that the project had not gone well didn't soften Seiji; it may even have made him resent it more that so many of us had advised him so strongly against it.

Still, there were plenty of happy moments to outweigh the

negatives. Among other things, Tanglewood received an important bequest: the 140-acre estate adjacent to the campus. This enabled us to make significant improvements. After a long bout of fund-raising and construction, the showpiece of the new Tanglewood was unveiled that same summer, 1994: Seiji Ozawa Hall, a new theater for recitals and chamber concerts. Building a new theater can be a bit of a crapshoot, since all the acousticians in the world don't seem able to consistently deliver good results, but this one, with its clean lines of brick and wood and glass, turned out to be an architectural and acoustical gem that enhanced the whole Tanglewood experience.

Also in 1994, I received a professional recognition that meant a great deal to me. The magazine *Musical America* named me Instrumentalist of the Year. Not conductor, not musician, not teacher: instrumentalist. It's an award I would have been proud to have been given as a pianist with two functioning hands. Instead, I had earned it—and earned it dearly—with just one.

I was still a pianist.

And I was working on something even better. I was about to start playing with two hands again.

Master Class 5

FRANZ SCHUBERT: SONATA IN B-FLAT MAJOR, D. 960 (1828)

Schubert's B-flat sonata is, to me, an ultimate piece. And I feel a particular connection to it. It's all mine.

That is, I learned it myself. I never worked on it with Schnabel, though I heard him give some lessons on it. The B-flat sonata was the piece I learned when I was discovering my ability to make my own decisions about music, to find my own answers to its questions. I learned it during a short period when I was living in Doda Conrad's building in Paris, before I got married—that is, I started learning it then, since the learning lasts a lifetime. Pretty much all of the solutions I've come up with about that piece I've arrived at on my own. Including the stupid wrong note in the first recording I made of it—my first recording with Columbia, before I started working with Szell—when I played a C-sharp instead of a B in the melody of the second movement. That wasn't entirely my fault; I had a badly edited edition of the score. But I should have been able to figure out that it wasn't right.

It's a gorgeous sonata. It's an absolutely ethereal piece of music.

There's a gentleness, an otherworldliness to Schubert. Beethoven is always shaking his fist at the heavens, but Schubert is just the music of the spheres. It's music of nature. There's something sublime about it. It's both poignant and serene. Sometimes it's suffused with pure joy. And there's wit, and humor, to be found in there as well. He likes to yodel, Schubert does.

The B-flat sonata is the ultimate illustration of Schubert's gift for a certain wistful kind of melody. Schubert writing in a major key can come up with melodies that are more poignant and sad than anyone else's melody in a minor key. He had that ability. Some of his major-key melodies can break your heart. Much more so than the minor melodies.

The biggest challenge of the piece: finding the right sound. You have to find a sound that communicates the sublime. This isn't a technical challenge in the usual sense of the word, but it's a huge artistic challenge. Playing very, very quietly, and yet being able to evoke Schubert's cosmos at the same time, takes a tremendous amount of physical control. You have to know what you're doing and how to produce the moods you want. And you have to figure out, all the time, exactly when to play the next note: when the exact moment comes when that sound will make sense.

The first movement should sound, I think, like a memory from far away. Schubert gives you a chance to remember it, too: he repeats the entire exposition, which is a good four minutes of music. A lot of pianists don't take that repeat. Alfred Brendel, for example, doesn't, and I didn't, in my first recording of the piece; even without it, the movement is about thirteen minutes long, which to some people seems quite long enough. I've come to think, though, that the repeat is essential. For one thing, the first ending presents absolutely new material that you don't encounter anywhere else in the piece; the ominous distant rumble that's been sounding quietly in the left hand from the outset really wakes up there and comes into its own. For another, the proportions of the piece change totally when you take the repeat. After it, the second movement doesn't seem so long. That second movement is far easier to deal with if you've done the repeat in the first movement.

Finally, taking the repeat allows you really to explore that idea of memory. The opening becomes like a memory remembered: traversing something familiar that's already fading into the distance.

The second movement is also sublime, and also aching, and yet entirely different from the first movement. Time stops. You have to keep nudging it ahead, imperceptibly, to keep it moving just barely forward, while you're lost in contemplation. I think of it as like rowing a boat: you take a stroke of the oar, and the boat moves ahead but starts to slow down, until you take the next stroke of the oar to keep

it going. That's not a bad way of dealing with the tune and its accompaniment. Once you think of it like that, you can start to play with
where you think the main impulses—the strokes—need to come. It's
not just a steady progression of the same pulse. You can give the stroke
every two bars and then extend it to four bars, and I think that way
you start to get to the heart of what Schubert is doing. Eventually, this
leads you to a middle section, a B section, that's quite regular, with an
underlying carpet of sixteenth notes, and then triplet sixteenths, that
carries the melody along in quite a different way. Then you return to
the A section, the recapitulation.

What happens next, in that recapitulation, is to me one of the
most divine moments in all of music. The movement is in the key
of C-sharp Minor, but Schubert takes it into the dominant, G-sharp
Major for a while. Then he pauses. And then the music comes in in
the key of C Major, radiant, suspended, angelic. It's heart-stopping. It's
one of the great, great inspirations in all of the music I've ever played
or ever heard. It certainly is a vision of heaven.

So the sonata arcs from heaven to heaven to a palate cleanser of a
third movement: *con delicatezza*, Schubert writes. Then there's a wonderful fourth movement full of surprises and sly deceptions. Schubert
keeps punctuating the movement with a little horn call on a G octave
that sounds at the start of the main theme and every time the theme
comes back. Then, suddenly, in the coda at the end of the movement, he lets that octave slip down to an F-sharp. Eyebrows have to
be raised. What is that? Oh, he says innocently, that's nothing, look:
that's just a passing tone that resolves into an F. You can hear his eyes
twinkle behind his glasses. Just kidding. Then he grabs you up and
races the whole thing pell-mell to a rousing close.

CHAPTER 10

RENAISSANCE MAN

Two hands. Fred Dufour (AFP/Getty)

Botulinum toxins are the most poisonous poisons in the world. And they're everywhere. They lie dormant until they get into an environment without any air: then they flourish. In, for example, a can or jar of preserves that has been improperly prepared. Or in sausage casings. Or in your body. The term *botulism* comes from the Latin word *botulus*, which means sausage.

The doctor who first worked with botulinum toxins in a medical capacity had no idea that they would become ubiquitous in cosmetic surgery as a treatment for wrinkles. He was trying to paralyze chicken embryos. His name is Dan Drachman, and he's not a psychopath: he was just looking for a cure for a congenital disease called arthrogryposis, which creates a kind of extreme clubfoot effect in all of a baby's limbs, and he needed to test his theory that movement in utero (or, in the chickens' case, in the egg) was key to proper joint development. He tried several different poisons before he discovered that a fractional dose of botulinum toxins didn't have to be fatal. Indeed, it eventually wore off. This discovery laid the foundation for the now-flourishing use of minute doses of botulinum toxins—Botox, in common parlance—in the offices of cosmetic surgeons and other doctors around the world. Had Drachman patented his discovery, he would have become fabulously wealthy. He settled for spending his career pursuing cures for life-threatening neuromuscular diseases (like ALS) instead.

Dan happens to be a friend of mine. I met him soon after he

moved to Baltimore in 1969 to head a new department of neurology at
Johns Hopkins. I never dreamed, then, that he might hold the keys to
helping me play with two hands again. It took us a couple of decades
to figure that out.

Actually, I met Dan's wife, Jephta, first. Jephta is the daughter of
the great cellist Gregor Piatigorsky, with whom I played Schubert and
Brahms in California so many years before, and when I met her the
musical link created an instant connection. Dan fully shares his wife's
love of music. He's a very respectable clarinet player. His father-in-law
called him "the best amateur musician I know." The night that he
proposed to Jephta, he spent the evening playing chamber music with
what had been described to him beforehand as an informal group
consisting of Piatigorsky and some friends. Those friends turned out
to be Jascha Heifetz and Artur Rubinstein.

So Dan and Jephta are fixtures on the Baltimore music scene. They
are regulars at BSO concerts. Jephta has long served on the board,
and has been president, of the Shriver Hall Concert Series, which
is Baltimore's main chamber music presenter, bringing major artists
to Baltimore every season. And the Drachmans' New Year's parties
are a tradition that has been going on for years: big gatherings with
wonderful food and an evening of chamber music. I play, and so do
Kathy and Dan and other friends from Peabody (Berl Senofsky played
when he was still alive) and Dan and Jephta's son Evan, a cellist, like
his grandfather, and the founder of the Piatigorsky Foundation, the
organization Kathy plays with from time to time. Evan usually brings
a few Piatigorsky Foundation artists along to New Year's as well. Then
there are people like Jeffrey Solow and Nathaniel Rosen, world-class
cellists who were students of Piatigorsky's; they come occasionally as
well. So the level of music making at those gatherings is pretty high.
And we have hats and balloons and confetti at midnight.

Because of the Drachmans' musical involvement, Dan sees quite a
number of musicians as patients. And yet for a long time I didn't even
think of consulting him. Whatever was wrong with me didn't seem to

have much to do with his high-end research into genetic abnormalities. I didn't, I couldn't, have a neurological problem. I had already been tested six ways to Sunday.

Privately, though, Dan had his own theory about what was wrong with my hand. He thought it was a form of dystonia.

Dystonia is a neurological disorder that causes contraction or spasm of the muscles. Basically, it means that the part of the brain that signals to a muscle that it can relax simply stops working properly, leaving the muscle in a near-perpetual state of contraction. Certain forms of dystonia develop in childhood, others in adulthood. Some forms affect the neck and head; some people find they can't control their eyelids; sometimes the vocal cords are affected. No one is quite sure what brings it on. But there are certain forms of focal dystonia that seem to be definitely related to specific, repeated tasks of the motor muscles. One is writer's cramp. And one affects the hands of musicians.

It was probably desperation that led me to consult Dan. The problem was not only music making. My hand was affecting all different aspects of daily life. Over the years, the contractions had been sometimes better, sometimes worse. Usually, I was able to relax the hand when I was at rest, but when I started playing the piano, those last two fingers would begin to curl up, until they were rock hard against my palm. At particularly bad times, the fingers would curl when I tried to do anything. Forget about playing the piano: sometimes I couldn't write my name. Kathy learned to forge my signature on checks. Sometimes I had trouble simply washing my hands. And Dan was one doctor I hadn't gone to yet.

When Dan mentioned dystonia to me, I mentally filed it away with all the other diagnoses I had received over the years. Dystonia was one I had heard before. I've already mentioned that, back in the 1970s, some NIH doctors had suggested that I might be suffering from torsion dystonia and had put me on L-dopa. It hadn't worked. As a result, dystonia was something I had pretty much ruled out.

But Dan had an idea for something concrete that I might do that I hadn't tried. The medical use of Botox was in its infancy at that point, but a colleague of Dan's at the National Institutes of Health, Mark Hallett, was conducting a pilot program to see whether injections of small amounts of Botox might be a viable treatment for various forms of dystonia. The idea was that Botox might shut down the overactive flexor muscles and allow the opposing extensor muscles to do what they were supposed to do. Dan suggested I go to Mark and have some Botox shots and see if it helped. He didn't think it could hurt.

So I went to the NIH yet again. This time, to have poison shot into my arm.

It was March of 1991 when I sat, somewhat nervously, in Dr. Hallett's office and let my arm be probed with a needle that detects electrical activity in the body. When it locates a site with abnormally high activity, the doctors know where to inject. The muscles they were looking for were actually located not in my hand but in my forearm; that's where you find the flexor muscles that control the contraction of the fingers. The needle probed. Electrical activity located. Injection needle inserted. Plunger depressed. And then—nothing. A Botox injection is utterly without drama. Nothing happens. It takes a few days for the poison to take effect. That made me nervous, too.

Dr. Hallett and his team sent me home and said to call and let them know how I was progressing, and if the hand was able to open up at all, and if I had any more functionality. We weren't looking for miracles. If I was able to wash my hand normally again, they would see it as a success. So I went home and waited to see if anything would happen.

I was always testing my hand, of course. I had never stopped testing it. I had never stopped trying to play around the problem. I tested it all the more after the Botox shot. Was I getting more movement in the fingers? It seemed to me I was. At the end of the first week, I could open my hand. It wasn't exactly what you would call flexible. But it seemed, more or less, usable, for longer periods of time.

Was it worth the risk of putting poison into my body for a benefit that could only be, at best, temporary? I wasn't sure. I waited about a year to go back to the NIH. I certainly had some benefits from that shot, especially for the first five or six months. When I went back to Dr. Hallett and his team, I was able to report that I had even been playing the piano again, which was a lot more than they expected. They were delighted. They gave me another injection and sent me home again, and that, too, had some effect. On some days, I actually felt I could play with two hands at the keyboard without too much adjustment.

And yet I had strong reservations about the whole thing. I wasn't sure that temporary shots, like Band-Aids, were really the kind of solution I had been looking for. I wasn't entirely sure that the improvement I was seeing was related to the Botox. And I didn't like the thought of injecting a deadly poison into my body, however small the dose: nobody really knew about the long-term effects. Kathy and I had been focused for a long time on eating better and living more healthily. Putting poison into my arm didn't quite seem to accord with that.

Furthermore, I still wasn't sure about the diagnosis. I had been living with my problem for a long time, and I had heard a lot of doctors suggest a lot of things, and I didn't think, by then, that I had a neurological condition. Dystonia, as I said, was something I had ruled out. It seemed pretty clear to me that what had happened to me was a result of overpracticing—of doing the same thing over and over too many times. A number of other doctors had suggested that what I had was repetitive strain injury, or overuse syndrome. That was a perfectly logical diagnosis.

One thing that complicated my diagnosis was that so many of these disorders and syndromes were only just beginning to be recognized for what they were. Both focal dystonia and repetitive strain injury (there are a lot of names for that one) were historically often characterized as psychosomatic problems: all in the patient's head. Not until the last couple of decades have they started to become recognized for what they are and to be moved from the realm of the psychologist to the realm of the neurologist or physiologist. Repetitive strain injury is actually an umbrella term that has been used to cover a whole spectrum of problems, sometimes even including focal dystonia.

The main symptom of what is today recognized as repetitive strain injury is pain. And I had never had any pain. But it was so obvious to me that it must be what was wrong with me. I had practiced too much and lost the use of my hand. Now, there was a syndrome that described exactly what had happened. How could it possibly be a neurological problem? And the idea of the poison just turned me off. So after the second injection I abandoned Dr. Hallett's program. It was almost ten years before I tried Botox again.

All this while, the music had been ripening, and deepening, in me.

The music wasn't in my fingers. It was in my mind and heart. And as I got older, I was less and less hung up on the idea that it had to come out with technical perfection. The intention of the music, the reason for making it, lies much farther below the surface.

Relationships are about compromises. It had taken me a long time to learn that, too. Not every day is ideal. You accommodate. You get by. Some days are better than others. That was true of my relationship to music and, even more, of my relationship to the piano. I was learning to live with my problem. Even to play the piano with my problem. Of course, I had to focus almost entirely on the simple mechanics of physical production. At the peak of my career, I'd say that 90 percent of my concentration went to the music. Now, that same amount of concentration went to making my hand work. I had to trust the music to come out on its own. In a way, there's something liberating about that.

I knew I had done it in 1982. I also knew that what I had done wasn't enough to support the exigencies of a solo career. But it was possible for me to make sounds at the keyboard, and the more I

worked the more I learned to navigate, to deal with my physical limitations. There were times—there always had been times—when I could
play my way through a piece. As I got older, I felt less and less that I
needed it to be perfect. I had established who I was; I didn't need to
drive myself at each performance to demonstrate my abilities, to try
to prove myself as one of the best pianists in the world. I didn't even,
any longer, need a big comeback. I just wanted to see what I could
do. I wanted to find that particular relationship to a piece, that sense
of having expressed it in the best way one can possibly express it at
that moment in one's life, that only comes through playing it in public.
And I felt that I had something to express that other people might be
able to find worthwhile.

In the winter of 1993, my old friend, colleague, and Theater Chamber Players stalwart Pina Carmirelli died at her home in Italy. We
promptly and wholeheartedly turned the next Theater Chamber Players concert, in April, into a tribute and memorial for this wonderful
musician and friend.

I wanted to make a special gesture. I played Bach's "Jesu, Joy of
Man's Desiring," in the same arrangement I had used when I performed it for Gary Graffman and the doctors at Mass General in 1981.
It's special music, mantra music, music that sounds as if it had the
power to wash away all of the dirt and evils and complications of the
world. It's very good for the mental health. It took me a long time
to grow into Bach and to reach an understanding of the music and a
feeling that I could play it with what I felt it required. "Jesu, Joy of
Man's Desiring" is particularly healing. It requires an almost childlike
simplicity, but it takes a lifetime's experience, I feel, to express it.

It's also a piece for two hands.

Playing with two hands was the biggest gesture I could think of
to honor Pina. It was between her and me. The other people who
were there—Kathy and Dina and the cellist Evelyn Elsing and the
conductor Joel Lazar and many others both on the stage and in the
audience—understood. The outside world hardly even noticed. But I

did it. I played with two hands, and I don't think I disgraced myself. And it felt pretty wonderful.

I'd lived through all the stages of grief about what had happened to my hand and what I had lost. I had been through the denial at the very beginning: this isn't really happening to me, I can overcome it, I thought, as I practiced harder and harder. There was always anger, flickers of rage: it was so horribly unfair. Depression, too, came and went over the years. My ability to bargain lay far behind me. "Just let me make it through the next concert" was hardly efficacious when there weren't any more two-handed concerts to make it through.

The final stage is acceptance. I was who I was, and I had this problem, and it was part of me. There were a lot of good things about the path I had taken. And there were still a lot of obstacles. I was in my mid-sixties, and there weren't going to be any great changes in my life. It was up to me to make the most out of what I had and to learn how to live with it. Maybe it wasn't so important to be the greatest concert pianist in the world. The most important thing now was just to be able to make the music I wanted. Because hand or no hand, I knew I still had something to say.

So I kept trying things, anything, that could help me out. I tried a course of something Kathy had gotten turned on to called chelation therapy, a three-hour IV drip of a combination of vitamins and other substances that cleans the heavy metals from your body. We visited a homeopathic doctor named Chandra Sharma in London, who treated people like Tina Turner and George Harrison, very fancy company; and before the actual treatment I submitted to a checkup and a routine series of questions about my health. One question had to do with what kind of shape I was in sexually. "I'm as fit as Big Ben," I said, in a nod to the host country.

"Currently under repair," observed Dr. Sharma drily. He was right. Big Ben was out of commission for several months. Fortunately I was doing better than that.

I went to a chiropractor. I also began a regular regime of stretching, something that grew out of my ballet lessons. I had watched Kathy stretching, before and after dance classes, practice sessions, jogging, any time she used her muscles. Stretching made a lot of sense. Muscles tend to contract after a workout; stretching keeps them limber. Well, my muscles were contracting more than anyone's. I stretched.

Then I started working with a Rolfer.

I had, as I said, already been Rolfed during one of my exploratory phases in the 1970s. It was all very well, but I hadn't felt especially transformed by the experience. There's a lot more to Rolfing, however, than the rhetoric of pain and self-transformation. Rolfers have had some amazing results working with specific injuries: curing a bad limp, for example, after a car accident. And the Rolfer that Kathy found this time round, in 1994 or so, focused particularly on my right hand. Kathy hadn't actually been looking for a new treatment for me, but the Rolfer, Tessy Brungardt, was recommended to her as someone who might help with some physical difficulties she was having due to taking on a new instrument, the flute. Since Kathy is open to every kind of approach in learning more about the body, she was curious enough to give Tessy a try, and she liked the results so much that she thought I might want to check it out.

The muscles of my hand had been in a near-constant state of contraction for decades. They were rigid, and they were used to being rigid. Tessy was impressed by my state of inflexibility. She hadn't, she said, seen anything quite like it; she compared my forearm to a piece of petrified wood. We started working together regularly, first once, then twice a week, focusing almost exclusively on my arm. It took Tessy more than a year of twice-weekly sessions to reestablish the plasticity of those muscles. She was as stubborn as I was. Together, inch by inch, we fought our way back. But I could feel a definite difference. Slowly, my arm and hand were coming back to life.

I would sit in my studio, on the third floor of our house, with the dogs barking beneath me at every passing car, and Kathy moving around downstairs, and the leaves rustling all along the hilltop, in the sun, and I would play my battered old piano, with the ivories springing from the keys. I wasn't so much wrestling with the music as working to let it come out, working to find a way that my hand could get to it. I couldn't play a certain note? I would refinger the passage. Sometimes those refingerings seemed to make even more expressive sense than what I had originally had. There were ways to work around problems. It wasn't an easy process. Some days were exercises in intense frustration. But others felt like I had climbed a mountain and was able to stand, at least briefly, on the top.

There wasn't a moment when I said to myself, "There. You've arrived. It's back." I wasn't back. I knew that. But I was learning to live with it. And the only way for me fully to understand where I was, how far I had or hadn't come, was to try playing a piece in public.

My friends knew I was playing with two hands. Dan Gustin, at Tanglewood, heard me practicing in my studio, and Seiji knew, as we worked together on our concerto recording, and Dina and all the Theater Chamber Players knew, because they had heard me play that "Jesu, Joy of Man's Desiring" at the concert for Pina. They all were eager for me to try it in public. Try it at Tanglewood, Dan urged. Try it at the Theater Chamber Players, Dina ordered.

I wasn't going to make a big splash. I didn't want the press, the cameras, the inevitable to-do about a Leon Fleisher comeback. I just wanted to see if I could do it. After a couple of months of working with Tessy and months of sitting at the piano and teasing the music out of it, note by note and line by line, I thought I had Mozart's K. 414 pretty well in hand. I didn't pick an earthshaking piece. K. 414 is a beautiful little concerto that Mozart wrote shortly after his marriage, when he was living in Vienna and trying to put himself on the map. It's sparer and more direct than some of the pieces he wrote while he was still living in Salzburg and trying to break out of provincial life there. It's relatively modest in scale; in fact, you can play it with a string quartet, though in my opinion it sounds a lot better if you add a double bass on the bottom. That was the version we played with the Theater Chamber Players in April 1995.

The Theater Chamber Players was like family. It felt as if even our audience knew us—knew our foibles, knew our strengths. I felt nothing but support. It felt so natural to sit there, among my colleagues, back at the middle of the piano bench where I belonged, and lift both hands to the keys, and enter Mozart's graceful, elegant world, proportioned on a human scale, so that everything feels like it just fits.

And it worked. Despite restrictions, limitations, refingerings, and finger curl, I was able to make it work. I could play Mozart. With two hands. It wasn't perfect. But it was me. Nothing ever felt sweeter than the feeling of those notes falling into place, the right hand singing, the left hand balancing it on the lower part of the keyboard, and the piece growing into something whole and complete, a dream become reality, in a way it never could when I played it alone at home.

I knew I wasn't "back." Technically, I wasn't playing the way I had played thirty years ago. But I was somewhere much farther along than I had been for a long, long time. And musically, I think, I had moved well beyond where I was thirty years before.

I must have been a little intoxicated by the wonder and sweetness of it all to do what I did next. Because it was nothing short of an act of hubris. A couple of weeks after that TCP concert, I was scheduled to play with the Cleveland Orchestra—George Szell's orchestra, the orchestra that had meant so much to me and my career for so many years. I was to play the Prokofiev Fourth, once again, with Christoph von Dohnányi, who was then reigning as the orchestra's music director. There had been a couple of other music directors since Szell, including Lorin Maazel (some of us dubbed Szell "Pa Szell" to distinguish him from "Maazel" in conversation), but Dohnányi, a handsome, patrician German, turned out to be the most worthy successor. Quite in Szell's spirit, he upheld the orchestra's legendary high standards, maintained its reputation for precision, and ushered in a second Golden Age for

Cleveland. Dohnányi and I went way back. I had played Beethoven's
B-flat Major concerto with him when he made his American debut in
1961, with the St. Louis Symphony.

If it hadn't been the Cleveland Orchestra, I might not have dared.
But the orchestra seemed like a perfect place for a homecoming. And
I was flying with the thrill of having played with two hands with the
TCP. So a couple of weeks before the concert, I called up Christoph
and asked if he would mind making a program change.

Christoph hesitated. He was concerned I might want to spring
something obscure on him, like the Korngold left-hand concerto, at
which the players were likely to protest.

Would he mind very much, I continued, if I played Mozart's K.
414 instead?

Christoph wasn't quite sure he had heard me right. I wanted to
play something with two hands? With the orchestra? After thirty
years?

Yes, I said, that was what I was asking.

And I was asking if he minded? I could hear his big smile right
over the phone line.

No press, I insisted. That was my one condition. No hubbub. No
fanfare about comebacks or returns. Just me and the music.

And so, almost exactly thirty years after I had played the Mozart
K. 503 with Szell in Severance Hall, at the concert before I stopped
playing with two hands for what I had thought might be forever, I
found myself on stage with Christoph von Dohnányi, preparing to
play Mozart's K. 414. There had been so little fanfare that some people
who saw the program change listing me as the soloist in the Mozart
assumed there had been some kind of mistake.

It wasn't a mistake, but I was so terrified that I felt, in the days
leading up to the concert, that it might be.

Be careful what you wish for, I kept telling myself, sitting in my
dressing room waiting to go out. I had what I wanted. I was about to
play, again, a regular piano concerto with one of the greatest orchestras

in the world. But it didn't feel quite like it had in my dreams for so many years.

Playing the piano certainly didn't feel the way it had in the years before my hand problem struck. I didn't have the same kind of control. It was a whole new adventure: each time, things came out a little differently. I didn't have the fluency, the ease that I had had when I was young. I had to remain keenly aware of my hand, and what it was doing, and what I needed it to do, every second I was on that stage. It was a very different sensation from what I remembered. And surrounded by that amazing orchestra—with, even, a few faces I remembered from thirty years before—I wondered if I had been crazy to take the plunge.

Christoph didn't make it any easier, either. He was thrilled that I was playing with him again. But he wasn't going to compromise his standards as a musician. He had very specific ideas about how K. 414 should be played, and they didn't always agree with mine. He may have meant it as a compliment. He wasn't going to give me special treatment just because I had been away for so long. He was going to treat me just as he would any other soloist. I had probably been hoping for a little more accommodation. I had been struggling for years to be able to express what I had to say in music. Finally, I was at a point where I was able to get it out. I hadn't really expected to have to debate it or be asked to modify it. So for me, Christoph's attitude added to the fear and tension that surrounded those concerts.

But I was sitting in Severance Hall again. I was playing a concert again. I was highly self-critical and filled with doubt and anxiety. But as we danced through the final movement, I and that fantastic orchestra, I could feel my heart singing along.

I could do it. I could play. I could.

I didn't stop playing left-hand performances. On the contrary, I had more left-handed performances than ever. I had my solo recital at

Carnegie Hall. I did the premiere of Bill Bolcom's "Gaea" with Gary. And I kept up a steady diet of the Ravel left-hand concerto. I wasn't going to be so foolish as to throw out my meal ticket. After all, it really is a great piece. And my right hand was nowhere near ready for a full battery of concerts, week in and week out.

But the world tingled with new possibilities.

For one thing, I was able to make music with my colleagues again. Of course, I had been playing left-handed things like the Schmidt and Janáček and Schuller chamber pieces and conducting all along. But I felt that all my work over the years had given me a better understanding of other musicians and of collaboration, and I was able to capitalize on that. One of the first projects I took on was as a collaborator with two Peabody colleagues through the Theater Chamber Players: Phyllis Bryn-Julson, with whom I had been working for so long, and John Shirley-Quirk. We did Schumann song cycles: "Liederkreis" and "Dichterliebe" for John and "Frauenliebe und -Leben" for Phyllis. I hadn't played those songs for a long time, but they were still in my fingers; I had learned them with Marjorie, my long-ago teenage love. Now, Phyllis and John and I performed them on TCP concerts and made a recording. It was my first two-handed recording in decades, and I took it as a compliment that one reviewer called my playing the strongest thing on it, without seeming to realize that I'd ever been away.

That was the year Tanglewood did one of its big galas. Someone realized that Seiji Ozawa was turning sixty, Itzhak Perlman fifty, and Yo-Yo Ma forty all in the same year. The result was a massive Tanglewood event called the "Three Birthdays," with special guests like Teddy Kennedy and James Taylor and John Williams to help celebrate the birthday boys. As chance would have it, I was the only real birthday boy: I turned sixty-seven the day of the concert. And I may have gotten the biggest present of all. I played the first movement of the Brahms B-Major piano trio with Itzhak and Yo-Yo. Yo-Yo was kind enough to say that he had dreamed of playing with me all his life. It was a very moving moment. I also, at Seiji's urging, played K. 414 at Tanglewood that summer. "Not only is he back," one woman in the audience said after the concert, in the hearing of a critic, "but he's better than ever." That was very sweet of her. I try not to pay too much attention to that kind of thing. But now I felt I was basking in the warmth of it all.

As for my own lifelong dream, I had been dreaming it for so many decades that it had become imprinted into my brain, like a shadow image burned into a television screen. I dreamed of play-ing the Brahms D Minor again. To sit with an orchestra and feel the fist shaking at the heavens and play all of the heroic drama and the shadows and the lyrical beauty of that monumental, touchstone piece. It was my piece. It was in my blood. It was so familiar, such an old friend, it seemed impossible that it would let me down. I wanted it so badly that I almost didn't care if it did. I wanted it so badly that I was precipitate. I agreed to open the San Francisco Symphony's 1996–97 season with a performance of the Brahms D Minor, with Michael Til-son Thomas conducting.

The Brahms D Minor concerto is about human will. I never felt it more truly than I felt it at that moment, on the stage where I had made my debut at fifteen. I can't describe how it felt to hear that open-ing snarl of defiance from the orchestra, with adrenaline and emotion flooding every pore of my body. It was one moment in my life that seemed too good to be true, and if I made mistakes, it was almost the equivalent of pinching myself, making sure I was still on earth.

It wasn't a perfect performance, I know. There were things I couldn't do as well as I could when I had first played that concerto on the same stage in 1944. There were fine points I may not have been able to bring off quite as I might have wanted. I might not have thun-dered as much as I did when I was young. And I overcompensated, by overplaying, in places.

But I think I brought more to it, too. I was bringing decades of experience. My relationship with music had evolved. The problems no longer seemed so frustrating; I knew I could find answers. I knew more in general than I had known when I first played that concerto. I knew something more about tone, and sound, and how to think about them. I knew something more about pain. I knew something more about defiance of the gods. And I think I knew something more about beauty, or about raising an awed prayer of thanks to the woman you love.

There were deficits in that performance. But oh, it felt wonderful. The wild dance of the final movement. Or the slow, silvery second movement, its music rising to the stars.

The "Three Birthdays" concert was a Tanglewood highlight. There were others, too. Physical developments on the campus were continuing. A year after the opening of Ozawa Hall, the TMC opened a new administrative center in a renovated building that was officially named the Leon Fleisher Carriage House. It was a touching tribute. But I said, only half in jest, that I trusted that the plaque with my name on it was removable.

For storm clouds were gathering over my summer idyll. Tanglewood was changing. The change was actually abrupt, and it was painful. What really happened, I think, is that Seiji briefly lost his mind.

It really began with the Wynton Marsalis debacle. For a lot of us—including the kids who were involved in playing the project—that was kind of a lost summer. But Seiji was infuriated at our resistance, and even more infuriated that we turned out to be right. The series was edited and released and broadcast, but it didn't exactly set the world on fire. For Seiji, it began a kind of me-against-them mentality that was ultimately to bring irrevocable change to all of Tanglewood.

It's always hard to know what's going on with Seiji. When he was young, he was the epitome of a new wind in classical music: long hair and flower-child beads and a special kind of crackling energy. He was also Japanese at a time when there weren't a lot of

Asian conductors in the West. In short, he was a real trailblazer, a role model. By the 1990s, however, he was an elder statesman. He'd been at the head of the BSO for years. His strengths and weaknesses were known. As in any relationship, some complacency had set in. And it was still difficult to know exactly what he was thinking. For all of his years in the West, Seiji has remained very Japanese: he has remained closely bound up with his country, his culture, and even his language. His lack of English skills made it difficult for him to express what he wanted. Add to this a deep-seated dislike of confrontation and an avoidance of the word *no*, and you can run into serious difficulties in communication.

Seiji was restless. He knew there were people who felt he was overstaying his welcome in Boston. But he didn't have any other big offers coming in; there was no logical next step for him. And he felt the need to do something new. That something new, it appeared, was going to be Tanglewood. For decades, Seiji had been very happy to let Tanglewood, specifically the TMC, hum along under Gunther Schuller, under me, and under all the other administrators who kept it operating. He was supremely uninvolved. But suddenly, in the mid-1990s, he decided the school was his chance to leave his mark and create a legacy. The opening of Ozawa Hall may have inspired him. And the reaction to the Marsalis project was a further goad. He decided that the school had grown stagnant. And he decided that it was up to him, as the BSO music director, to step up, get more involved, and start to make some of the changes he thought were necessary.

We could all tell that Seiji wasn't happy. There were sinister looks. There were mutterings. But it was hard to tell exactly what kinds of changes he was looking for. New ideas? Different programs?

I asked him one day, point-blank. "What do you want, Seiji?"

"I don't know," he said. There was a long pause while he thought. Finally he said, "Tabasco sauce."

I think that he was actually talking about himself. His own reputation had changed, and he wasn't bringing the Tabasco sauce any more.

His performances were no longer seen as a burst of spice in the cultural buffet. He was aware of this on some level, and he didn't like it.
He wanted the Tabasco back. So he took it out on Tanglewood.

By 1996, I had been at Tanglewood for eleven years. Most of the
core faculty and administrators had been there longer than I had. It's
true that we were largely a group of white males (with a couple of
women) of an older generation. But as an institution, the school was
doing wonderful things. The contemporary music festival was going
great guns, first under Ollie Knussen and then, after he left, under
Reinbert de Leeuw, who did every bit as good a job as Ollie had done.
We even realized our long-held dream of mounting an opera, putting
on *Peter Grimes* for the fiftieth anniversary of the work's first Tanglewood performance. And we had top people teaching every year.

For me, the main issue was about upholding tradition. Tanglewood represented a certain standard of excellence. In my view, it was
important that it be free from the constraints of the outside world,
a place where students could explore and learn and grow. But Seiji
was very aware of the modern world. He kept wanting to open the
school up a little bit to other influences. Marsalis. Or James Taylor. Or
Marcus Roberts, a jazz pianist. Seiji had Marcus Roberts come in and
do a version of Gershwin's "Rhapsody in Blue" arranged for his jazz
trio. I thought that kind of thing was atrocious. I love jazz and I love
Gershwin, but I have no patience for someone coming in and making inferior arrangements of great music in the name of winning over
a public. Let the public hear the real thing and make up their own
minds. That's how I see it.

I may have had a certain complacency myself. By now, Tanglewood was so much a part of the fabric of my life that I simply couldn't
imagine anything changing in my relationship to it. I remember Seiji
looking around at a faculty meeting and saying, aloud, "Just because
you have a house here doesn't mean you're going to be at Tanglewood
forever." I heard him say it, and it registered. I just never dreamed it
could mean me. I thought he was referring to everybody else.

His meaning was brought home, though, when in the fall of 1996 he fired Richard Ortner.

None of us could figure out why. Richard had tried to support Seiji. He had tried to reconcile us all to the Marsalis project. But he had also tried to let Seiji know about some of our concerns, and Seiji apparently saw this as disloyalty. He viewed Richard as the ringleader, in effect, of what he was coming to regard as the faculty clique. The firing left us all reeling, and Seiji didn't make any attempts to reassure anybody when we reconvened the following summer. He informed us, "This summer will be a test for us all." I suggested to him later that his attitude was making people anxious and afraid. "A little fear is a good thing," he said. This was something out of a bad movie, not the Tanglewood I loved.

It was a devastating test. A lot of us had given a huge chunk of our professional lives to the school. Gil Kalish had a chart in his office where he kept track of all the students, their lessons, their coachings, to make sure their needs were being met. It was hard to hear that somehow we were seen as failing the school. Still, we tried to address Seiji's concerns. We held faculty meetings and attempted to figure out what he wanted, and how to give it to him, through all of that long, sad summer. We were, all of us, perplexed. One thing Seiji emphasized was that he wanted BSO musicians to take a more active role in teaching at the TMC. We all thought this was a reasonable idea, and in fact we had already taken steps to implement it before the summer began. It wasn't clear, though, that Seiji noticed.

Our efforts were pretty much a waste of everybody's time. Seiji had made up his mind. Something was wrong with the way things were. Those of us who had been there for a long time appeared, in his mind, to represent the problem. It did no good to point out that there hadn't seemed to be any problem until he made one.

By the end of the summer, everything was strained to the breaking point. It wasn't really a surprise that things started to snap.

First, Gil Kalish resigned. He felt he had been treated outrageously, and he saw the writing on the wall. He wrote Seiji a blistering letter of resignation, and he made it public. Most of the faculty felt he was speaking for them.

Almost immediately after that, Seiji announced that a new position had been created. A woman named Ellen Highstein was now the director of the Tanglewood Music Center, and all faculty would report to her. Gil's resignation seemed prescient: neither he nor I had been consulted about this appointment. There were no explanations, either publicly or in private, about what happened to my role as artistic director if Ms. Highstein was now director. I was as much in the dark as anybody. Nobody had made any effort to reach out to me, or explain, or talk to me about it. It would have been hard to send any clearer a signal that I wasn't wanted.

All those long years of collaboration, mutual respect, and something that had felt almost like a friendship appeared to count for nothing. I wouldn't have minded so much if Seiji had told me he wanted me to go away. But to hear about it at second hand, in effect, was humiliating. In person, Seiji couldn't even talk openly about what had happened. He just said he wanted me to stay on in an advisory capacity, as a teacher and chamber music coach.

I worked for a long time on my letter of farewell—as long as I had worked on any of the Tanglewood opening addresses. That was fitting enough: after so many greetings, this was a final good-bye. I didn't consider it a resignation letter; I felt I had already been unceremoniously fired. It took a number of attempts just to start to channel my fury. I couldn't believe that a colleague would treat me like this. I couldn't believe that my hard work was ignored, dismissed, denigrated. The orchestra had gone on the defensive by making veiled reference to some of my weaknesses: the implication was that I wasn't a great administrator, that I wasn't a great conductor, that students complained about playing under me. And this from Seiji, who had brought me in to conduct his orchestra in Japan for years because he thought I had so much to offer. From Seiji, who had helped convince me to take a job I wasn't, at first, sure I wanted.

Now he was asking me to stay on in some kind of ceremonial puppet role. I told him in my letter what I thought of that. It was, I wrote, "somewhat akin to having my legs chopped off at the knees, you then gently taking me by the arm and inviting me for a stroll. I must decline the invitation."

I was devastated at the loss of Tanglewood. It had become a cornerstone of my identity, a way that my life made sense to me. It represented to me one component of the balance and equilibrium that I had come to, with Kathy, relatively late in life. I had put so much of myself into the school. To have to uproot myself, sell our house, leave town, lose the regular connection to so many people I had come to respect and even love was deeply painful. It wasn't the first time in my life that something I loved deeply was ripped away from me without warning. It was no easier to take at sixty-nine than it had been at thirty-six. Of course, there was no dip in my outside activities. I kept right on performing, and playing, and teaching around the globe. But the pain was intense. For the first time, I felt a tinge of something wintry, the onset of old age.

It's funny how joy and sadness can be juxtaposed in life. At the same time as I was mourning the loss of Tanglewood, I was fulfilling some of my greatest dreams. I was playing again. Playing real concertos. Fiercely exhilarated to be sitting again, on stage, communing with the music I loved. I had never thought it would happen. Nobody had ever thought it would happen. People would approach me backstage with tears in their eyes: people who remembered hearing me play in the 1950s, people who had grown up on my recordings and never heard me play at all.

I worked like a dog, tenaciously, ferociously, patiently. It took work and focus to play now, almost beyond anything I'd mustered before. It would be a lie to say that I had figured out how to deal with my hand. I was still learning how to deal with my restrictions, in performance, to work around the things I couldn't do, to understand that what worked on one day might not work the next. Every performance was an adventure into the unknown. I was excited, and stubborn, and took on a ridiculous amount: both Brahms concertos and Beethoven's "Emperor" concerto, the things I'd wanted to play again before I died. I was seventy years old. What did I have to lose?

I played the Brahms D Minor concerto in Florida. I played it in Hartford. I played it in Vancouver, with my old friend Sergiu Comissiona—one of the few active conductors who had already conducted me in a two-handed performance. I played it under Danny Barenboim in Berlin. There were missed notes. But I knew I was getting to things in the music that I'd never reached before as a young man. A lot of my listeners knew it too.

Brahms seemed to sit well with my hand. His music tends to focus on chords more than on passages of rapid scales: a lot of the playing is about solidity rather than virtuoso fireworks. The chamber music became particularly rewarding. I was able to start performing rather a lot of that. I would take it one piece at a time: the C Major trio, the C Minor quartet, the F Minor quintet. Communicating with my colleagues through those scores was music making at another level—one I couldn't reach in the practice room at home or even on the podium in front of an orchestra. I felt I had grown up with Brahms, and now I was growing old with him. There's a famous picture of Brahms in his sixties, bearded, sitting raptly at the piano, arms outstretched. I could identify with that.

My solo recitals had evolved, too. I wasn't about to subject my hand, or my listeners, to a whole evening of two-handed music. Instead, I let my programs reflect me: the years of left-handed repertory, and the two-handed pieces encroaching, little by little. I would open with "Jesu, Joy of Man's Desiring," because I thought that everybody should be able to hear that music at least once a day, and I often played Brahms's Opus 39 waltzes. But I also kept some of the left-handed pieces that had been written for me. For my seventieth birthday, George Perle wrote me a left-handed solo piece called "Musical Offerings." The reference was to Bach's Musical Offering, a set of pieces he wrote for Frederick the Great that are full of games and allusions and intricate tricks of counterpoint. George's title played with the ambiguity of the word *offering*, which can mean "gift" but also "sacrifice." The work was in three short movements, and each was dedicated to one of my "fallen" colleagues at Tanglewood: Richard Ortner, Gil Kalish, and Dan Gustin, who had finally lost his job at the festival as well. It was a beautiful and bittersweet piece, and I was happy to play it.

My summers were hardly empty. When I left Tanglewood, there were plenty of institutions ready to welcome me with open arms.

I had played at the Aspen Music School and Festival a few times over the years. Now David Zinman, the BSO's music director whom I admire so greatly, had become artistic director there as well. David gave me carte blanche at Aspen. He invited me to come out and stay and teach and just be an éminence grise during the summers. I quite enjoyed that. Aspen, a thriving ski resort in the winter, is stunningly beautiful: all jewel-like greens and blues and snow-capped mountains glinting in the thin, crystalline air. That air is a little too thin: the altitude can give some people problems. One summer I played the Brahms D Minor there, and I definitely felt I was at a disadvantage. The next week, I played the concerto at Ravinia—under the same conductor, Iván Fischer—and I had no problem at all. After that, I told my manager that I play only at sea level or lower.

But if you can take the air, Aspen is another one of those flashpoints where musicians gather and great performances happen. There's a sense of freedom about a festival: you're outside the normal working constraints, the pattern of rehearsal, rehearsal, concert. The word *festival* has been rather misappropriated in the United States, in fact. In Europe, the great festivals—Salzburg, Glyndebourne, Bayreuth—used to be even better prepared than regular season concerts, but in the States, sometimes a "festival" seems merely like an excuse to have fewer rehearsals. I can remember back to when there were hardly any festivals at all—just Ravinia and Tanglewood and the Hollywood Bowl. And Aspen came along in 1949. Now there are festivals everywhere. It's great when they're able to keep them small and exclusive, like Marlboro, where you are working to the very highest standard. The problem with a place like Aspen, which doesn't have an orchestra keeping it up like Tanglewood does, is that they have to accept a lot of students in order to make it financially viable, and it's gotten very big.

But I loved my time in Aspen. And now that I was able to use two hands, I was able to really enjoy musical encounters with my colleagues as I hadn't been able to before. I remember playing one of the Brahms piano quartets with Michael Tree, of the Guarneri Quartet, on viola, and Cho-Liang Lin on violin, and Lynn Harrell on cello. Lynn got his start in the Cleveland Orchestra, but I knew him best as the son of Mack Harrell, who was a wonderful singer in New York when I was young. The group that Schnabel was involved with, New Friends of Music, would put on one of the Bach Passions every year, and Mack always had a prominent role. He died, tragically, very young, when Lynn was only fifteen, and Lynn, who lost his mother two years later, ended up in Cleveland as a protégé of Szell, who had worked with his father at the Met. Lynn left the orchestra and began a solo career in 1971, but when we met we immediately bonded through our memories of Szell. What I remember most about playing with him is the extraordinary, massive sound that comes out of his cello. Sitting at the piano, I could hardly hear Michael: it was as if Lynn's playing had erected a wall of sound between us.

I met young artists, too, at Aspen, like the conductor Alan Gilbert, who was already making waves then and has now taken over as music director of the New York Philharmonic. Alan is a great guy. He would literally give you the shirt off his back. And I mean that. One time when I was in Aspen, my dinner jacket didn't come back from the cleaners in time for my performance. Alan lent me his.

All of the playing I was doing was tremendously exciting. But the more I played, the more aware I was that my hand wasn't actually cured. In fact, I was more eager than ever to find new solutions.

One summer I went over to Switzerland to work in a program headed up by a doctor named Ed Taub, along with a physical therapist named Victor Candia, who was doing research on musicians with disabilities. Victor had been a classical guitarist until he was incapacitated by what appeared to be a crippling hand problem very much like mine. He responded by getting a degree in psychology and starting intensive research into the condition. Ed and Victor wired me up with all manner of electrodes in some kind of earthquake-proof, tornado-proof, everything-proof chamber, until I felt like a character from the movie *Alien*. They also had an exoskeletal device that I wore on my hand, which immobilized certain fingers and left other fingers free. They were quite convinced of its efficacy but said it would take time. They were talking in terms of a year or two, to retrain the brain. And time, as I moved into my seventies, was one commodity I didn't feel I had that much of.

I needed something that would work more quickly. My hand was still curling. Even after several years of playing with it, it wasn't doing what I wanted. With Rolfing and with fierce concentration, I was able to bring my fingers into submission, for limited periods of time. It was an act of pure will. Playing was not easy for me, and it wasn't getting any easier. Sometimes I toyed with giving it up altogether: I had had my two-handed fling. Maybe that was enough.

But I found myself thinking more and more of Dr. Hallett's program at the NIH.

By now, Botox was in common use in cosmeticians' offices the world over. Clearly I didn't need to be scared of it. I had also observed that more musicians were coming up to me and thanking me for being outspoken about my problem. Indeed, I knew other musicians who were being sidelined with it. It wasn't only Gary Graffman. Peter Oundjian, first violinist of the Tokyo Quartet, began having trouble with his left hand in the 1980s and by 1995 had to leave the quartet. The diagnosis: focal dystonia. Peter did the logical thing, throwing himself into developing a career as a conductor. Reinhard Goebel, the German violinist who founded the ensemble Musica Antiqua Köln: same thing. Today he's a conductor as well.

I had been uncomfortable with the focal dystonia diagnosis. But more and more, it looked like focal dystonia was the best description for what I had—especially when I met other people with the same problem.

I had been reassured countless times over the years that whatever was wrong with me, it wasn't in my head. In my heart of hearts, though, I had been dogged with a recurring terror that my problem was somehow of my own doing. It was so mysterious, so elusive. It wasn't consistent. Sometimes I could play for a little while before the fingers began to curl. Sometimes they were intractable. I had worked, over and over, to free myself from the shame, the sense of stigma. When Gary Graffman developed the same problem, I was briefly reassured. But it was hard to silence the demons within, poking at me with questions about whether I had somehow made the whole thing up.

But focal dystonia was real. If it were purely psychosomatic, there wouldn't be, there couldn't be so many other musicians suffering from the same thing.

I think I reached the final stage of acceptance when I embraced the name for my condition. I had focal dystonia. There was no cure. But there was something I could do about it. I went back to the NIH and started getting Botox shots again.

At first, of course, nothing happened. I went home and waited. The first day, little movement. The second day, some more. By now the years of Rolfing, and of playing, had opened up my hand. The muscles were no longer rigid. And by the end of the week, I could hold my hand outstretched. It looked almost like a normal hand. It felt almost like a normal hand. I began to play. It was there. It was back.

Botox is a poison that cures. It's the best metaphor I can think of for something bad that ends up doing something good. Thus it's a perfect symbol for what happened with my right hand. It was a horrible, devastating blow. Yet ultimately it changed my life—and changed me—for the better.

I will never be cured. I have focal dystonia; I am dystonic. Even Botox doesn't entirely take away the problem; I have to accommodate to what my hand can do, every time I play. But I can live with it. Over the years, my affliction had been a heavy burden and then a burden I had learned to shift, and carry, in smaller and smaller segments. Botox melted the rest of it away. Some days are better, some days are worse. Every few months, the Botox wears off and my fingers curl up and I go back to get another shot. But there's no more affliction. There's just the way I am.

And there's the music. I can access the music. In the end, for me, that's what really counts.

Life became richer than ever. And it's stayed that way. I travel the world. I've led student orchestras in Singapore and master classes in Shanghai; I've played Brahms in the Swiss Alps and in the center of Paris. I've run into Manny Ax in a restaurant in Tokyo; I've played Mozart in Mozart's hometown of Salzburg, with its narrow cobblestone streets and Baroque churches very much as they were in his day. In 2002, I went back to Cadenabbia, on Lake Como, for a piano institute that was created on the model of Schnabel's, in his memory. It was as if the clock had been turned back, with the blue water and the Alps in the distance and the sounds of pianos wafting out over the veranda. The only difference was that I had a harder time climbing the steps.

When I'm home, I crowd my days with back-to-back lessons with my Peabody students, making up for all the time that I'm away. When we can, Kathy and I go out to dinner, or try to take in a play—we love the theater—or go for long walks with our dogs. Of course there are social engagements: dinners with friends, benefit fund-raisers for animal rescue or our political beliefs—we were involved in an Obama benefit at the Meyerhoff that brought in more than $1 million—or family gatherings like the big bashes we had for my seventieth and then my eightieth birthdays. For the latter, Julian had T-shirts made up with the familiar iconic image of Che Guevara, the bearded revolutionary, slightly altered so that instead of Che's face, you saw mine.

At home, I watch a certain amount of TV. I'm a *Law and Order* addict. I think those shows are very much akin to Bach fugues in their self-contained elegance. I work on my scores for conducting engagements, like Ligeti's *Aventures* and *Nouvelles Aventures*, which I found myself doing again thirty years after I first did them with the Theater Chamber Players. It was funny how the music had continued to develop within me all that time. And of course I still practice. I keep meaning to have my old piano fixed. It's about to fall apart.

I've made a point of taking on projects that sound like fun.

Every year or so, I play with Jaime Laredo, on his series at the 92nd Street Y in New York. That has been a way to keep indulging my love of chamber music. Michael Tree was one of his regular violists, and I think it was Michael who came up with the idea of putting together a concert based on the Brahms trio for horn, violin, and piano. Michael had a special relationship to that trio. Back in the days of Marlboro, he and Rudi Serkin and Myron Bloom (who became the first horn in Cleveland under Szell) made a recording of the piece that's still widely seen as definitive. Now he had the idea that David Jolley, who's a first-rate horn player, and he and I could get together for a program with that trio and a couple of other pieces. I thought it sounded like fun. I think that's the ideal way to approach making music: a few colleagues exploring an idea just for the heck of it, without any real thought of the commercial benefits. So we formed the Fleisher-Jolley-Tree-O, and took it on the road.

It was indeed a lot of fun. With Michael, it was guaranteed to be fun, because Michael is one of the great raconteurs. He's like Scheherazade—one story after another, leaving you in stitches. We were sitting in an airport once waiting for our flight, and Michael was regaling us with anecdote after anecdote. Finally the gate agent asked us where we were going, and we told him, and he let us know that our plane had already left the gate. We hadn't heard the announcement because we were laughing too hard. They couldn't bring the plane back to the gate, because they would have had to unload all the baggage, so we had to walk out across the tarmac. The other passengers were not amused.

I wish I had that gift. I can't tell stories well. I always mess up the punch line.

I played a few times with my kids. My kids have grown up to be amazing people. I am in awe of them: their variety, their depths, their accomplishments. Julian is a terrific nightclub-cabaret-style singer in New York with a group he's dubbed the Rather Big Band. I find his skills just amazing. I brought him and the band down a couple of times to perform at benefits for the Theater Chamber Players, with, in Julian's parlance, "Papa Fleisher tickling the ivories." It was a lot of fun, though not enough to keep the TCP from disbanding a few years later. We had a good run of thirty-five years. It was just too much work to keep it going.

Then I went down to Florida for a concert in a synagogue with my Opus 1 kids: Deborah, Dickie (along with Kayo), and Leah. It was a moment of great pride for a father. Deborah and Dickie are both professional harpists. Deborah has her own harp studio and plays all manner of freelance gigs. Sometimes she comes up to Baltimore to sit in on my classes at Peabody, to gather information for her own lessons. It's a wonderful thing to have kids who are musicians, who understand where you're coming from. Occasionally Deborah and I will talk before a concert and I'll confess my potential feelings of nervousness. She always says, "Well, better you than me." And I find that very reassuring. It really does help somehow.

Dickie has played with the Naples Philharmonic for years. Once, the pianist Jeffrey Kahane came to Naples to play the Brahms D Minor concerto and Dickie went up to him at a break in the rehearsal and asked him what his favorite recording was. Jeffrey said that it was the Fleisher/Szell recording, and Dickie said he could tell from the way he played the second movement. He suggested, though, that if Jeffrey really wanted to emulate that recording, he should play very softly, rather than mezzoforte, on the second chord of that movement. Jeffrey thanked him, and did, and the result, Dickie said, gave him goose bumps. But he never told Jeffrey who he was.

Leah lives the closest to me of any of my children. She's a physical therapist in the D.C. area. She specializes in—of all things—occupational injuries to musicians. It's wonderful to have an in-house therapist in the family. It's very useful. She writes out exercises for me to do, and I do them assiduously for several days at a time, and then gradually abandon them. If I kept to the program, I'd probably be in amazing shape by now. She and I are sometimes invited to travel together professionally, I to teach, she to give workshops. It turns out to be a great partnership. But she still plays a fine harp.

We've even done a couple of family appearances with all five kids. The first one was at Aspen. The four harpists—Deborah, Dickie, Leah, and Kayo—played some four-harp arrangements, and Julian sang, and Kathy and I played four-hand piano duets. Paula was the emcee. Paula stayed out of music, which was probably wise. She works at the University of California, devising ways to connect researchers and projects with community centers and clinics where their efforts can be of direct use. One project she's involved in is trying to develop a curriculum that will help train doctors to communicate better with patients, because it is apparent that there tend to be difficulties in that area and there's a need to bridge the gap.

Up on that stage, we looked like one big happy family. I'd dare to say we even felt that way.

And Kathy and I began performing together more and more. For a long time, it seemed we couldn't play well together at all. I had a lot of stress about my hand, and on days when it wasn't working well, I think Kathy sometimes got the brunt of my anxiety. At one particularly argumentative rehearsal, we couldn't agree on the pedaling in a four-handed piece. It's always a bit of a debate: Who pedals? Do you take turns? And when you pedal, do you tend to favor your own part over the other person's? We had sufficient discussions about this that Kathy finally suggested the creation of a new tort law for divorce on the grounds of irreconcilable pedaling.

Eventually, though, we found a way to come together, to let go of our own issues and respect each other. After that, performing together started to be a lot of fun. In fact, we now regularly perform four-hand piano concerts around the world as the "Fleisher Duo." After one performance in Calgary, a reviewer wrote that it was impossible to tell us apart by ear, which made us both very happy.

I kept working on my solo recitals, refining the program to take advantage of my increased flexibility. I wanted to gather pieces that had meant a lot to me personally over the years. I had a scrapbook of left-hand pieces that were very important to me. In addition to George Perle's "Musical Offerings," there was Dina's "Messages" and there was Leon Kirchner's "L.H." After my first, unhappy experience with that piece, I had a bit of a bee in my bonnet about getting it right on stage, and it really is a terrific piece. Then there was the Brahms arrangement of the Bach Chaconne that had sustained me for so long.

I balanced these out with touchstones of the two-handed repertory. I started with another Bach piece that's like a mantra for me, "Sheep May Safely Graze." I kept the Sessions "From My Diary" pieces that had been with me since the beginning of my career. And on the second half of the program, I claimed a piece that was entirely my own: the Schubert B-flat sonata.

I played the recital a few times before I tried it out at Carnegie Hall. I had avoided talk of a "comeback" all these years. I had been careful to temper expectations, to explain that my two-handed play-ing was very much a work in progress. But playing with two hands, alone, on the stage at Carnegie Hall was a pretty definite statement. Not "I'm back." Just "Here I am." All of my friends were there. My family was there. This time, it was a joyous occasion. It was one big celebration.

We even got a little goofy. The concert took place on Halloween. My son Julian wasn't going to pass up the opportunity to dress up just because his father was giving a concert in Carnegie Hall. (I should note that Julian was thirty-seven years old at the time.) He turned up in a gorilla suit, complete with flashing red eyes. I think some people were a little shocked. He was persuaded, or compelled, at least to take the head off while he was listening to the music.

I also wanted to do something fun for the encore, though my efforts were a little thwarted. My original idea was to repeat "Sheep May Safely Graze" and have all my students come with portable tape players containing recordings of sheep baaing, which they would switch on at the appropriate moment so that gentle bleats would rise from every corner of the hall. We were all ready to go with this idea, but it turned out that one wasn't allowed to bring such devices into Carnegie Hall, so we had to scrap it. Instead, I got a big basket of Tootsie Rolls and other Halloween candy and set it out at the front of the stage and told the audience to come help themselves. I was con-sidering grabbing handfuls of candy and throwing them out into the auditorium, but I worried about putting somebody's eye out.

It's important to remember to have fun.

And counterbalancing all the levity was the Schubert sonata, which has its joyful moments, too, but is somehow wiser, looking deeper into the heart of things than the average glance can penetrate. I can't quite let myself go when I play with two hands. I have to be quite clinical about the way I go about it and to plan every move. That keeps me on the ground. But the Schubert sonata is still something special, and playing it gives me a great deal of pleasure.

Dan Gustin, my old colleague and friend from Tanglewood, who now runs the Gilmore festival and prize for talented pianists, came to town for the occasion, and he took me out for a drink the next day. He was very flattering in his praise. He seemed deeply impressed with the Schubert, in particular. "Oh, Leon," he said, "it's better than ever."

"Well, I hope it's better," I said. "The music is not in my fingers. It's in my mind. Of course it's been growing as I've been evolving all these years. I don't need my right hand for that."

After that recital, I felt secure enough to record a solo album—my first solo album of "regular" piano repertory in forty years. It was called, simply, *Two Hands*.

Playing music is a state of grace. It's an ecstasy. And it's a privilege. After I began playing again, I never took it for granted. In all of my rich and varied life, there's still nothing I love more.

I kept going for Botox shots and for Rolfing. My results weren't typical of either treatment. Neither Tessy Brungardt nor the NIH doctors ever had quite the same degree of success with other patients.

I've developed plenty of other problems over the years. I have what they call boutonnière deformity on the index finger of my right hand: the first joint bends down and the second joint, nearest the fingertip, pulls up. It's highly unattractive. It doesn't hurt, but it means that when I try to use that finger it tends to pull the rest of the hand out of balance. So I have to deal with that all the time when I play. Then there's a touch of arthritis. And then there's a problem in the joint of my right hand, at the base of the thumb. The cartilage is gone, so when I move it's basically bone on bone. It hurts like hell, especially when I cross over and cross under, and I have to take lots of aspirin every time I play. At this point, I have so many things wrong with my hand that it's almost as if the dystonia were of secondary importance. I keep thinking I won't need any more Botox injections, because the fingers kind of stay out on their own now. But then there comes a time when my hand gets tired and the fingers start to curl under, and I go in for another shot.

It's a nuisance. But it hasn't held me back. I've been able to play, and record, and perform. I made another solo album, *The Journey*, a title that seemed to describe what I've been through pretty well. Then, in 2009, I released my first two-handed concerto album since the 1960s. I went back to Mozart. Now, thanks to the ubiquity of pirate recordings, you can compare my performance of K. 488 with Bruno Walter in 1949 with the way I sound now, sixty years later. I tend to think that I played much too fast, in general, on my early recordings. I can't say how I sound on my later ones. But to me they hold a kind of joy.

Inevitably, my two-handed comeback did eventually attract a lot of attention. Once I'd been playing for a while, I stopped avoiding the media. I was even quite willing to talk about the problem and became a spokesman for focal dystonia, a kind of poster boy to draw attention to the problem. I hoped that by speaking out I could help save people from some of the doubt and shame and fear I had gone through; just having dystonia is bad enough without feeling stigmatized by it. I appeared on National Public Radio a few times, talking about my return. I was the subject of a couple of documentary films, including *Two Hands*, by Nathaniel Kahn, which was nominated for an Oscar. (Walking down the red carpet, I was flattered to hear cries that sounded like "Leon! Leon!" I was just about to raise my hands in acknowledgment, when I turned around and saw behind me the actual object of the adulation: Leonardo DiCaprio.) And I made a number of appearances on various national television shows. They all wanted to know about my comeback.

Media attention, on that scale, has a way of reducing all the nuances of a story to its basic outlines. I wasn't particularly invested in correcting anybody about details of exactly what happened when. I couldn't keep track of it all myself. I got a Botox shot, and I was cured. That's pretty much what happened. The main thing was that I got to play again, which is a miraculous gift. Every story leaves some things out.

In 2007, I was awarded the Kennedy Center Honors, the highest award that the United States of America can give to an artist.

I did a lot of soul-searching about the Kennedy Center Honors. I didn't agree at all with the policies of the leadership in the United States at that time. I was concerned about appearing to accept an award from an administration I abhorred. I knew I would have to shake hands with President George W. Bush, and, a die-hard liberal all my life, I felt strongly that this would not send a message I wanted to transmit.

But the honor wasn't from my president. It was from my country. My country has given me so much, and I'm proud to be an American. I've tried to give something back over the years. Now this award appeared as a sign that I had made some contribution and that other people recognized it as worthy. It was a symbol of everything I'd worked for all my life.

After days of deliberation, I made my decision. My political feelings were important, but my country was more important. I was proud to accept the Kennedy Center Honors.

I made two gestures to show my feelings toward the regime. I sported a purple ribbon in my lapel as a sign of my dedication to my own beliefs. And I wrote an open letter about my difficulty with the decision, which was later published in the *Washington Post*. I wrestled with that letter for some time, with a lot of input from my children, who understood my feelings very well. To me, that letter was more than an explanation: it was a kind of manifesto of who I am.

I am a musician, one of five artists—the others being Brian Wilson, Steve Martin, Diana Ross and Martin Scorsese—honored recently by the John F. Kennedy Center for the Performing Arts.

The event, a deeply moving and gratifying tribute to the performing arts and artists in America, was broadcast to our nation. But what you couldn't see in that broadcast was how conflicted I felt about being there.

Let me be frank: I was flattered to be included in so distinguished a group and to be recognized for whatever contributions I may have made to American life. I was pleased to be part of an event that raises money for an institution as vital as the Kennedy Center and to be with my family and to see their joy at the ceremony.

What made me unhappy and continues to trouble me was that I was required to attend a White House reception on the afternoon of the gala. I cannot speak for the other honorees, but while I profoundly respect the presidency, I am horrified by many of President Bush's policies.

In the past seven years, Bush administration policies have amounted to a systematic shredding of our nation's Constitution—the illegal war it initiated and perpetuates; the torturing of prisoners; the espousing of "values" that include a careful defense of the "rights" of embryos but show a profligate disregard for the lives of flesh-and-blood human beings; and the flagrant dismantling of environmental protections. These, among many other depressing policies, have left us weak and shamed at home and in the world.

For several weeks before the honors, I wrestled with this dilemma, deciding in the end that I would not attend the reception at the White House. That decision was met with deep, if understandable, disapproval by the powers that be. I was informed that I was hardly the first honoree to express such reserve; cited to me, among others, were Arthur Miller and Isaac Stern during the Reagan years and several during the present administration. I was asked to attend all of the scheduled events and to follow the well-established protocol of silence.

While this might have made for a glamorous experience, it also presented a profound irony. Turning a blind eye to the political undercurrents of the event dismantles the very force of art in this country that the honors celebrate: the freedom, nay, the obligation to express oneself honestly and without fear. Ultimately, there is no greater honor than that freedom.

In the end, I decided to attend wearing a peace symbol around my neck and a purple ribbon on my lapel, at once showing support for our young men and women in the armed services and calling for their earliest return home. My family did the *same, as did a number of fellow attendees who, over the weekend's various events, asked me for ribbons of their own.*

I had no wish to pressure or embarrass the other honorees. I did not want to disappoint my family, and I certainly did not want to embarrass or injure the Kennedy Center, where I have performed for decades and which is named for an American whom I greatly admired. As President John F. Kennedy said, "The life of the arts, far from being an interruption, a distraction, in the life of a nation is close to the center of a nation's purpose—and is a test of the quality of a nation's civilization."

I can't say yet whether these small gestures were or will be sufficient to neutralize the sense of regret that came with having agreed to follow protocol. Time, one hopes, will tell. And there is, of course, much more to do.

I am nearly 80 years old and have been making music for almost all of that time, sustained by the belief that, in the words that Beethoven inscribed in his copy of the "Missa Solemnis," the purpose of music is to communicate from the heart to the heart. Beethoven's vision of music as a force capable of reconciling us to each other and to the world may today seem remote, but that renders it an ever more crucial ideal for which to strive.

Therefore I am making known the dilemma I faced during my most celebrated hours. Perhaps speaking about my internal struggle will loosen the ties that bind future honorees—not to mention the generations of artists they mentor and for which they serve as models—from the code of silence that has pervaded this pinnacle of artistic recognition.

Some seven decades separate the time when older people would tell me that I played very well for my age from the occasions nowadays when younger people say the same thing. That time seems to have flown by, and I have come, perhaps inevitably, to understand the aphorism "Ars longa, vita brevis." Yes, art is long. And life is short. And I am waiting most impatiently for Jan. 20, 2009.

Letter or no letter, not all of my friends agreed with my decision. After I shook hands with President George W. Bush, my old friend Dina Koston, by now frail and aging but no less committed to her liberal political views, hardly spoke to me again for the rest of her life. I made my peace with the decision, though. It was an honor to be recognized by the country I loved. It was one of the happiest days of my life.

My whole family gathered at the Kennedy Center in Washington for the ceremony. Kathy and all of my children were there, sporting purple ribbons. They made me even prouder than I was already. My two grandchildren were there as well: Deborah brought her beautiful daughter, Lena, then just at the beginning of her teen years, and Paula and her spouse, Lucy, brought their son, Harry, the baby of the family. My children and I have had a chance to get even closer as I get older. As my eightieth birthday approached, the kids and Kathy got together and agreed that I shouldn't travel alone, so they all take turns going with me on my various trips. It's been a wonderful chance to have some close time with them all. Harry particularly looked forward to a trip to Taiwan we all took one winter, when I participated in a chamber music workshop that the cellist David Finckel and pianist Wu Han set up in emulation of Isaac Stern's Encounters in Jerusalem, which we had all enjoyed so much. Harry, who was nine at the time, looked forward to it not just because it was a big trip but because it gave him a chance to speak Chinese. He attends a bilingual Chinese school in San Francisco, and he's quite fluent. It was a wonderful trip. Not only was Harry generally adored as the only kid in the group, but he caused general astonishment on a regular basis when he, a little fair-haired Caucasian boy, would address the people around us in fluent Chinese.

Somehow, we've all become one family. Somehow, we all love one another. Somehow, my children seem to have been able to forgive me for everything I wasn't able to be for them when they were young. They may see me the way I see the current state of my hand. It's not perfect but it's yours, and if you make the best of it, you can find quite a lot of happiness in spite of all the flaws.

And of course Kathy, my anchor, was at my side, greeting, conversing, beaming: my radiant, beautiful wife.

The weekend passed in a blur. We all got red-carpet treatment.

There were receptions. There were dignitaries. We kept seeing people like Teddy Kennedy and Colin Powell and Condoleezza Rice, who at one function got up and said, "I want everybody to know that when I was a sophomore in college I wanted to be a piano major, and then I listened to Leon Fleisher's recording of the Brahms D Minor concerto, and it was better than I could ever hope to be, and that's why I decided I didn't want to be a piano major any more." I was touched.

The sense of being in a movie only intensified when we entered the Kennedy Center Concert Hall and took our places of honor to receive tributes honoring our life's work.

I was seated in a concert hall filled with a glittering, glamorous crowd, as I had been so many times before. I was used to the hum of voices, and the adrenaline, and the TV cameras panning over the crowd. This time, though, I wasn't on stage. It wasn't up to me to perform. This time, I got to sit back and receive, rather than prepare to give, as the lights went down.

And suddenly there I was, up on the stage, aged seven, with a bright-eyed smile.

They had prepared short biographical films about each of the honorees. So I sat in the Kennedy Center, on national television, and watched my life literally pass before my eyes. San Francisco. My mother and me on the boat to Italy. Me and Schnabel. Me making my Philharmonic debut. Playing with George Szell. Conducting. Teaching. Learning to play again.

The film was introduced by a member of classical music's elite, the cellist Yo-Yo Ma. In his remarks, he mentioned one thing that wasn't covered in the film but that was so central to my life: the Brahms D Minor concerto. I was glad he managed to include that. He said that when he heard me play it, he felt me physically grappling with primal forces while drawing upon the deep regenerating energy of the universe. That sounded like a description of my life, too.

Or lives.

In conclusion, Yo-Yo looked up at me, in the box, with an impish smile.

"They say that cats have nine lives," he said. "You've had at least three, Leon. I look forward to the next six."

"Three?" I wanted to say. "I've had a lot more than three lives already."

But it didn't matter. Three, six, or nine: it was a lot of wonderful life. And any protest I might have raised was washed away in the roar of my country's applause.

DISCOGRAPHY

The authors have compiled a group of highlights of specific musical excerpts discussed in this book at the Web site http://knopfdoubleday .com/leonfleisher

STUDIO RECORDINGS

Original release information is given here; release date does not necessarily reflect the date of the recording. Many of these recordings have been reissued many times since the original release date and are currently available from other labels. On compilation albums, only works featuring Leon Fleisher are listed. Leon Fleisher is the piano soloist except where otherwise indicated.

In 2008, for Leon Fleisher's eightieth birthday, Sony rereleased six of his classic recordings on Arkivmusic.com. At the time of publication, all six were still for sale on the Arkivmusic.com Web site; the recordings in question are marked in the list below with an asterisk (*).

Columbia ML 5061*
Franz Schubert: Sonata for Piano in B-flat Major, D. 960
Franz Schubert: Deutsche Tänze, D. 790
(1956)

Epic LC 3356/Philips A 00365
Szymon Goldberg, Netherlands Chamber Orchestra
Paul Hindemith: *The Four Temperaments:* Theme with Four Variations for Piano and Strings
(1956)

Epic LC 3330
George Szell, Cleveland Orchestra
César Franck: *Symphonic Variations* for Piano and Orchestra
Sergei Rachmaninoff: Rhapsody on a Theme of Paganini in A Minor for Piano
    and Orchestra
(1957)

Epic LC 3331
Johannes Brahms: Variations and Fugue on a Theme of Händel, Op. 24
Johannes Brahms: Waltzes, Op. 39
(1956)

Epic LC 3484/BC 1003
George Szell, Cleveland Orchestra
Johannes Brahms: Concerto No. 1 in D Minor, Op. 15
(1958)

Epic LC 3554
Claude Debussy: Suite bergamasque
Maurice Ravel: Sonatine
Maurice Ravel: Valses nobles et sentimentales
Maurice Ravel: Miroirs: Alborada del gracioso
(1959)

Epic LC 3574/BC 1025
George Szell, Cleveland Orchestra
Wolfgang Amadeus Mozart: Concerto No. 25 in C Major, K. 503
Ludwig van Beethoven: Concerto for Piano No. 4 in G Major, Op. 58
(1959)

Epic LC 3584*
Wolfgang Amadeus Mozart: Piano Sonata in C Major, K. 330
Wolfgang Amadeus Mozart: Piano Sonata in E-flat Major, K. 282
Wolfgang Amadeus Mozart: Rondo in D Major, K. 485
(1959)

Epic LC 3675/BC 1066*
Franz Liszt: Sonata for Piano in B Minor, S. 178

Carl Maria von Weber: Sonata No. 4 in E Minor, Op. 70
(1960)

Epic LC 3689/BC 1080
George Szell, Cleveland Orchestra
Edvard Grieg: Concerto for Piano in A Minor, Op. 16
Robert Schumann: Concerto for Piano and Orchestra in A Minor, Op. 54
(1960)

Columbia ML 5636/MS 6236
Benita Valente, soprano; Marlena Kleinman, alto; Wayne Connor, tenor; Martial
    Singher, bass; Rudolf Serkin, piano
Johannes Brahms: Liebeslieder Walzer, Op. 52
(1961)

Epic LC 3788/BC 1136
George Szell, Cleveland Orchestra
Ludwig van Beethoven: Concerto No. 1 in C Major, Op. 15
(1961)

Epic LC 3789/BC 1137
George Szell, Cleveland Orchestra
Ludwig van Beethoven: Concerto No. 2 in B-flat Major, Op. 19
(1961)

Epic LC 3790/BC 1138
George Szell, Cleveland Orchestra
Ludwig van Beethoven: Concerto No. 3 in C Minor, Op. 37
(1961)

Epic LC 3791/BC 1139
George Szell, Cleveland Orchestra
Ludwig van Beethoven: Concerto No. 5 in E-flat Major, Op. 73, "Emperor"
(1961)

Epic LC 3853/BC 1253
George Szell, Cleveland Orchestra (Jules Eskin, cello)

Johannes Brahms: Piano Concerto No. 2 in B-flat Major, Op. 83
(1963)

Epic LC 3862/BC 1262*
Aaron Copland: Piano Sonata
Leon Kirchner: Piano Sonata
Ned Rorem: Three Barcarolles
Roger Sessions: From My Diary
(1963)

Epic LC 3865/BC 1265*
Juilliard String Quartet
Johannes Brahms: Quintet in F Minor for Piano and Strings, Op. 34
(1963)

Epic LC 3874/BC 1274
Franz Schubert: "Wanderer" Fantasy in C Major, D. 760
Franz Schubert: Piano Sonata in A Major, D. 664
(1963)

Desto DC-7168
Sergiu Comissiona, Baltimore Symphony Orchestra
Benjamin Britten: *Diversions* for Piano (Left Hand) and Orchestra, Op. 21
(1973)

Vanguard Classics VA 25014
Sergiu Comissiona, Baltimore Symphony Orchestra
Maurice Ravel: Concerto for Piano (Left Hand) in D Major
(1982)

Sony Classical 47188
Seiji Ozawa, Boston Symphony Orchestra
Maurice Ravel: Concerto for Piano (Left Hand) in D Major
Sergei Prokofiev: Concerto No. 4 for Piano (Left Hand) in B-flat Major, Op. 53
Benjamin Britten: *Diversions* for Piano (Left Hand) and Orchestra, Op. 21
(1993)

Sony Classical 48081
Piano Works for the Left Hand
Johann Sebastian Bach, arr. Johannes Brahms: Chaconne from Partita II for
    Violin in D Minor, BWV 1004
Felix Blumenfeld: Etude for Piano Left Hand in A-flat Major, Op. 36
Leopold Godowsky: Symphonic Metamorphoses of Themes from Strauss's *The
    Gypsy Baron*
Camille Saint-Saëns: Six Etudes for Piano Left Hand, Op. 135
Robert Saxton: Chacony for Piano Left Hand
Alexander Scriabin: Two Pieces for Piano Left Hand, Op. 9
Jenó Takács: Toccata and Fugue for Piano Left Hand, Op. 56
(1993)

Mode 42
The Musical Railism of Anne LeBaron
The Kennedy Center Chamber Players (Leon Fleisher, conductor)
Anne LeBaron: The Sea and the Honeycomb
(1995)

Arabesque 6700
Phyllis Bryn-Julson, soprano; John Shirley-Quirk, bass-baritone
Robert Schumann: Liederkreis, Op. 24
Robert Schumann: Frauenliebe und -Leben, Op. 42
Robert Schumann: Dichterliebe, Op. 48
(1997)

Sony Classical 48253
Jaime Laredo and Joseph Silverstein, violins; Michael Tree, viola; Yo-Yo Ma, cello
Erich Wolfgang Korngold: Suite for Piano Left Hand and Strings, Op. 23
Franz Schmidt: Quintet in G Major
(1998)

Vanguard Classics 1551
Two Hands
Johann Sebastian Bach: "Jesu, Joy of Man's Desiring" (arr. from BWV 147)
Johann Sebastian Bach: "Sheep May Safely Graze" (arr. from BWV 208)
Frederic Chopin: Mazurka in C-sharp Minor, Op. 50, No. 3

Frederic Chopin: Nocturne in D-flat Major, Op. 27, No. 2
Claude Debussy: Suite bergamasque, 3rd movement: "Clair de Lune"
Domenico Scarlatti: Sonata for Harpsichord in E Major, K. 380/L. 23
Franz Schubert: Sonata for Piano in B-flat Major, D. 960
(2004)

Vanguard Classics 1796
The Journey
Johann Sebastian Bach: Capriccio in B-flat Major, "On the Departure of a
    Beloved Brother," BWV 992
Johann Sebastian Bach: Chromatic Fantasy and Fugue in D Minor, BWV 903
Wolfgang Amadeus Mozart: Sonata in E-flat Major, K. 282
Frederic Chopin: Berceuse in D-flat Major, Op. 57
Igor Stravinsky: Serenade in A
Ludwig von Beethoven: Bagatelle No. 25 in A Minor, "Für Elise"
(2006)

Deutsche Grammophon 000871802
Emerson String Quartet
Johannes Brahms: Piano Quintet in F Minor, Op. 34
(2007)

Ondine ODE 11412
Christoph Eschenbach, Curtis Symphony Orchestra
Paul Hindemith: Klaviermusik mit Orchester, Op. 29 (world premiere recording)
(2009)

Sony 88697435052
Stuttgart Chamber Orchestra
Wolfgang Amadeus Mozart: Piano Concerto No. 7 in F Major, K. 242
    (with Katherine Jacobson Fleisher)
Wolfgang Amadeus Mozart: Piano Concerto No. 12 in A Major, K. 414
Wolfgang Amadeus Mozart: Piano Concerto No. 23 in A Major, K. 488
(2009)

LIVE RECORDINGS

These recordings—mainly from old radio broadcasts—are not all available in the United States. Several of them have been released on more than one label and can thus be found in other incarnations and collections than those cited below. The dates given are those of the original performances.

Dynamic IDIS Historical IDI6369
Bruno Walter, Los Angeles Philharmonic
Wolfgang Amadeus Mozart: Piano Concerto No. 23 in A Major, K. 488
(June 12, 1949)

Cypres Records CYP9612
50 Years of Emotion: The Queen Elisabeth International Music Competition
Franz André, Belgian National Orchestra
Johannes Brahms: Piano Concerto No. 1 in D Minor, Op. 15
(May 26, 1952)

West Hill Radio Archive WHRA6012
Pierre Monteux, Boston Symphony Orchestra
Johannes Brahms: Piano Concerto No. 1 in D Minor, Op. 15
(January 28, 1954)

Orfeo C774083D
George Szell, Berlin Philharmonic (Salzburg Festival)
Wolfgang Amadeus Mozart: Piano Concerto No. 25 in C Major, K. 503
(August 3, 1957)

Medici Arts/WDR MM036-2
Otto Klemperer/Hans Rosbaud, Cologne/WDR Radio Symphony Orchestra
Ludwig van Beethoven: Piano Concerto No. 2 in B-flat Major, Op. 19 *(Rosbaud)*
Ludwig van Beethoven: Piano Concerto No. 4 in G Major, Op. 58 *(Klemperer)*
(November 18, 1957 and February 27, 1956)

Library of Congress concert (release information not available)
Budapest String Quartet

Franz Schubert: "Trout" Quintet, D. 667
(April 21, 1961)

Relief CD (release information not available)
George Szell, Orchestre de Festival du Lucerne
Ludwig van Beethoven: Concerto No. 2 in B-flat Major, Op. 19 (second and third
    movements only)
(August 29, 1962)

LWO 3876 (Library of Congress)
Juilliard String Quartet
Wolfgang Amadeus Mozart: Piano Quartet in E-flat Major, K. 492
Johannes Brahms: Piano Quintet in F Minor, Op. 34
(November 1, 1962)

LWO 4274 (Library of Congress)
Juilliard String Quartet
Alberto Ginastera: Quintet for Piano and String Quartet
Johannes Brahms: Piano Quartet in G Minor, Op. 25
(May 1, 1964)

Disco Archivia 409
Leon Fleisher in Concert
Frederic Waldman, Musica Aeterna Orchestra
Ludwig van Beethoven: Piano Concerto No. 3 in C Minor, Op. 37
Wolfgang Amadeus Mozart: Piano Concerto No. 23 in A Major, K. 488
(November 22, 1964)
Leon Kirchner, New York Philharmonic [presumably]
Leon Kirchner: Piano Concerto No. 2
(December 1964)

Audiofon CD 72018
New England Conservatory Orchestra; Leonard Shure, piano (Leon Fleisher,
    conductor)
Ludwig van Beethoven: Piano Concerto No. 5 in E-flat Major, Op. 73, "Emperor"
    (Leonard Shure, soloist)
Robert Schumann: Fantasia in C

(The concert, a memorial to Artur Schnabel, also included Schnabel's
   Duodecimet.)
(1982)

NOTABLE REISSUES
Sony Classics 721581
The Essential Leon Fleisher
George Szell, Cleveland Orchestra
Ludwig van Beethoven: Concerto No. 5 in E-flat Major, Op. 73, "Emperor" (1st
   movement)
Johann Sebastian Bach, arr. Johannes Brahms: Chaconne from Partita II for Vio-
   lin in D Minor, BWV 1004
Johannes Brahms: Quintet in F Minor (3rd movement)
Johannes Brahms: Piano Concerto No. 1 in D Minor, Op. 15 (1st movement)
Franz Schubert: Sonata in B-flat Major, D. 960 (1st movement)
Wolfgang Amadeus Mozart: Piano Concerto No. 25 in C Major, K. 503 (3rd
   movement)
Edvard Grieg: Concerto in A Minor, Op. 16 (2nd movement)
Erich Wolfgang Korngold: Suite for Two Violins, Cello, and Piano Left Hand,
   Op. 23 (3rd movement)
Maurice Ravel: Concerto for the Left Hand in D Major
Maurice Ravel: Alborada del Gracioso

Sony Classical Masterworks 63225
Leon Fleisher Plays Brahms
George Szell, Cleveland Orchestra
Johannes Brahms: Piano Concerto No. 1 in D Minor, Op. 15
Johannes Brahms: Piano Concerto No. 2 in B-flat Major, Op. 83
Johannes Brahms: Variations and Fugue on a Theme of Händel, Op. 24
Johannes Brahms: Waltzes, Op. 39

CBS Masterworks 42445
George Szell, Cleveland Orchestra
Ludwig von Beethoven: The 5 Piano Concertos
Wolfgang Amadeus Mozart: Piano Concerto No. 25 in C Major, K. 503

WORKS COMPOSED FOR LEON FLEISHER

IN CHRONOLOGICAL ORDER
Leon Kirchner: Concerto for Piano No. 2 (1963)
Robert Saxton: Chacony for Piano Left Hand (1988)
Gunther Schuller: Concerto for Piano Three Hands (two pianos and chamber orchestra) (1990)
Curtis Curtis-Smith: Concerto for Left Hand and Orchestra (1991)
Jean Hasse: Silk Water (for piano left hand) (1992)
Lukas Foss: Concerto for the Left Hand (1993)
Gunther Schuller: Sextet for Flute, Oboe, Clarinet, Bassoon, Horn, and Piano Left Hand (1994)
Leon Kirchner: L.H. (1995)
William Bolcom: Gaea (for two pianos left hand and orchestra) (1996)
George Perle: Musical Offerings for Left Hand Alone (1998)
Dina Koston: Messages I (2002)

ACKNOWLEDGMENTS

This book would never have happened without Steve Rubin, who, when still the publisher of Doubleday, had the idea for it, brought the coauthors together, and worked with considerable energy to get them, literally, on the same page, and who has since continued to provide invaluable advice. To him we owe a tremendous debt of gratitude.

Gerald Howard, our editor, is an ideal reader whose thoughts about the way to shape a book are a constant source of reference and inspiration. We thank him for keeping us moving in the right direction, allowing us time for our thoughts to percolate, providing essential feedback, and—encouragingly—purchasing, and listening to, a considerable number of Leon Fleisher recordings.

The book would also never have happened without the active help of Joy Harris, agent extraordinaire, and Robert Perlstein, pit-bull lawyer. Frank Salomon has been a wonderful manager for several years and a dear friend for much longer than that; he contributed both his expertise and his memories.

A life isn't lived alone. The story of this one was enhanced by contributions from family, friends, and colleagues who accompanied it along the way.

This is particularly true of the members of the Fleisher family. Dot Fleisher, Risselle Rosenthal Fleisher, Katherine Jacobson Fleisher, Deborah Fleisher, Dickie Fleisher, Leah Fleisher, Paula Fleisher, and Julian Fleisher went beyond the pale in their candor, openness, and honesty. In more senses than we can enumerate, this book would not have been possible without them. To them all, our deepest thanks and a father's and husband's love.

Many thanks are also owing to Gary and Naomi Graffman, Shirley Perle, Marta Istomin, Jaime Laredo, Lynn Harrell, Phyllis Bryn-Julson, Yefim Bronfman, Jonathan Biss, Dominique Weber, Julian Martin, Arno Drucker, Dr. Dan Drachman, Dr. Mark Hallett, Dr. Barbara Karp, Anthony Tommasini, and Tim Page for their time, friendship, and willingness to talk.

We are grateful to those who helped us track down facts and photos: Ann Schnabel Mottier and François Mottier of the Schnabel Foundation, Jennifer Schlosser and Deborah Helfling of the Cleveland Orchestra, Donald Manildi and Leahkim Gannett of the International Piano Archives at the University of Maryland. Nell Mulderry, top-notch publicist, was as always invaluable in making sure everything was done properly.

The Peabody Institute of the Johns Hopkins University has for more than fifty years been a second home. Thanks are owed to the many, many administrators, colleagues, students, and friends who have helped to create and preserve this haven as a place where good creative work can be done. Margaret Bell provided welcome assistance for many petty book-related details.

Many thanks are due to the editors and colleagues at the *Washington Post* who were understanding and supportive of the time and effort involved in producing this book: Lynn Medford, Ned Martel, Joe Heim, John Pancake and Ann Olson, Deborah Heard, Steve Reiss, Rich Leiby, Peter Kaufman, Philip Kennicott, Blake Gopnik, Manuel Roig-Franzia, and Allison Schweitzer, among many others (you know who you are).

We couldn't have written the book without the support of our wonderful families and many friends. But our spouses were its life's blood. Greg Sandow was by turns a patient sounding-board, insightful editor, astute critic, cheerleader, and companion whose knowledge of both writing and music, and remarkable willingness to read manuscript drafts, helped prevent many an error. Katherine Jacobson Fleisher lived the story, then told the story, then shepherded us through the writing of the story—all with her consummate blend of intelligence, support, and insight. Without them, none of it would be possible.